United Nations Economic Commission for Europe

PROMOTING INNOVATION IN THE SERVICES SECTOR

REVIEW OF EXPERIENCES AND POLICIES

UNITED NATIONS
New York and Geneva, 2011

NOTE

The designations employed and the presentation of the material in this publication do not imply the expression of any opinion whatsoever on the part of the Secretariat of the United Nations concerning the legal status of any country, territory, city or area, or of its authorities, or concerning the delimitation of its frontiers or boundaries.

ECE/CECI/9

UNITED NATIONS PUBLICATION
Sales No. **E.11.II.E.3**
ISBN 978-92-1-117039-9

FOREWORD

Services play a growing role in modern economies. The development of services is a major source of productivity growth, as it provides critical inputs for other activities and facilitates the development of new business models. Information and communication technologies, in particular, have a direct impact on organizational innovation capabilities in manufacturing.

A well performing services sector is therefore increasingly seen as a key dimension of an effective innovation system. However, innovation policies and strategies relating to the services sector are less developed than those targeting manufacturing. The recognition of the importance of a dynamic services sector has been accompanied by efforts to ensure that the promotion of innovation in services is duly acknowledged in innovation policies.

This publication presents a collection of contributions by experts involved in the UNECE work on innovation and competitiveness policies carried out under the UNECE Committee on Economic Cooperation and Integration (CECI). The publication addresses a wide range of issues related to the promotion of innovation in the services sectors as well as policy lessons learned in this area drawing on the experiences of different countries.

The issues discussed in this publication refer to a relatively new policy area. Countries are at different stages in the conceptualization and implementation of relevant strategies. Overall, there is a need to further develop the understanding of innovation in services and increase policy awareness of the importance of innovation in the services sector. This creates significant scope for policy learning and the exchange of experiences through international multilateral initiatives.

I hope that this publication will contribute to the dissemination of good practices in the promotion of innovation in services and provide a useful reference for policymakers and other innovation stakeholders in their activities.

Ján Kubiš
Executive Secretary
United Nations Economic Commission for Europe

ACKNOWLEDGEMENTS

This publication was prepared in the context of the programme of work of the UNECE Committee on Economic Cooperation and Integration, which includes the activities of the Team of Specialists on Innovation and Competitiveness Policies (TOS-ICP). It was compiled on the basis of the contributions of members of the TOS-ICP and other experts participating in the Applied Policy Seminar "Promoting Innovation in the Services Sector". This Applied Policy Seminar was part of the third session of the TOS-ICP, which was held in Geneva on 25-26 March 2010.

The UNECE Secretariat would like to express its deep appreciation to all the experts who contributed articles for this publication.

CONTENTS

LIST OF TABLES

LIST OF FIGURES

ABBREVIATIONS

AI	Artificial Intelligence
BMBF	Federal Ministry of Education and Research (Germany)
BMWi	Federal Ministry of Economics and Technology (Germany)
BRDIS	Business Research & Development and Innovation Survey
BSP	Business Service Providers
CDP	Continuous Professional Development
CEC	Commission for Environmental Cooperation
CIS	Community Innovation Survey
CPS	Cross Pollination Space
EC	European Commission
ECTS	European Credit Transfer and Accumulation System
EINT	Economics of Innovation and New Technology
EPO	European Patent Office
EPISIS	European Policies & Instruments to Support Innovation in Services
ESR	Embedded Science Renewal
EU	European Union
EUROSTAT	Statistical Office of the European Commission
EVD	Private Sector Development Support (the Netherlands)
FBS	Flash Barometer Survey
FDI	Foreign Direct Investment
GATS	General Agreement on Trade in Services
GD Logic	Goods-Dominated Logic
GDP	Gross Domestic Product
ICT	Information and Communication Technology
IETF	Internet Engineering Task Force
IIP	Create – Innovation Platform for Media/Creative Industries (NL)
ILO	International Labour Office
INNO	Pro INNO Europe, an initiative of the EC's Directorate-General for Enterprise and Industry acting as a focal point for innovation policy analysis and policy cooperation in Europe
IPC	Inter-Process Communication
IPPS	Innovation Policy Project in Services
IPR	Intellectual Property Rights
ISIC	International Standard Industrial Classification
IT	Information Technology
ITC	International Trade Centre
KIBS	Knowledge-Intensive Business Services
KIS	Knowledge-Intensive Services
KISPIMS	Knowledge-Intensive Services in the Planning, Installation, Maintenance and Scrap services for renewable energy production systems
LDC	Less Developed Country
MDG	Millennium Development Goal

MERCOSUR	Economic agreement between Argentina, Brazil, Paraguay and Uruguay
MIT – CCI	Massachusetts Institute of Technology: Centre for Collective Intelligence
MMES	Micromechanical Engineering Systems
NACE	The Statistical Classification of Economic Activities of the European Community
NIST	National Institute for Standards and Technology
NMS	New Member State (EU)
NSF	National Science Foundation
OASIS	Open-source Ad Serving Inventory System
OECD	Organisation for Economic Co-operation and Development
OGF	Open Grid Forum
OSEO	Public agency for Innovation Financing and Guarantee Support (France)
PATSTAT	EPO Worldwide Patent Statistical Database
R&D	Research & Development
R&E	Research & Experimentation
RTD	Research & Technical Development
SD Logic	Services-Dominated Logic
SEPA	Single Euro Payment Area
SIDS	Screening Information Datasets
SII	Service Innovation & ICT (the Netherlands)
SME	Small/Medium-sized Enterprise
SSME	Service Science, Management and Engineering
TEKES	Finnish Funding Agency for Technology and Innovation
TRIPS	WTO Agreement on Trade-Related Aspects of Intellectual Property Rights
UNCTAD	United Nations Conference on Trade and Development
UNDP	United Nations Development Programme
UNESCO	United Nations Educational, Scientific and Cultural Organization
VC	Venture Capital or Venture Capitalist
VINNOVA	Sweden's innovation agency
W3C	World Wide Web Consortium
WIPO	World Intellectual Property Office
WTO	World Trade Organization

PART I

INNOVATION IN THE SERVICES SECTOR: CONCEPTS, MEASUREMENTS AND POLICY CHALLENGES

1. THE CHALLENGES FOR SERVICE INNOVATION AND SERVICE INNOVATION POLICIES[1]

Luis Rubalcaba, University of Alcalá, Spain

A. INTRODUCTION

This paper presents the main challenges for service innovation and service innovation policies. On the one hand, the chapter introduces the reader to the concept of innovation as a key factor in the service economy. On the other hand, it discusses some key issues concerning service innovation in a European context: recognition and importance, specificities and conceptualisation, measurement and policy implications.

B. INNOVATION AND SERVICES: A PATHWAY TO GROWTH

Since the beginning of economic science, economists have linked innovation with economic growth, Joseph A. Schumpeter being the author who placed it at the forefront. As a growth factor using processes of creative destruction, innovation has taken shape as one of the most significant explanatory factors for long-term growth. According to Schumpeter (1942), innovation is the essential force behind an evolving capitalism, provided that it maintains its underlying entrepreneurial nature. After Schumpeter, the developing growth theories used Solow as their basis, placing technological progress – and therefore innovation processes – at the core of economic analysis. With new theories of endogenous growth (Romer, 1986, 1990, Lucas, 1988), technological progress is fully integrated as an endogenous variable, which is explained by learning- and knowledge-related elements, among others. The value of intangibles, and therefore the related services, would form part of these elements.

In recent years, an alternative approach to the neoclassical theories has come to light. Evolutionist growth models stress another concept of innovation within growth by looking at the integration of economic and non-economic factors (culture, institutions and sciences). Evolutionist theories have been the preferred field of service innovation specialists. Services have developed within innovative systems as another dimension linked with the wider economic system, especially by means of knowledge-intensive services. In this respect, important contributions have arisen, such as those by Antonelli (1999), Miles (1999), Boden and Miles (2000), Metcalfe and Miles (2000), Muller (2001a) and Zenker (2001).

Service innovation affects growth by means of three key mechanisms:

- As services comprise around 70% of activity in advanced economies, their innovation process will be essential for the group of innovative systems and their impact on growth.

---

[1] This paper is largely based on previous contributions dealing with services innovation (Rubalcaba, 2007; Gallego and, 2008; Den Hertog and, 2010) and service-innovation related policies (Rubalcaba, 2006; et alt., 2010). Acknowledgement is given to the co-authors of these works and the permission given by publishing houses to reproduce part of the text.

- Certain services were and are essential in the development of some technological innovations.
- Business services, especially KIS (Knowledge-Intensive Services), are used as intermediate inputs in production, due to their positive effects on innovation in those companies that make use of these services. This includes impacts on manufacturers that provide products for the service sector.

The remainder of this chapter refers to the first of the aforementioned mechanisms. The third mechanism was discussed and summarized in previous work (Rubalcaba, 1999). The strategic role of business services in industry is associated with their innovative nature. This function can be better understood by analyzing the five types of innovation that promote business services: technological, organizational, strategic, commercial and operational (see Table I.1.1). Some of these terms are the modern expressions of the innovative aspects as defined by Schumpeter. According to Schumpeter, innovation includes new products, new processes, new forms of organization, new markets and new sources of inputs to production (Schumpeter, 1939).

We will take technological innovation as an example, where the incorporation of technologies and their improved usage are the first consequences of innovation produced by business services. IT services are those most related to technological innovation, although electronic communication, engineering, computer-assisted design and certain telecommunication services could also have the same or higher importance. All these business services contribute to a real and effective technological innovation: real because such technology would otherwise likely remain outside of those companies failing to understand its potential use, due to a lack of accompanying services; and effective because if there were no services linked to new technologies, they would be under-used.

Business knowledge-intensive services have achieved an important role in modern economies and national innovation systems (Kox and Rubalcaba, 2007, Windrum and Tomlinson, 1999), and favour the modernization of a country's knowledge base. This achievement becomes evident in two ways: on the one hand, due to technological innovations (in subsectors with high levels of intensity in R&D such as engineering, software and research), including those of an organizational type and those related to business strategy, marketing and management of human resources (Boden and Miles, 2000); and on the other hand, due to the diffusion of knowledge for developing best practices for solving the most common business problems encountered by different customer organizations, and for orientating them towards a relevant efficiency. Knowledge-intensive services provide the intangible elements (know-how, software, organizational skills, R&D capabilities, and so on) which have become the key motivating elements for the creation of value, since according to Grubel (1995), a substantial part of growth in total factor productivity can be explained by increased specialization in the production of inputs.

From a service economy perspective, it is understood that innovative processes do not form, transmit or produce the same effects as those generated in a manufacturing environment, which are much more linear and relate directly to products or productive processes. Intangible aspects, resulting from the interactive nature of services help to explain the peculiar way in which services innovate, are innovative, or enable other sectors to take advantage of innovation capabilities. All in all, the wide ranging possibilities of technological change opened up by an appropriate system of innovation are reinforced by the service economy (Miles, 2000), although some differences persist, depending on the type of services involved (Howells, 2001). Advanced services do not generate innovation in the same way or with the same intensity as do more traditional or operational services.

At international or interregional levels it is clear that there is an existing correlation between knowledge innovative business services and economic dynamism, as Figure I.1.1 points out. A high concentration of innovative services is located in rich and dynamic areas like the South East of England, the Benelux area, the Rhine areas in Germany or the capital-regions of Paris in France, Madrid in Spain, Copenhagen in Denmark, and so on. Services innovation matters in economic growth.

Figure I.1.1. Distribution of knowledge-intensive business services in Europe

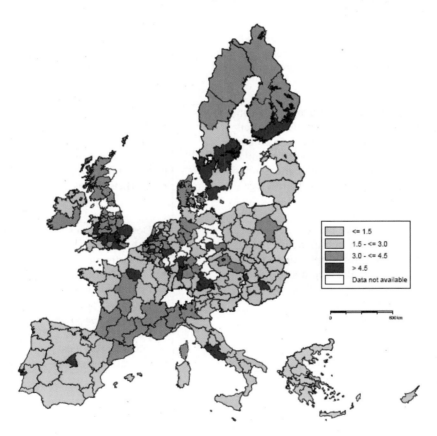

Table I.1.1. Business services innovative functions

Innovative Functions	Main innovation components	Business services (some representative activities)
Technological Innovation	<ul><li>Major technology incorporation</li><li>Major utilization of existent technology</li><li>Technological adaptation to the business necessities</li><li>Efficiency in the information and communication advanced processes</li><li>Automation of routine processes</li><li>Enhanced flexibility of productive structures</li><li>Improvement in quality</li></ul>	<ul><li>Computing services</li><li>Engineering services</li><li>Design services</li><li>Communication services</li><li>Electronic on-line communication services</li><li>Quality control services</li></ul>
Organizational Innovation	<ul><li>Efficient internal organization</li><li>Integration of control and coordination processes</li><li>Improved selection, training and utilization of human factor</li><li>Improvement in different functional specializations</li></ul>	<ul><li>Management consultancy</li><li>Legal audit and services</li><li>Personnel services (selection, training and part-time jobs)</li></ul>
Strategic Innovation	<ul><li>Flexibility for dynamic environments</li><li>Positioning in complex markets</li><li>Strategic information on alliances</li><li>Information on product adequacy</li><li>Information on allocation and markets</li><li>Defence in an adversarial legal environment</li></ul>	<ul><li>Management services</li><li>On-line services</li><li>Audit services</li><li>Legal services</li><li>Fair and exhibition services</li><li>Market studies</li></ul>
Commercial Innovation	<ul><li>Competitive product design</li><li>Innovative commercialization</li><li>Major utilization of opportunities</li><li>Business development</li><li>Innovative Marketing</li><li>Image and branding</li></ul>	<ul><li>Design services</li><li>Exhibitions</li><li>Advertising</li><li>Direct marketing</li><li>Public relations</li><li>After-sale services</li></ul>
Operative Innovation	<ul><li>Functional work division</li><li>Focus on core activities</li><li>Operative consideration</li><li>Image consideration</li></ul>	<ul><li>Language services</li><li>Courier services</li><li>Security services</li><li>Operative services</li></ul>

Source: Rubalcaba (1999).

C. CONCEPT AND FEATURES OF SERVICE

There are many definitions of service innovation. For example, van Ark et al. (2003) establish a lengthy definition of innovation in services, including its main kinds: 'A new or considerably changed service concept, client interaction channel, service delivery system or technological concept that individually, but most likely in combination, leads to one or more (re)new(ed) service functions that are new to the firm and do change the services/goods offered on the market and do require structurally-new technological, human or organizational capabilities of the service organization'.

First, there is a need to distinguish between innovation in services and service innovation (Table I.1.2). The first concerns the innovative change within the service activity or sector itself. The latter refers to the innovative change in those organizations or companies that use innovative services or those engendering innovation. It is worth highlighting that the majority of the approaches conducted to date refer to modes I and III, and that there are few examples relating to modes II and IV. However, quantitative approaches are based on mode I, and some of them on mode II; the lack of data regarding service activities hinders quantitative approaches to the analysis of modes III and IV.

Table I.1.2. Modes of service innovation: supply or demand approach

	Innovation in services (supply approach)	Service innovation (demand approach)
Service companies	Innovative services companies (Mode I)	Use of innovative services companies (e.g. external KIS) (Mode II)
Service activities (any sector)	Innovative services activities (Mode III)	Use of innovative services activities (e.g. internal or external KIS) (Mode IV)

Note: KIS = Knowledge-intensive services.
Source: Rubalcaba (2007).

In recent years, the literature regarding innovation has explored different taxonomies. The categorization to product, process and organizational innovation first emerged from Schumpeter's work (1934). Specifically for services, Miles and Howells distinguish between product innovation (goods or services), process innovation, organizational innovation and innovation in client interaction as a specific type. Gallouj (1994) distinguishes between vaporization, anticipation and objectification innovation processes, on the basis of the function carried out by each type of innovation.

Van Ark et al.'s work (2003) develops the difference between several types of technological profiles, and also distinguishes among three types of non-technological innovation: new services conceptions, new interfaces with clients and new systems of service delivery. These authors also drew a distinction between innovation guided by the supplier, the client, the company itself, the use of services or by paradigmatic changes. In this respect, the customer-supplier duality is found in the delivery of services, where customers are suppliers of significant inputs to the innovative process (Fitzsimmons et al., 2004). Another approach, based on that of Soete and Miozzo (1989), is developed further by Hipp and Grupp (2005). This approach shows the differences between four key categories on the basis of their intrinsic characteristics and their innovation processes: knowledge-intensive, network-intensive, scale-intensive and external innovation-intensive.

These taxonomies for the service economy, be they analytical or sectoral in nature, recognise the strong interaction between producer and consumer in service activities. This interaction begins to blur the distinction between product and process innovation, which is more evident in manufacturing (Miles, 1995). The relationship with clients constitutes one of the basic and typical elements of service innovation; its co-productive nature is preserved in the processes generated by many service innovations (Miles, 1999). As a result of its co-productive nature, this feature is upheld in processes generated from many services innovations. Some business services channel their innovations from externalization and outsourcing.

Some consumer services, in turn, direct a share of their innovation towards self-service, in line with the statement of Gershuny (1978) many years before. The interactions required in service co-production may imply that innovation has its own features, conducts and needs, such as an emphasis on human and organizational factors as competitive elements, in comparison to the manufacturing sector (Evangelista et al., 1998; Tether, 2005). Services require greater consideration of the organizational aspects, beyond the traditional product and process innovation methods (F. Gallouj, 1994, 2002 and C. Gallouj, 1996; Gadrey et al., 1995; Sundbo, 1998). This is due to the significant intangible and informative elements associated with these service products and processes, through the transmission of knowledge and skills rather than through the purchase of machinery or technology (F. Gallouj, 2002).

Service innovation is related to goods innovation through a process of 'encapsulation', as described by Howells (2004), whereby non-technological factors and information intermediaries are of greater importance. As a consequence, service innovation can be considered to be multidimensional in developing new concepts, new interfaces with clients, new systems of provision and new technological options (den Hertog and Bilderbeek, 1999). Accordingly and from a multidimensional approach, services are more innovative than generally believed.

D. STATISTICAL SOURCES AND THEIR LIMITATIONS

In the statistics regarding innovation, the conventional definitions of the Oslo Manual[2] are used. These definitions are problematic when considering services, as the wide range of their characteristic innovation sources are not taken into consideration. This can be seen in taxonomies in which there are serious difficulties in the measurement of organizational innovation. In addition, an added difficulty in the case of services exists when differentiating between the three types of basic innovation, as the frontiers are not always delimited. The Frascati Manual (OECD, 1993) defines R&D as creative work undertaken on a systematic basis in order to increase the stock of knowledge (including knowledge of humans, culture and society), and the use of this stock of knowledge to devise new applications.[3]

It is not easy for services companies to identify and to define the 'systematic base' in the absence of R&D processes formalization. In services, a part of R&D is not statistically registered (for example, because it is not conducted in an R&D department or because such a department does not exist), and many programmes of innovation investment are not included in R&D. At present, there are debates on whether the definition of R&D is appropriate or

---

[2] Product innovation: any change in the product leading to the improvement of features offered to the client (with or without a technological dimension). Process innovation: the provision of an important change to the manufacturing processes of a product. Examples include new equipment, new management and organizational methods, or both types together.

[3] Three activities are observed: basic research, without any particular application or immediate use on sight; applied research, with a specific practical objective; and experimental development.

whether it should be modified or re-created specifically for services. It seems there is at least some margin for its revision, so that the level of recognition of innovative activity in services can be improved. However, more research appears to be necessary (Miles, 2005a).

In general, the statistical difficulties in studying innovation in services can be summarized as follows: problems in the definitions and their coverage; difficulties with identifying innovation in services in the same way as the majority of academic studies regarding innovation in services and related typologies; over-orientation of the Community Innovation Survey (CIS) toward manufacturing, which excludes the analytical and statistical needs required to meet the key aspects of innovation in services (Rubalcaba, 2004)[4]; lack of statistical sources complementary to the CIS; lack of statistical continuity in the use of KIS as an innovative source; bias of the current approach toward supply rather than demand; statistical ignorance with regard to internal service innovation within manufacturing and services companies; lack of distinction between product-innovative services and goods; non-existence of a vertical approach specific to certain services sectors; sparse knowledge and a limited range of statistics regarding organizational and non-technological innovations; absence of statistical continuity regarding modes, conductors, obstacles and impacts of different types of service innovation; insufficient disaggregation of R&D statistics (concepts, programmes, companies, etc.); limited knowledge of the service area (services activities and services companies) participating in national and EU R&D programmes; and problems of statistical coverage (countries providing only limited data, and comparability issues).

E. CHARACTERISTICS OF SERVICE INNOVATION IN EUROPE

R&D expenditure is a classical indicator of the innovative potential of a country. Despite the fact this is only one of the inputs necessary to achieve innovation, and although its approximation is relatively limited in the services domain, R&D continues to be the most comparable and widely used statistical indicator in the field of innovation.

As a whole, the intensity of services R&D remains below the levels registered in manufacturing. However, as shown in Figure I.1.2, between 1995 and 2003 R&D business expenditure grew to a greater extent in the services sector than in manufacturing. This trend has been influenced by the role played by some business services, particularly computing services, which experienced exceptional growth during this period, as well as distributive trades. This statement holds true for all the countries considered, with the exception of Greece, partially as a result of the reduction in R&D investment in the distribution sector.

Data extracted from Figure I.1.3 suggests that the behaviour of R&D growth in services varies considerably between European countries. Between 1995 and 2003, German computing business services presented an outstanding R&D growth rate (above 30%), whereas in southern regions R&D efforts were concentrated in the distributive trades. In Scandinavian countries, transport services decreased their R&D expenditure level, in contrast with what occurred in the two other observed areas. The development of services R&D has been particularly relevant in southern regions in comparison with Scandinavian countries, where

---

[4] The CISIII represents a substantial improvement on previous surveys, which initially focused only on manufacturing companies. It introduced some organizational elements, but many issues relating to innovation in advanced services are not yet covered, and indicators remain biased towards the traditional innovation sources.

this development has been much less notable. Thus, this tendency may reveal, to a certain extent, a convergence process in business innovation between northern European countries, with a more advanced development of R&D, relative to southern regions with traditionally lower levels of investment.

Figure I.1.2. Annual growth rates of internal business expenditure in the manufacturing and service sectors, 1995-2003 (%)

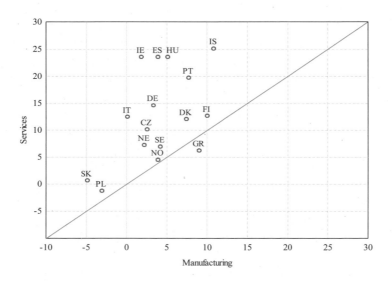

Note: Exponential growth rates in R&D spending at constant prices.
Sources: Gallego and Rubalcaba (2008) based on the ANBERD database, OECD.

Figure I.1.3. Average growth rate of the R&D internal business expenditure in three European areas by services sectors, 1995-2003 (%)

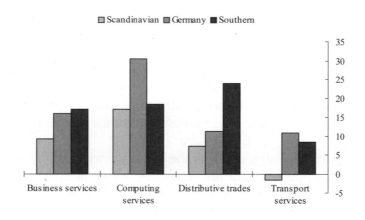

Notes: Nine countries have been included as representative of the three areas. Scandinavian=Denmark, Finland, Norway and Sweden; Germany; Southern=Greece, Italy, Portugal and Spain. Figure I.1.3 includes Germany in the comparison since it is the largest European economy.
Sources: Gallego and Rubalcaba (2008) based on the ANBERD database, OECD.

Finally, the increasing role of services in R&D reflects at least four key factors:

- *More research*: Firstly, the service sector is increasing the use of new technologies and developing increasingly complex services functions and processes within companies.
- *Companies outsourcing*: Manufacturing companies sometimes purchase (or externalize) R&D when locating their laboratories in a distinct corporate entity or when they purchase R&D services from another private company.
- *Government outsourcing*: Frequently, governments purchase R&D instead of conducting it themselves.
- *Measurement*: R&D statistics in the service sector have notably improved in some countries. The increasing role of services in R&D is partly the result of changes undertaken in statistical practices, and partly the result of better sampling. In addition, an important statistical bias is related to those primarily manufacturing companies that recently surpassed the 50 per cent mark of their turnover in services. Their activities, including R&D, are classified currently as integrated in the service sector.

Focusing on KIS firms, R&D expenditures and employment are observed to be highly concentrated in a few firms, most of which have formal and distinct R&D departments - an organizational arrangement that is uncommon in the services sector. However, the share of total R&D accounted for by services continues to grow. Furthermore, R&D investments by large individual firms represent only a part of the total innovation effort. This is particularly relevant for the services sector, which accounts for a greater number of small- and medium-sized enterprises than the manufacturing industry. However, during the last decade, R&D business expenditures grew faster in the service sector compared to the manufacturing sector. This trend is influenced by some business services, particularly computer services and related activities that experienced exceptional growth during this period.

Tables I.1.3 and I.1.4 sheds some light on this phenomenon, presenting data for the top 15 European computer service and software companies with regard to their R&D investments. The figures have been extracted from the '2007 EU Industrial R&D Investment Scoreboard', which presents data on the top 1,000 R&D investing organizations with registered offices in the EU. The figures are derived from company accounts and represent the R&D invested by companies' own funds, independent of location of the R&D activity. The computer services sector includes 32 enterprises among the top 1,000 R&D investors. Their R&D efforts are greater than €900 million, and provide employment for more than 190,000 workers in Europe. The five top-ranking European firms within this sector are among the 10 world leading enterprises by R&D investments. On the other hand, almost 10 per cent of the major European R&D investors refer to the software services industry. Within this sector, there are 95 firms among the top 1,000 R&D investors, whose R&D efforts total €3.5 billion. This particular service sector exhibits R&D investment levels above those achieved in more traditional manufacturing sectors such as food and beverage production or industrial machinery.

Table I.1.3. Europe's largest computer service enterprises/groups, ranked by R&D investment (2006)

Rank	Company	Country	R&D Investment €m	Net Sales €m	Employees Numbers
1	Telent	UK	206.30	1,452	9,000
2	Fujitsu Siemens Computers	The Netherlands	145.10	6,952	10,757
3	Indra Sistemas	Spain	96.44	1,407	10,611
4	Wincor Nixdorf	Germany	87.44	1,948	7,444
5	TietoEnator	Finland	72.50	1,782	14,414
6	LogicaCMG	UK	59.66	3,956	32,425
7	Sopra	France	31.10	898	9,602
8	Northgate Information Solutions	UK	24.26	494	3,232
9	F-Secure	Finland	23.38	81	439
10	Anite	UK	21.48	248	1,387
11	Torex Retail	UK	18.74	248	2,285
12	IONA Technologies	Ireland	12.09	59	351
13	Teleca	Sweden	11.51	327	3,940
14	SciSys	UK	10.38	93	770
15	Cegedim	France	9.87	541	4,968

Table I.1.4. Europe's largest software enterprises/groups, ranked by R&D investment (2006)

Rank	Company	Country	R&D Investment €m	Net sales €m	Employees Numbers
1	SAP	Germany	1,298.12	9,402	38,053
2	Dassault Systemes	France	281.04	1,158	6,840
3	Business Objects	France	147.91	951	5,402
4	Amdocs	UK	141.63	1,881	16,234
5	Sage	UK	140.85	1,389	10,510
6	Misys	UK	131.50	1,343	6.081
7	Ubisoft Entertainment	France	130.66	547	3,240
8	SCI Entertainment	UK	85.19	266	900
9	Symbian	UK	80.86	170	1,047
10	Infogrames Entertainment	France	65.50	391	982
11	Software	Germany	44.86	483	2,621
12	Autonomy	UK	41.60	190	903
13	Gameloft	France	41.21	68	2,635
14	IBS	Sweden	35.16	252	1,873
15	ISOFT	UK	34.55	299	3,224

Source: R&D Investment Scoreboard 2007.
http://iri.jrc.ec.europa.eu/research/scoreboard_2007.htm

In addition to R&D, other indicators have been analysed in a previous work (Den Hertog and Rubalcaba, 2010). In this work, the authors highlighted the heterogeneity of the services sector in relation to various key characteristics. Some variables have been selected for policy purposes. The percentage of innovative enterprises is of interest in order to promote policies to spread and to disseminate innovative behaviour and attitudes among the business society. In this case, business services and financial services are characterised by high proportions of innovative companies, unlike distributive trade and transport services (Table I.1.5). Concerning intramural and extramural ratios, business services use more of both R&D categories than other services branches, except financial services which also draw quite heavily upon extramural R&D. In R&D, only business and financial services offer similar or higher shares of companies than manufacturing, while other services show lower shares, in line with previous studies concerning the role of R&D in services (Miles, 2005b; RENESER, 2006).

Table I.1.5. Distinctiveness coefficient in some key policy related indicators: services versus goods, Europe-16

	Total goods industries	Manufacturing	Total services	Distributive trades	Transport and communications	Financial services	Business services
Innovative firms	1.00	1.004	0.773	0.699	0.625	1.204	1.070
Intramural R&D	1.00	1.060	0.791	0.601	0.627	0.815	1.213
Extramural R&D	1.00	1.017	0.964	0.932	0.873	1.142	1.112
Impacts on costs	1.00	1.005	0.677	0.656	0.841	0.888	0.576
Impacts on quality	1.00	1.010	1.033	0.907	1.063	1.118	1.170
Impacts on response time	1.00	1.007	1.227	1.250	1.330	1.307	1.113
Patents	1.00	1.033	0.517	0.575	0.254	0.125	0.825
Copyright	1.00	1.014	1.598	1.065	0.531	0.764	3.632
Obstacles	1.00	1.005	0.901	0.878	0.799	1.004	0.989
Total public funding	1.00	1.005	0.574	0.470	0.463	0.239	0.944

Note: Europe-16 refers to Belgium, Czech Republic, Denmark, Spain, France, Italy, Cyprus, Lithuania, Luxembourg, Hungary, the Netherlands, Poland, Portugal, Romania, Slovakia and Norway.
Source: CIS4 database, Eurostat.
Source: Den Hertog and Rubalcaba (2010).

In relation to impacts, it is clear that innovation in service industries is less oriented towards cost-related outcomes when compared with innovation in manufacturing industries, while the outcomes relating to capacity to respond to customer needs is higher in service industries. In terms of quality related outcomes the situation is more balanced between sectors. This suggests that the orientation of particular R&D and innovation funding should take into account the various outcomes that such funding can be expected to result in. Possible specific approaches may follow, even where the generic challenges for innovation are the same across both goods and services (a similar balance is obtained in relation to the perceived obstacles to innovation). In other words, evidence on impact suggests that policies should not solely take account of the volume of public spending addressed to services, but also of the design of public programmes. The design of the latter may need to take account of the characteristic features of service innovation.

Differences are important in other policy-related variables such as the protection systems. As expected, patents are much more important in manufacturing than in services, while the opposite applies to the copyright system. It may be the case that IPR is underdeveloped in services, and/or that services require another approach for the protection of results. In any case, this empirical evidence should be taken into account at the stage of policy formulation. On the one hand, possible biases should be identified in order to assess explicit or implicit discrimination against services innovation in terms of the aggregate distribution of public funding, and the rationale behind any such biases discussed. On the other hand, attention should be paid to the qualitative design of innovation policies; the problem is more likely qualitative than quantitative. The appropriate policy mix might vary across industries, i.e. innovation policies – at least to some extent – need to be customized, even within service subsectors.

F. IDENTIFICATION OF CHALLENGES

Despite the fact that innovation plays a key role within the service sector, only recently has extensive theoretical and empirical work been conducted on this subject. In fact, the majority of studies relating to innovation have used the industrial sector as a reference, setting the tertiary sector to one side. This is based on the traditional idea of a limited scope in the service sector for the incorporation and use of technology, and hence a lesser margin for technical change and innovation, with the inevitable consequences for the development of this sector of the economy. From an empirical perspective, the lack of relevant contributions is associated with the difficulties that arise in the study of technological change and innovation in the service sector, and the lack of standard criteria to define these concepts.

Nonetheless, recent developments clearly undermine these arguments. Services companies are increasingly the subject of initiatives specifically targeting innovation, as a means of increasing levels of cost efficiency, quality standards or developing new service types. In this respect, there is a group of advanced services within the heterogeneous tertiary sector that, far from adopting a passive role in promoting economic competitiveness and modernization, become innovation-generating, innovation-driving and innovation-transmitting elements. This is the main point upon which numerous contributions regarding services and innovation are based, stressing the related innovative importance of other aspects beyond the strictly technological.

As previously stated, even though innovation in the service sector is founded mainly on organizational and information factors, R&D continues to be a significant indicator of its innovative activity in this sector. Although the intensity levels in service R&D are low relative to investment levels in the manufacturing sector, the annual growth rates of internal business expenditure of services in R&D have been higher than those registered in industry over the last decade. This phenomenon can be understood as a result of four possible actions: improvements in statistics and statistical bias; increased investment in technological and more complex processes within the service sector; increased outsourcing of R&D activities by the manufacturing sector; and similarly increased outsourcing by central governments.

In Europe, services sectors such as business services and the financial sector register a higher level of innovation density than manufacturing. Business services frequently outstrip the industrial sector in variables including, among others, the introduction of new products to the market, the protection of intellectual property through copyrights and trade secrets, the implementation of new corporate strategies, the improvement in the quality of products, or the percentage of people involved in R&D tasks. In this sense, it is also worth mentioning the relevant differences in innovation behaviours of the different sectors within the services field. Hence, more traditional or operational activities such as transport and communications will generally register lower propensities for innovative activity.

In any case, the manufacturing sector still registers the highest proportion of innovative companies in the market, despite the high levels of innovative activity in services sectors such as business services. The difficult task of measuring service innovation, in a sector with many diverse activities and different innovation processes, is an obstacle to the service organizations' acknowledgement of their own innovative operations. Moreover, statistical sources that facilitate the analysis of service innovation activity in the economy are sparse; they generally adopt a methodological approach that is more applicable to goods than to services. As a consequence, one of the main challenges that any innovation policy must tackle, including in relation to services, is the need to strengthen a deficient statistical and evidence base.

Significant institutional differences in the degree of financial support to the different sectors could also have a decisive impact on the results. Evidently higher levels of support provided to manufacturing, at least at both the European and national levels, to the detriment of some service sectors – politically considered as less productive and innovative – may influence the innovative potential of services. Similarly, recent works (Rubalcaba and Gallego, 2006) suggest that a pro-industrial and technological orientation of R&D programmes can explain the gap.

Cross-country analysis shows significant differences regarding levels of entrepreneurial innovation between northern and southern European countries. In this respect, northern European regions, in comparison with those in the south, develop more internal R&D; apply more for intellectual property protection; maintain an important innovative relation with external agents (clients, universities, R&D centres, etc.); and realise a larger number of innovations in the market. Southern European countries, in turn, register greater relative impacts as a result of the introduction of innovative elements in their productive systems. This latter characteristic may reflect a degree of productivity 'catch up' of southern regions, which are generally starting from a lower base in comparison to more highly developed regions.

Figure I.1.4 summaries some key challenges for service innovation from a policy perspective. The relatively low participation of services in R&D or pro-innovation activities is a key issue where potential increased innovation in services is foregone. The lack of formalisation and a related innovation culture can be a major challenge, together with market and systemic failures, an onerous regulatory burden and markets that may be fragmented and protected. All these obstacles affect productivity growth in services, the innovation profile of service economies and the capacity to face the global sourcing challenge. The section that follows will deal with the policy aspects of these challenges.

Figure I.1.4. Key challenges for services innovation

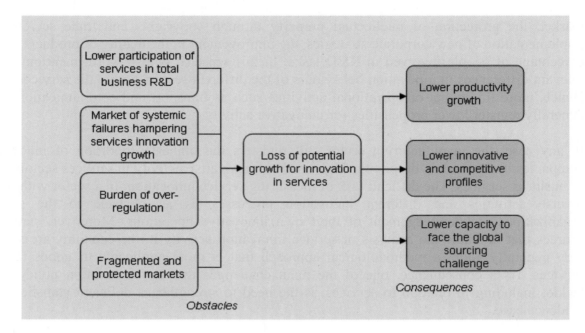

G. THE RATIONALE FOR A SERVICES INNOVATION POLICY: MARKET AND SYSTEMIC FAILURES

Existing policy approaches and rationales for policy intervention are generally less well developed and attuned to service industries and service innovation. According to previous results on public funding, on average 28% of innovative manufacturing companies versus 16% of service companies receive public funding. Figure I.1.5 displays a clear bias towards manufacturing in innovation funding - although this is more marked at the central/national level than at the regional or EU level. In particular, the EU's policies are rather balanced between services and manufacturing. This better European balance is mainly explained by the role of services in ICT policies, and the relative success of business services in obtaining EU funding.

The bias in the distribution of public funding can be observed at the various different levels at which innovation policies are active, i.e. at the local, regional, national and European levels. (Rubalcaba, 2007; Gallego and Rubalcaba, 2008). We should bear in mind, however, that this bias does not apply uniformly in all cases, countries and subsectors. Regarding the type of innovation funding, a more balanced distribution between services and manufacturing can be found in funding derived from EU sources, as previously observed by Resener (2006) from CIS3 and van Cruysen and Hollanders (2008) from CIS4 data.

**Figure I.1.5. The funding bias towards manufacturing and
the role of EU programmes**

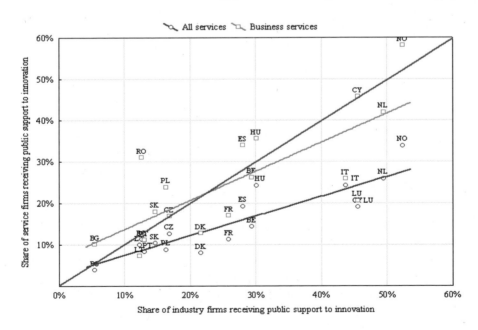

Source: Based on CIS4, Eurostat.

The more balanced sectoral distribution of EU funding is mainly explained by the active role of (mostly knowledge-intensive) business services in securing EU public funding. These business services in turn represent a dynamic sector that receives significant funding in all countries. Figure I.1.6 shows that there is a significant bias in public funding against the whole set of services, but also that this bias does not apply in the case of business services in a number of countries. Typical service industries with lower shares of public funding for innovation are the distributive trade, transport and finance sectors.

Figure I.1.6. Share of firms receiving public funding for innovation, by sector

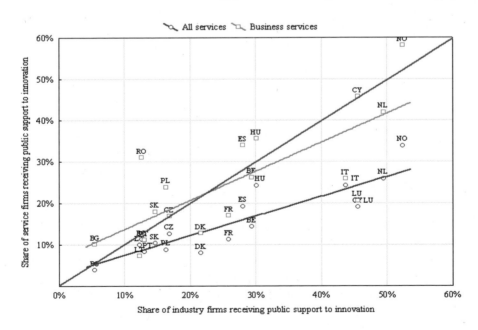

Source: Den Hertog and Rubalcaba (2010) based on CIS4 database, Eurostat.

In previous work (Rubalcaba, 2006), several ideas explaining the need for a policy in relation to service innovation were developed. There are many reasons supporting the idea of a service innovation policy which are similar to those underlying innovation policy in the industrial sector. There are three basic arguments: the macroeconomic; market failures; and systemic failures related to the dynamics of innovation systems. At the highest level, the following may be emphasized:

- Service innovation is a stimulant for innovation generally and for investment in intangibles and knowledge, important factors for endogenous growth and total factor productivity;
- There is a relatively low productivity performance in many service sectors and relatively low use of ICT in services in Europe;
- The relatively low participation of services companies – with some exceptions – in R&D programmes. This raises the question of the Lisbon strategy and the aim to achieve 3% of GDP in R&D investments in Europe;
- The lack of formulation and organization of service innovation, which requires the promotion of new instruments of business support;
- The recent deregulation and liberalization in many service sectors, which means that businesses forsaking protected market niches need to find new strategies to boost their competitiveness; and
- The current phenomenon of relocating services to lower-cost countries or countries with a higher specialization means that businesses in advanced countries must find new, competitive strategies based on innovation.

From the point of view of market failure, four arguments have traditionally been advanced: those concerning uncertainty and risk, externalities, scale economies and market power. In services, uncertainty is not only related to investment risk, but also and more particularly to imperfect and asymmetric information. Since innovation requires different means and levels of interaction between seller and purchaser, the problems of asymmetric information could hamper innovation, as one party might have concerns regarding unknown features of the other party (e.g. attitude, skills). The problem of uncertainty not only justifies public investment – to take risks derived from a potential failure – but also financial intermediation – e.g. soft credits and grants. The particular case of asymmetric information limits the demand for new services and requires public performance, with demand, market transparency and informational impacts. Additional action directed towards the supply side is also required.

Externalities are derived from the public nature of knowledge and its spillovers, which generate problems of appropriability and use of innovation without the need to pay a market value (free-riding). This market failure justifies the intellectual property protection policies (intellectual property rights) on the one hand, and direct government intervention, on the other. The latter, however, is only justifiable in the case where the intervention implies the maximisation of net social welfare. As far as services are concerned, appropriability problems seem to be even greater than in the case of goods, due to the limited use of patents and the insufficient level of protection offered by copyright systems.

Scale economies are related to the indivisibility of technological activities requiring a minimum critical mass. The problem of indivisibility in the world of services is probably less than in the case of goods, where R&D processes are better structured and require a higher quantity of inputs. As innovation processes are more diffused in services' production processes, it appears less problematic to reach a critical mass. On the contrary, when innovation effort concerning inputs is invested in qualified human capital, an active policy is justified in the field of education and training. At the same time, services are to a larger extent SME markets than is the case with goods markets. This reinforces the traditional justification for SME-oriented policies, where reaching a critical mass and sufficient human capital is more difficult.

And finally, market power is of particular interest in relation to services, where the lack of competition can act as a disincentive for generating innovation. As many services operate in highly segmented markets with a high degree of market power, this market failure is particularly important.

As a consequence of the above-mentioned failures, a lack of spatial convergence in the distribution of innovation activities and their effects can be expected. The strong regional and urban concentration of knowledge-intensive services (KIS) reinforces territorial imbalances and justifies an innovation policy to reduce these differences.

Observing the need to correct the systemic failures in services, the evolutionist theory suggests some innovation models or systems without simple one-way relationships between knowledge generation and absorption (O'Doherty and Arnold, 2003, Arnold and Kuhlman, 2001). Therefore, a systemic approach is necessary to understand the relationships between science, technology and innovation, as well as an evolutionist approach, indicating that there is a specific situation of relevance for each case according to the cumulative processes generating change in the systems. Within this body of understanding, it is worth identifying some ineffective elements particularly harmful to services within the innovation system:

- As regards industrial systems, circulation between SMEs and new technological businesses suffers from a lack of fluidity and transparency. The dominance of SMEs operating in segmented markets against larger innovative businesses frequently operating under oligopolistic conditions does not help the circular flow of knowledge within the service industrial system.
- Regarding intermediaries, technological institutes, technological transfer centres, universities or regional development centres, the orientation towards issues related to services is quite limited, with some exceptions, such as the Fraunhofer Institutes in Germany.
- In relation to infrastructure, financial and credit systems do not take adequate account of the assets of services companies. Such assets are mainly intangible and therefore are not often registered in businesses' financial accounts. Despite the present efforts towards accounting recognition of intangible assets, the current credit system penalizes uncertain or risky activities based on intangible assets, which are often treated as operating costs rather than capital investment.
- As mentioned above, protection systems are highly ineffective for services, and the lack of quality standards and regulations for service sectors makes transparency especially problematic.

- There is some degree of institutional failure: public agencies and governments are not yet fully aware of the importance of service innovation, which means a lower level of support, not only in public R&D programmes, but also in other initiatives relating to technological and innovation policies.

- A lack of demand is often highlighted as a key factor explaining low levels of service innovation, to which we must add a lack of awareness on the supply side concerning its innovative activities and potential. These aspects underline structural failures linked to available knowledge, training, information, culture and social values.

- There are some failures in the regional networks of service innovation systems. The high concentration of services in certain regions and cities favours the concentration of their innovation in such areas. Regional innovation systems have traditionally been oriented towards agricultural or manufacturing industries, and as such do not take account, except in special cases, the added value that could be achieved from a pro-innovative service system.

- And finally, as players and their context evolve simultaneously to attain a steady state – knowledge and innovation systems are never mature at the outset – and their success is to a large extent context dependent. This is particularly noticeable in the service domain, where information is fragmented, production and transmission mechanisms of innovation are uncertain and the heterogeneity of services themselves and their types of innovation increase asymmetries and delay adaptation.

Figure I.1.7. Different approaches to services innovation policy

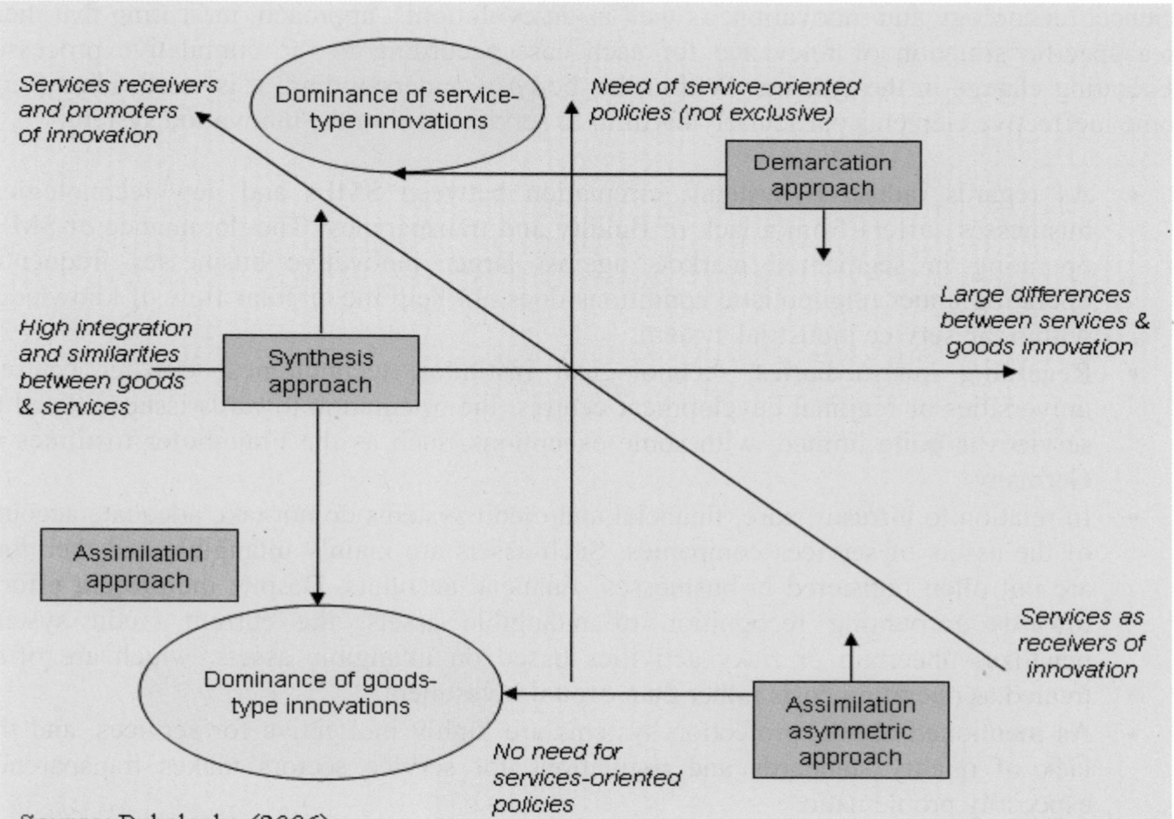

Source: Rubalcaba (2006)

Figure I.1.7 shows the most significant elements justifying a service innovation policy, not only from a neoclassical view point of market failures, but also from the contextual facts and the systemic or evolutionist approaches. Evidently, these three types of argument are interrelated, and cannot be understood in isolation. For example, asymmetric information creates a natural barrier that explains the degree of competition deficit in many service markets with attendant consequences for productivity and innovation. At an institutional level, these facts are not sufficiently recognised, and for this reason pro-innovative and pro-competitive actions are underdeveloped.

Many of the arguments discussed in this section apply also for other services-related policies, not only innovation policies. For example, employment and training policies or regulatory policies may be based on similar arguments (Rubalcaba, 2007). What is specific in justifying service innovation related policies is the uneven degree of certain market failures commonly used to justify public intervention in innovation (e.g. externalities and appropriation), and the specific neglect of service-related issues in the institutional systems, in R&D and innovation systems in particular.

At present, three distinct approaches to service innovation coincide, as analysed by Boden and Miles (2000), and previously by Gallouj (1996), from which varying implications of technological policy can be derived: "assimilation", "demarcation" and "synthesis". Extensions of these approaches have been carried out by Drejer (2002) and Rubalcaba (2006).

It is worth highlighting the fact that within the synthesis approach, complementarities between the most frequent service-type innovations (e.g. organizational) and the most frequent goods-type innovations (e.g. technological change) would be possible. There is some evidence regarding the complementarity between service innovation and new technologies (Licht and Moch, 1999, Gago and Rubalcaba, 2006), although this has not always been sufficiently considered, or the ICT is regarded as neither a necessary nor a sufficient condition for innovation (den Hertog et al., 2003).

A different typology of policies can be offered depending on the opinions in favour of or against the development of a specific innovation policy for services:

- *Pro-industrial status quo (goods and technological innovation issues alone).* Opinions fall within the assimilation approach, in favour of maintaining the status quo and denying the need of a service-related policy. This position is based on lines of argument such as: goods-oriented R&D is led by the most advanced countries; the intangibility of service innovation results prevents their evaluation; results are non-patentable, so there is an insufficient margin for IPR policy; aids to innovation could distort competition in the service sector, in addition to the obstacles already present; and, overall, innovation in the most productive sectors (the goods industries) is what is most important.

- *Extension to services (innovation "horizontal" policies should aim to cover services sectors).* Opinions in favour of a horizontal approach including services take the view that the starting point should be the inclusion of services in existing policies; and that there is no a priori theoretical justification to exclude services. Some horizontal measures that take greater account of the service role are required (this approach is the umbrella covering the majority of possibilities under the three-fold typology previously outlined: "deepening", "broadening" and "horizontalization").

- *Increased focus on service sectors (from specific manufacturing subsector-related policies to specific services subsector-related policies; policies that are needed to tackle services sectors in a vertical way: more specific actions with regard to financial, tourism, transport services, and so on).* There are also some views in favour of a specific focus on services. The degree of heterogeneity in the sector and the fact that not all services have the same problems or the same behaviour, would lead to the need for specific measures in particular markets. Even if services shared the same problems, different solutions could be required. It does not seem so straightforward to argue that a horizontal policy – beyond aids to businesses – is enough to fulfil the interests of sectors as varied as telecommunications, tourism, commerce or professional services. For instance, if there are whole sectors excluded from R&D programmes, the consequences of such a situation must be analysed together with the methods of promoting R&D in those specific sectors.

- *Services as a systemic dimension (existing and new policies should deal with the service dimension in any sector).* This claims to be a combination of the above-mentioned approaches, but it refers to a more integrated view of the service economy. It also includes two specific objectives. Firstly, the inclusion of intangible elements as objects of the innovation policies implies the acknowledgement that there are organizational aspects in all businesses, and that intangibles play a decisive role in innovation and growth. Secondly, its objective is not only to promote organizational improvements in goods companies or innovations in service companies, but also to improve the relationships between them, favouring the knowledge economy. In this context, KIS becomes an essential component of the innovative system, and more than simply one sector to be considered.

The final case tends to fit with evolutionist approaches, which stress the importance of systemic factors within the innovative process, and with results that are difficult to anticipate. Service innovation is understood as a horizontal element affecting the whole production system, and the lack of service innovation as a systemic failure. As stated at the outset, services are understood not only as an economic sector, but also as a dimension that needs to be reinforced. Services do not strictly require the extension of vertical innovation programmes similar to those launched by the public authorities with uneven results in manufacturing industries, but to be considered as another dimension – horizontal – of the innovation system.

The place of services as a dimension of innovation systems is justified by the role of advanced services in knowledge as a necessary intermediate input to improve the competitive and innovative capacity of any manufacturing or service company (Rubalcaba, 1999; Antonelli, 2000; Wood, 2001), their connections with new technologies, the e-service being a singular example (Sundbo et al., 2005), and especially their consolidation as part of the innovation system (Antonelli, 1999; Miles, 1999; Boden and Miles, 2000; Metcalfe and Miles, 2000; Muller, 2001b, Zenker, 2001, and Hipp and Grupp, 2005). The particular role of IT in service research and innovation has been recognised (Howells, 2006). An efficient performance of the KIS requires a broad reference framework that extends to the sectoral area, a framework encompassing the numerous ways in which these services influence current economic systems and their innovative nature.

Figure I.1.8 shows the main aforementioned positions compared with a specific policy for goods, as well as the position arising from the consideration of service innovation as a systemic dimension in the economy, of a horizontal nature.

Figure I.1.8. Approaches towards services innovation

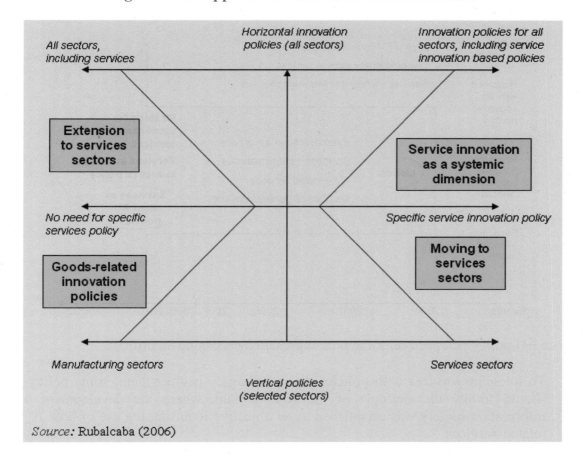

Source: Rubalcaba (2006)

H. FINAL REMARKS ON THE EU INNOVATION POLICY FOR SERVICES

This paper has shown the importance of service innovation in the European context, its specificities and differences with respect to manufacturing or goods innovation, its challenges and the reasons for sustaining policy support.

The inclusion of services innovation in the EU policy framework is very recent. As shown in Figure I.1.9, 2007-2008 is the period in which service innovation started to be clearly identified in the EU innovation policies. Although previous service and service innovation-related initiatives existed beforehand in the framework of the internal market for services, an EU information society policy where services were increasingly recognised together with ICT elements, the role of business-related services and the development of the services of general interest. All these policy areas either included services or focused upon them as a result of the Lisbon strategy in 2000. Before 2000, references to services were largely marginal, and focused on limited activities such as transport, health or business-support services. Nowadays, in 2010, services are relevant and present in an important set of EU policies. However, there is a still much to be done in order to fully integrate services in European policies.

Figure I.1.9. A route map towards recognising services innovation in Europe

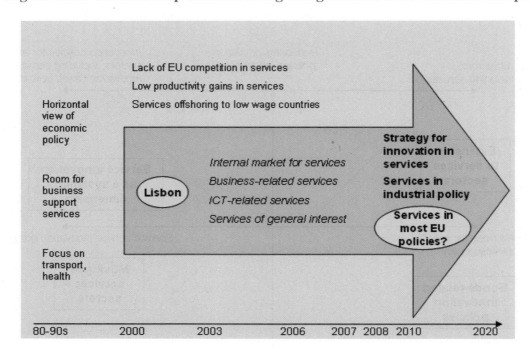

From an EU policy perspective, some pressing challenges can be identified:

- To integrate services with policies that still largely neglect them; some policy areas should follow the example of the ICT domain, where the development of the information society was established as an objective requiring the use of both ICT and related-services.
- To promote the development of services innovation policies at a national level. There are still many countries with no consideration of services within their innovation policies. Examples provided by the Innovation Policy Project in Services (IPPS), coordinated by the Finnish government, together with those of other countries presenting contributions in this volume, should be followed.
- To explore and profit from synergies between different policies affecting services innovation. As depicted in Figure I.1.10, services innovation involves the joint actions of several policy fields including internal market, competition, better regulation, employment, education, quality and regional policies, among others. A further coordination between regulatory policies and non-regulatory policies could be envisaged.

In short, recent years have provided some examples of best practices and meaningful developments in the area of services innovation. Significant progress has been made, both within the academic and research domain, as well as from the policy practice in certain EU Member States and some EU policies. However, there is no reason for complacency in the sense that there remains much to be done in terms of a full recognition of the importance of services innovation and the real integration of services into innovation policies. A final challenge may be added to this: current positive developments in the European context may be extended to other regions, including developing economies, where services innovation can act as a source of both economic growth and social development.

Figure I.1.10. Innovation and other service-related policies: potential synergies

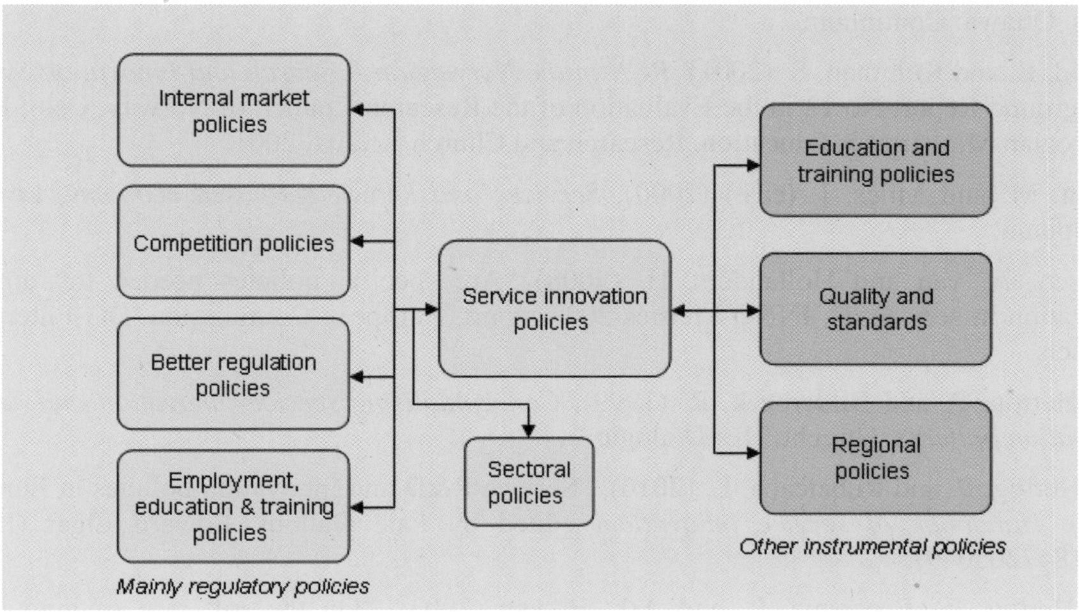

REFERENCES

Antonelli, C. (1999), *The microeconomics of technical change*, London and New York: Routledge.

Antonelli, C. (2000), "New information technology and localised technology change in the knowledge-based economy", in *Services and the knowledge-based economy,* eds. Boden and Miles, Ottawa: Continuum.

Arnold, E. and Kuhlman, S. (2001). *RCN in the Norwegian Research and Innovation System*, Background Report No 12 in the Evaluation of the Research Council of Norway, Oslo: Royal Norwegian Ministry for Education, Research and Church Affairs, 2001.

Boden, M. and Miles, I. (eds.) (2000), *Services and knowledge-based economy*, London: Continuum.

Cruysen, A. van and Hollanders, H. (2008) "Are specific policies needed to stimulate innovation in services?", INNO-Metrics 2007 report, European Commission, DG Enterprise, Brussels.

Den Hertog, P. and Bilderbeek, R. (1999), *Conceptualising service innovation and service innovation patterns*, Utrecht, NE: Dialogic.

Den Hertog, P. and Rubalcaba, L. (2010), "Service R&D and innovation policies in Europe", in the *Handbook of service innovation*, edited by Faiz Gallouj. Edward Elgar (ISBN: 978-1847205049).

Den Hertog, P., Broersma, L. and Ark, B. van (2003), "On the soft side of innovation: services innovation and its policy implications", *De Economist*, December, 151 (4), 433-452.

Drejer, I. (2002), "Business Services as a Production Factor", paper presented at the DRUID Summer Conference on Industrial Dynamics of the Old and New Economy, Copenhagen, 6-8 June 2002.

Evangelista, R., Sirilli, G. and Smith, K. (1998), "Measuring innovation in services", *IDEA Papers series*, STEP group.

Fitzsimmons, J.A., Anderson, E., Morrice, D. and Powell, G.E. (2004), "Managing service supply relationships", *International Journal of Services Technology and Management*, 5 (3), pp. 221–232.

Gadrey, J., Gallouj, F. and Weinstein, O. (1995), "New modes of innovation. How services benefit industry", *International Journal of Service Industry Management*, 6 (3), pp.4–16.

Gago, D. and Rubalcaba, L. (2007), "Innovation and ICT in service firms: towards a multidimensional approach for impact assessment", *Journal of Evolutionary Economics*, Volume 17, Number 1, pp. 25-44(20).

Gallego, J. and Rubalcaba, L. (2008), "Shaping R&D and services innovation in Europe", *International Journal of Service Technology and Management*, Vol. 9, Nos. 3/4, pp. 199–217.

Gallouj C. (1996), "Le commerce interrégional des services aux entreprises", Une revue de la littérature". *Revue d'Economie Régionale et Urbaine*, 3, pp.567-596.

Gallouj, C. and Gallouj, F. (1996), *L'innovation dans les Services*, Paris: Economica.

Gallouj, F. (1994), *Economie de l'innovation dans les services*, Paris: L'Harmattan / Logiques Economiques.

Gallouj, F. (2002), *Innovation in the service economy: the new wealth of nations*, Cheltenham: Edward Elagar.

Gámir, L. (1998), "Privatización, eficiencia y transparencia", ICE, 772, pp.27–44.

Gershuny, J. (1978), *After industrial society?*, London: Macmillan.

Grubel, H. (1995), "Producer services: their important role in growing economies", in Felli, E., Rosati, F.C. and Tria, G. (eds.), *The service sector: productivity and growth*, Heidelberg: Physica-Verlag.

Hipp, C. and Grupp, H. (2005), "Innovation in the service sector: the demand for service-specific innovation measurement concepts and typologies", *Research Policy*, 34 (4), pp.517-35.

Howells, J. (2001), *The nature of innovation in services. Innovation and productivity in services*, Paris: OECD.

Howells, J. (2004), "Innovation, consumption and services: encapsulation and the combinatorial role of services", *The service industries journal*, 24 (1), pp.19–36.

Howells, J. (2006), "Information technology research in the UK: perspectives on services research and development, and systems of innovation", *Science and Public Policy*, 33 (1), pp.17-31.

Kox, H. and Rubalcaba L. (2007), "The contribution of business services to European economy", in Rubalcaba, L. and Kox, H. (eds.), *Business Services in European Economic Growth*, London: MacMillan / Palgrave.

Licht, G. and Moch, D. (1999), "Innovation and information technology in services", *The Canadian Journal of Economics*, 32, pp.363-383.

Lucas, R. (1988), "On the mechanisms of economic development", *Journal of monetary economics*, 22, pp.3–42.

Metcalfe, S. and Miles, I. (eds.) (2000) *Innovation systems in the service economy: Measurement and case study analysis*, Kluwer Academic, London.

Miles, I. (1995), "Service, innovation, statistical and conceptual issues", Working group on innovation and technology policy, DSTI/ESA/STP/NESTI, 95/12, Paris: OECD.

Miles, I. (1999), "Foresight and services: closing the gap?", *The Service Industries Journal*, Volume 19, Issue 2, pp.1 - 27.

Miles, I. (2000), "Services innovation: coming of age in the knowledge-based economy", *International Journal of Innovation Management*, 4 (4), pp.371–89.

Miles, I. (2005a), "The future of R&D in services: implications for EU research and innovation policy", Foresight on services and R&D, Section 1, Main report, Platform foresight, Report prepared for DG Research, European Commission.

Miles, I. (2005b), "Knowledge-intensive Business Services: Prospects and policies", *Foresight – The Journal of Future Studies, Strategic Thinking and Policy*, 7(6), pp.39-63.

Muller, E. (2001a), "Knowledge, innovation processes and regions", in Koschatzky, K. Kulicke, M. and Zenker, A. (eds.), *Innovation networks: concepts and challenges in the European perspective*, Heidelberg: Physical-Verlag, pp.37–51.

Muller, E. (2001b). *Innovation interactions between knowledge-intensive business services and small and medium-size enterprises*. New York: Physica-Verlag, Heildelberg.

OECD (1993), *Proposed standard practice for surveys of research and experimental development – Frascati Manual*, Paris: OECD.

O'Doherty, D. and Arnold, E. (2003), "Understanding innovation: the need for a systemic approach", The IPTS Report, 71.

Reneser (2006), "Research and Development Needs of Business Related Service Firms", Final report to DG Internal Market and Services of the European Commission, Dialogic/ Fraunhofer/ PREST/ Servilab, Utrecht/ Stuttgart/ Manchester/ Madrid.

Romer, P. (1986), "Increasing returns and long-run growth", *Journal of political economy*, 94, pp.1002–1037.

Romer, P. (1990), 'Endogenous technical change', *Journal of political economy*, 98, pp.71-102.

Rubalcaba, L. (1999), *Business services in European industry: growth, employment and competitiveness*, Brussels / Luxembourg: European Commission DGIII-Industry.

Rubalcaba, L. (2004) "Innovation in services: current statistical needs and proposals for a better coverage", *Services sector statistics – Future needs and possible answers*, Workshop 29/30 June 2004, Luxembourg.

Rubalcaba, L. (2006), "Which policy for service innovation?", *Science and public policy*, Vol. 33, No. 10, pp. 745-756.

Rubalcaba, L. (2007), *The New Service Economy: Challenges and Policy implications for Europe*, Edward Elgar.

Rubalcaba, L. and Gallego, J. (2006), "The participation of business-related services in public R&D programmes: their particular role in EU Framework Programmes", Paper prepared for the European Commission project: *Evaluation of the R&D needs of business-related services enterprises*, Utrecht, the Netherlands.

Rubalcaba, L., Gallego, J. and Gago, D. (2010), "On the differences between goods and services innovation", *Journal of Innovation Economics*, Vol. 5, pp.17-40.

Schumpeter, J.A. (1939), *Business cycles: a theoretical, historical, and statistical analysis of the capitalist process*, New York and London: McGraw-Hill.

Schumpeter, J.A. (1942), *Capitalism, socialism and democracy*, London: Unwin.

Soete L. and Miozzo M. (1989), *Trade and Development in Services: A Technological Perspective*. Maastricht Economic Research Institute on Innovation and Technology (MERIT), Report No. 89–031.

Sundbo, J. (1998a), *The Organization of Innovation in Services*, Roskilde: Roskilde University Press.

Sundbo, J. (1998b), *The theory of innovation*. Cheltenham: Edward Elgar.

Sundbo, J. et al. (2005), *E-services within knowledge services – innovation, growth, employment and the consequences for business customers and citizens.* Proposal for the EU Commission (mimeo).

Tether, B. (2005), "Do Services Innovate (Differently)? Insights from the European Innobarometer Survey", *Industry and Innovation*, 12 (2).

Van Ark, B., Inklaar, R. and McGuckin, R. (2003a), "ICT and productivity in Europe and the United States. Where do the differences come from?", Research Memorandum, Groningen: GGDC.

Van Ark, B., Melka, J., Mulder, N., Timmer, M. and Ypma, G. (2003b), "ICT investment and growth accounts for the European Union 1980–2000", Research Memorandum, GD-56, Groningen: GGDC.

Van Ark, B., Broersma, L. and den Hertog, P. (2003c), *Services innovation, performance and policy: a review. Synthesis report in the framework of the SID project (structural information provision on innovation in services)*, The Hague: Directorate-General for Innovation, Ministry of Economic Affairs.

Windrum, P. and Tomlinson, P. (1999), "Knowledge-intensive services and international competitiveness: a four country comparison", *Technology Analysis and Strategic Management*, 11 (3), pp.391–408.

Wood, P. (2001), *Consultancy and innovation: the business services revolution in Europe*, Routledge: London and New York.

Zenker, A. (2001), 'Innovation, interaction and regional development: structural characteristics of regional innovation strategies', in Koschatzky, K., Kulicke, M. and Zenker, A. (eds.) *Innovation networks: concepts and challenges in the European perspective*, Heidelberg: Physica-Verlag, pp.207–222.

2. FROM UNDERSTANDING TO EXPLOITING SERVICE INNOVATION – THE PERSPECTIVE OF TRANSITION ECONOMIES

Metka Stare, Faculty of Social Sciences, Ljubljana, Slovenia

A. INTRODUCTION

Innovation has long been recognised as a key driver of economic growth, although in a way that was shaped by the approaches developed for innovation in manufacturing, which focused on technological breakthroughs enabled by research and development investment. The last decade has seen a growing awareness and acknowledgment of innovation taking place in service sectors and service activities throughout the economy and society. In addition, horizontal concepts of innovation are evolving that reach beyond traditional sectoral boundaries. These concepts result not only from the dominant role of the service sector in advanced economies, but also reflect the profound integration and complementarity of service activities with other sectors of economy and society. Innovation is becoming a systemic activity with the participation and contribution of actors from different areas. The omnipresence of information and communication technology (ICT), high speed broadband internet connections and the diffusion of social networks enhance the arrival of new services, new ways of organizing businesses and citizens and of connecting them with users. In parallel, ICT establishes the infrastructure for open, participative innovation with the potential to drive social innovation and pave the way for improving the welfare of citizens (Service Innovation, 2010).

Discussions regarding services innovation[5] have contributed in an important way to the economic literature on innovation. They have also come gradually to influence both strategic and policy considerations towards a greater focus on enhancing service innovation at the regional, national and international levels. Recent actions by the European Commission in the preparation of the EC innovation plan, the OECD Innovation Strategy's incorporation of broader concepts of innovation, as well as the policies of the most advanced countries with regard to services innovation, bear witness to the utmost importance of exploiting the potential of services innovation to address serious issues relating to economic crises, environmental problems, aging populations, climate change, etc. It is now increasingly evident that these emerging trends are important drivers of innovation and confirm that innovation impacts reach far beyond the traditional concept of 'competitiveness' to include welfare, environmental and societal problems (CEC, 2009, OECD Innovation Strategy, 2010). In this context, the challenges are yet more significant for transition economies, where innovation is still largely perceived through the lens of technological innovation. In particular,

---

[5] A Report of the Expert Group on Innovation in Services defines 'innovation in services' as innovation processes within service industries (as specified by the NACE and ISIC definitions); whilst 'service innovation' covers any innovation activity with service-like attributes that can occur in any part of the economy: manufacturing, agriculture, services or even informal parts of the economy. Thus, service innovation is used to denote both elements associated with innovation and services (Fostering Innovation in Services, 2007). We acknowledge the interpretation and apply it throughout the chapter.

there is a need for policymakers to fully consider the multi-dimensional nature of service innovation, which calls for a comprehensive and systemic approach to shaping the policies that would adequately address service innovation. This chapter aims to contribute to a better understanding of service innovation in transition economies[6] by highlighting the key properties of service innovation, shedding light on its complexity and identifying some of the key barriers to service innovation. In conclusion, some guidelines are presented for ensuring that innovation policy in transition economies adequately reflects service innovation.

B. DISTINCTIVE FEATURES OF SERVICES INNOVATION AND TYPOLOGY

The traditional approach to innovation is to treat it as a technical change, derived from a radical new or improved technical solution to a manufacturing problem. Within such a conceptual framework, services as limited users of traditional technologies were generally regarded as non-innovative. However, Schumpeter already defined innovation as "the introduction of new elements or a new combination of elements in the production or delivery of manufactured and service products" (Schumpeter, 1934). Such a concept of innovation embraces different areas of innovation activity, some even more service sector specific (for example market and organizational innovation). It is argued that the "Schumpeterian scheme provides a framework for studying manufacturing and services on the same terms, giving services the attention that the volume and growth of service activities justifies" (Drejer, 2004).

Due to the pervasive role of services in advanced economies and the central role played by innovation in economic development, a wider understanding of service innovation is gradually emerging. There has been a growth in the scale and scope of analyses dealing with services innovation, and these reveal the key features distinguishing innovation in services from that in manufacturing, as well as the similarities. According to Gallouj (2002), there are three principal approaches to research on innovation in services: the technologist approach, the service-oriented approach and the integrative approach. While the first approach focuses on the introduction of technology into service organizations, the second broadens innovation in services to include service-specific forms of innovation (e.g. ad hoc innovation, intangible processes and products), as additions to technical innovation. The integrative approach, however, suggests there is no need to treat innovation in services separately from innovation in manufacturing due to the growing convergence between the two. Other scholars confirm the need for a synthesis approach to innovation by the inadequacy of the traditional, technologist approach even in manufacturing, where non-technological innovations also occur (Drejer, 2004). They argue that services innovation is multi-dimensional and to a large extent characterised by organizational changes, which include new service concepts, new client interfaces and new service delivery systems (Van Ark et. al., 2003; Howells, Tether, 2004). They do, however, establish that technological and non-technological innovations are complementary, with individual dimensions differing in importance between various service activities (Van Ark et. al., 2003). As argued by Sundbo, the types of innovations in services are mainly social in comparison to manufacturing, where they are more focused on physical

---

[6] We apply the term transition economies especially to the former socialist countries of East and Central Europe that have become new EU member states in 2004 and in 2007 (Bulgaria, Czech Republic, Estonia, Hungary, Latvia, Lithuania, Poland, Romania, Slovakia and Slovenia). These countries share certain similarities in past socio-economic development, which form the environment for innovation policy and could be to some extent generalized to other transition economies as well.

objects, and more radical in their nature[7]. Further insights into the discussion on service innovation properties were brought about by the concepts of user innovation and open innovation. Innovation is being democratised, with end users playing a crucial role in the innovation process by co-creating new products and services (von Hippel, 2005). While these concepts apply to innovation in general, they are of particular relevance to service innovation, where interactivity between suppliers and users is essential. Nevertheless, the analysis of service innovation has so far been focused on supply-driven characteristics.

Features distinguishing services from the manufacturing sector (intangibility, interaction between suppliers and customers, information-intensity, informational asymmetries) make the conceptualisation of service innovation a difficult task. In addition, service innovation is usually incremental as opposed to radical in nature, and consequently less visible. Finally, service innovation is less formalised and is rarely carried out in research and development departments. It occurs along the whole value chain, and with cooperation and interaction between different actors, including suppliers, intermediate and final customers. User-driven innovation thus presents enormous potential for driving service innovation in different activities.

Further complexity in the conceptualisation of service innovation comes from its multi-dimensional character (technological and organizational innovation), and the terminology used to define it. The distinction is often made between technological and non-technological innovation, in which case the latter may assume an ambiguous or pejorative connotation, in contrast to technological innovation. In addition, the term 'non-technological innovation' does not clearly allude to organizational and marketing innovations providing new solutions to customer needs (business models, distribution channels, customer interfaces). Service sectors and service functions assume various roles in the innovation process that need to be fully acknowledged. Service sectors innovate and generate new services based on information and communication technologies (e.g. e-banking), or applying new organizational approaches (e.g. door-to-door delivery). Owing to the increased inter-linkages between services and other sectors, knowledge-intensive services facilitate innovation elsewhere (e.g. university research input to new drug development in the pharmaceutical sector, or marketing and design in the production of standardised goods, such as cars or home appliances).

The boundary between different types of service innovation is, however, much less clear cut, and in many instances service innovation appears at the intersection of different types of innovation that address the needs of businesses or end users. The complementary nature of various types of service innovation is further confirmed by practices at the firm level, where firms will simultaneously generate, adopt and implement multiple forms of innovation[8]. For example, firms that introduce product or process innovation are very likely to also introduce innovation in organization and marketing. The Community Innovation Survey (2006)

---

[7] Social innovations, as opposed to technological innovations, are intellectual or behavioural (Sundbo, 2001).
[8] The launch of iPod by Apple is considered to have used quite a few types of innovation. The company adopted the iTunes software platform developed by another firm; launched innovative design which turned an MP3 player into an elegant device without lots of buttons, but one wheel to serve all the same functions; introduced a novel business model by signing an agreement with music companies to sell their songs online, etc. The result of a series of innovations is the outstanding market success of iPod.

confirms that, on average, 77% of firms engaged in innovation activity[9] in EU27 also introduced organizational and/or marketing innovation (Eurostat Statistics in focus, 2009).

Table I.2.1 seeks to capture the complexity of services innovation via a simplified typology, and illustrates it with concrete examples of different types of services innovation. The reality of service innovation is, however, richer and more diverse.

Table I.2.1. The typology of service innovation

	Service sectors	Service functions
Technological innovation	Banking services: ATM services, e-banking; Retail trade: on line shopping; Education and training: e-learning.	Satellite monitoring of fertiliser use in farming; Design in automotive industry.
Organizational innovation	Air transport: low cost carrier services; Catering services: door-to-door delivery of food.	Direct marketing in selling tourist products; Outsourcing of human resource management in construction.
Combination of innovation	E-commerce via internet; Public administration : one stop shop services for company establishment via e-platform	

The multi-faceted nature of service innovation (as illustrated in the table above) makes it difficult to fully capture the phenomenon at play in official innovation statistics which, despite significant improvements, remain insufficient. In particular, current approaches facilitate the measurement of service innovation exclusively in the service sectors, while service innovation in other sectors remains hidden. Innovation surveys such as the Community Innovation Survey (CIS) are the most widely used source of comparative data on innovation in the EU, and have also gradually incorporated statistics relating to innovation in the service sectors[10]. The data tend to focus on the technological dimensions of innovation in products/services and process innovation. Starting with CIS2 a group of market services was included in innovation surveys, and with CIS3 an indicator for non-technical change and innovation was introduced to reflect advanced management techniques, new or significantly changed organizational structures or significant changes in the aesthetic appearance or design of a product. However, firms that introduced non-technological changes were not counted as innovators. The 2005 revision of the Oslo Manual finally resulted in the incorporation of organizational and marketing innovation into the CIS 2008, which will facilitate the improved capture of broadly defined innovation activity in companies[11], thereby addressing the current under-representation at the aggregate level. The provisional data of CIS 2008 for Slovenia[12] confirm a substantial difference in the share of innovation-active companies. When both technological and non-technological innovators are taken into account, the share of companies engaged in innovation activity amounted to 50.3% in 2008, while the share of companies that introduced only technological innovation (new products, processes or services) accounted

---

[9] Those that introduced new products, services or processes.

[10] Transition economies, most notably new member states of the EU joined the innovation surveys with CIS3, except for Poland and Slovenia who have even earlier conducted surveys similar to CIS2.

[11] The Oslo Manual (2005) defines four types of innovation: product innovation, process innovation, marketing innovation and organizational innovation.

[12] SORS, 2010.

for 34.4 % of the total population of companies[13]. Even though the CIS 2008 data represent a significant breakthrough in innovation statistics, the improved measurement of innovation activity needs to remain firmly on the agenda of national and international institutions. The OECD proposes some key actions including, for example, improved measurement of broader innovation and its link to economic performance, the measurement of innovation in the public sector, the integration of outcome measures of innovation activity, etc. (OECD Innovation Strategy, 2010).

Service innovation is a dynamically evolving phenomenon that gains momentum with the rapid diffusion of new technologies, and growing pressures from environmental and social challenges. It remains to be fully understood, and its potential for increased competitiveness and welfare are not fully grasped. While some advanced economies are now actively addressing new challenges for service innovation, the transition economies have only recently begun to explore them. The following section addresses the major weaknesses that remain for transition economies in embracing service innovation.

C. THE CONTEXT OF TRANSITION ECONOMIES AND SERVICES INNOVATION

Historical background and services innovation

In the last two decades, the service sector has acquired a dominant position in terms of value-adding and employment in most transition economies. There are a number of transition economies where services surpass the 60% share. Moreover, services are key inputs to all sectors of the economy, and contribute to enhancing economic efficiency and welfare. Services are also deemed essential in manufacturing's renewal process, facilitating the introduction of new products to the market. Nonetheless, previous shortcomings in innovation policy with respect to services in transition economies could not be overcome in such a relatively short timescale. Services 'catch up' was faster in traditional areas such as distribution and transport, while knowledge-intensive services lag much farther behind relative to standards in advanced economies. Modest quality and low efficiency, as well as slow internationalization of the service sector appear to be further weaknesses in service sector development, reflecting on the one hand insufficient competition in service markets, and weak innovation activity in services on the other (Stare, 2007).

Transition economies have historically neglected the innovation potential of services as a determinant of growth and competitiveness. This neglect has its origin in the ideological view of services as unproductive labour, and in the material concept of valuing production (Kostecki, 1996). Consequently, the understanding of innovation was limited to technological changes in manufacturing with a tradition or history, while an understanding of the specificities of innovation in services was lacking. Transition economies, which have in the past overlooked the importance of services for enhanced efficiency, have difficulties in fully recognizing the innovative potential of services. In services, innovation is seldom achieved by formal R&D, but mostly through organizational change and innovative marketing methods (Van Ark et al., 2003), and also extends beyond the service sector. It is therefore perhaps

---

[13] Preliminary data based on CIS 2008 questionnaire for European countries are expected to be published by Eurostat in June 2010.

unsurprising that service innovation is not easily understood and integrated into innovation policies in transition economies.

The latest available data on innovation activity[14] in new member states indicate that they perform less strongly than most EU15 countries both in services and manufacturing, with the notable exception of Estonia (Figure I.2.1). This is the only new member state whose innovation activity in services exceeds the EU27 average. Innovation activity in manufacturing[15] is on average more intensive than in services in all EU27 countries, with the exception of Latvia, Greece and Portugal. There exists, however, a positive correlation between the intensity of innovation activity in manufacturing and in services[16], pointing to common set of factors that underpins innovation activity in particular countries, irrespective of the sector. Based on the data from Figure I.2.1, the gap in innovation activity between the new member states and more advanced EU countries does not appear to be significantly greater in services than in manufacturing. In the next section we assess the barriers to service innovation in transition economies that might provide additional justification for this.

Figure I.2.1. The share of enterprises engaged in innovation activity: manufacturing and services, EU27*, 2006

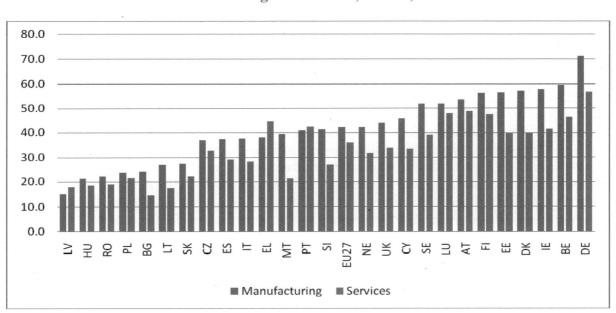

*Data for France not available.
Source: CIS5, Eurostat.

---

[14] Even though we rely on a single indicator we believe that the latter is the end result of a variety of factors in enterprises and in a wider innovation environment that impacts the intensity of innovation (from skilled workforce and management strategy of the enterprise to innovation support mechanisms and efficient market competition).

[15] Scholars suggest caution in cross-country comparisons of innovation capacity in services and in manufacturing on account of the different character of innovation in both sectors. Innovation in manufacturing depends on accumulated capacity and know-how to a far larger extent than is the case in services. Accordingly, service firms progress much faster in innovation activity than manufacturing firms (Kanerva et al., 2006).

[16] Rank correlation of innovation intensity in manufacturing and services amounts to 0.89 for EU27 (excluding France).

Obstacles to services innovation in transition economies

A growing awareness of the importance of innovation in services prompted investigation of the key factors deterring it. The relative importance of barriers to innovation in services identified by different studies and surveys varies across service industries, size of service enterprises and across countries (Preissl, 1998, Kuusisto, Meyer, 2003, Van Ark et al., 2003). The third Community Innovation Survey (CIS3 data refer to 2000) represented the most comprehensive investigation to date of the barriers to innovation in services in the new member states (NMS), and did not find significantly differing obstacles to innovation in services across countries. High innovation costs, a lack of appropriate finance, a perception of excessive risks and the lack of qualified personnel were ranked as the most important barriers to innovation by service firms (Eurostat, 2004). The comparisons of barriers to innovation in services between the EU15 and the NMS do, however, reveal some differences. In particular, a higher proportion of enterprises in the EU15 perceive economic risk as a highly important barrier to innovation in services than in the NMS. Similarly, the lack of qualified personnel is seen as a highly important barrier to innovation in services to a larger share of enterprises in the EU15 than in the NMS. While innovation costs are assessed as a highly important barrier to innovation by a high proportion of service enterprises in both the EU15 and in the NMS, the relative importance of this barrier appears greater in the EU15. The only barrier that seems more pronounced for service enterprises in at least some of the NMS compared to the EU15 is access to finance for innovation[17].

The above results, together with the substantial variability in the perceived relative importance of the various factors limiting innovation in services in some NMS, question the reliability and consistency of responses obtained in the NMS by the survey[18]. Nevertheless, the results may accurately reflect the perception in the NMS enterprises that lack of finance and high innovation costs are the major barriers to innovation in services. Other barriers (e.g. the availability of qualified personnel, organizational rigidities), do not yet affect innovation to a noticeable extent due to a lower level of innovation activity. However, we argue that the obstacles affecting innovation in services in the NMS and possibly also in other transition economies are related to specific patterns of socio-economic development, and to the overall business framework. Some of the barriers refer to innovation in general, while others are service innovation-specific.

General barriers

Peculiarities of the business environment and related cultural determinants, knowledge and skills deficiencies, institutional and systemic impediments are seen as the most relevant general barriers to innovation in NMS (Bučar and Stare, 2002). Notwithstanding significant improvements in enhancing entrepreneurship in the transition economies, the dismantling of cultural barriers and changes in the value systems (e.g. risk-aversion) may take much longer to achieve. This requires a systematic approach, integrating the knowledge on innovation,

---

[17] This indicates that financial markets in the NMS are less developed and insufficiently equipped to provide different types of support to innovating firms.

[18] In Lithuania, for example, only 1% of innovation active enterprises in services report innovation costs as a highly important barrier while in other NMS this amounts to at least 15% of innovation active enterprises in services (Statistics in Focus, 2004).

innovation policy and the management of innovation. Deficiencies in adequate knowledge and skills are one of the key remaining barriers to innovation activity in the transition economies, particularly when we consider that knowledge rapidly becomes obsolete, and needs to be updated on an ongoing basis. A major shortcoming in the transition economies seems to relate to the question of how to translate invention into innovation. Here, aside from the lack of appropriate financial mechanisms, other factors come in to play. It is our educated guess that poor commercialization of inventions has to do both with the narrow (technical) understanding of innovation and with the legacy of central planning, which focused on "how to produce" issues, while "how to market" issues were not important. Moreover, a predominant supply orientation on the part of businesses and policymakers impedes uptake of the demand driven innovation paradigm. Despite the progress achieved to date, the lack of managerial and marketing competences and skills required for a successful innovation process continues to restrict the dynamics and efficiency of innovation activity in transition economies.

Development of national innovation policy was not regarded as a priority issue in economic policy in these economies during the transition, and even when it entered the policy agenda, a narrow view of the national innovation system was taken. As highlighted by Mickiewicz and Radošević (2001) for the transition countries as a group: "innovation policy was considered secondary to the transition related concerns". Also, under the influence of EU innovation policy, the NMS have introduced a number of instruments and mechanisms to support innovation, but policies have largely concentrated on the institutions that promote the acquisition and dissemination of knowledge, and are the main sources of (technological) innovation. They have tended to disregard mechanisms, which provide support through managerial knowledge or financial schemes (Bučar, Stare, 2002).

Service-specific barriers

These largely reflect the shortcomings of service markets' development in transition economies, and deficiencies in policymakers' understanding of the complexity of the services innovation process. Insufficient competition has a specific impact on innovation in services, where transition economies experienced much weaker competitive pressures even after the introduction of market-oriented reforms. This is the result of a slow deregulatory process (dismantling barriers for new entrants to the services market), as well as insufficient institutional and human capacity to effectively implement new regulations. Taking account of the fact that the degree of competition significantly influences the capacity to generate demand for innovation (Radosevic, 2004) lower levels of competition in the transition economies imply less pressure on the service enterprises to invest in innovative activity. FDI inflows to the service sectors and progressive liberalization of services have to some extent contributed to improving the situation.

Even though the services sector witnessed impressive overall growth in value added during transition, the structure of the sector did not undergo a similarly dynamic change. The lagging of the NMS and other transition economies behind the EU15 remains particularly troublesome in the knowledge-intensive service sectors, such as various business services (innovation management, consultancy, testing, design, marketing, etc.), which play a critical role in turning new ideas into marketable innovation[19]. These services generate new knowledge, process it and diffuse it within the innovation systems (Miles, 2001 Muller, Zenker, 2001). Not only are these services highly 'innovation active', they also serve as a catalyst for the dissemination of innovation throughout the economy[20]. This is clearly illustrated by Figure I.2.2, which displays the strong correlation between the share of employment in knowledge-intensive services and the countries' innovation capacities, as proxied by the summary innovation index[21] (correlation coefficient 0.81). Hence, the deficient supply of knowledge-intensive services presents both a general impediment to innovation in all sectors, and a specific obstacle to services innovation.

Figure I.2.2. Knowledge-intensive services and innovation in Europe, 2008

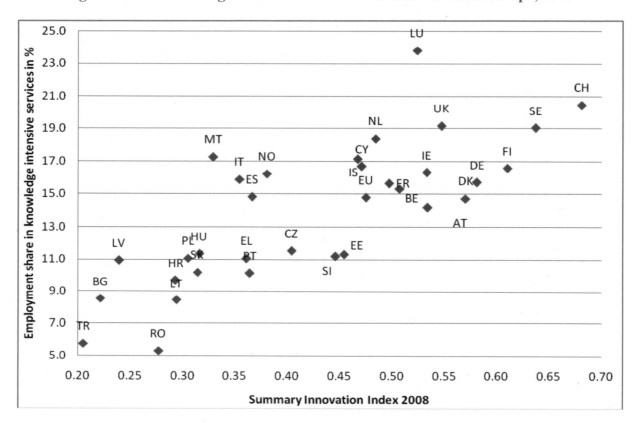

Source: European Innovation Scoreboard, 2008.

The level of development of knowledge-intensive services determines the intensity of interaction between services and other sectors of the economy. Further, the role of

---

[19] The lag of transition economies in this regard has its origin in the pre-transition economic system where business services were commonly internalized within large manufacturing enterprises. The latter did not dispose with specialized knowledge and skills for individual service functions such as marketing, advertising, quality control, management, technical services, consulting.

[20] As revealed by CIS5 data the share of innovative enterprises in business services is higher or similar to the share of innovative enterprises in manufacturing in most EU27 countries.

[21] Summary innovation index is a composite of 29 indicators that depict enablers of innovation activity, firm activities and outputs of the innovation activity. It provides comparative assessment of the innovation performance of EU27, as well as of Croatia, Turkey, Iceland, Norway and Switzerland.

knowledge-intensive services must be viewed from a service innovation specific perspective, which is driven more by non-technological or organizational innovation. The implementation of this type of innovation depends critically upon the availability and sophistication of knowledge-intensive services. The present level of knowledge-intensive services development in the transition economies, coupled with insufficient competition, neither requires nor encourages innovation. As innovation in knowledge-intensive services is critically related to the diffusion of ICT, and given that the latter was slower in the transition economies compared to the EU15, it held back service innovation at the same time.

Nevertheless, innovation is emerging in the transition economies in the service sector and in service activities[22]. Services and manufacturing companies are increasingly aware of the need to extend their innovation activities beyond R&D, and make use of innovation potential throughout the value chain. Service innovation is frequently occurring implicitly via the introduction of information-communication technology platforms that generate new services and solutions for customers. As seen in the cases of Estonian and Latvian knowledge-intensive service firms, as well as creating new services they also generate high-income employment and increase value added in manufacturing (Regional KIS, 2010). Another important channel of service innovation in transition economies is the diffusion of innovative management techniques, the introduction of new organizational models, new distribution channels and changes in the relationship with customers. Even so, a critical mass of firms undertaking service innovation in individual transition economies is lacking, and therefore failing to exert a stronger influence on competitiveness. As a result, the innovation potential in services has been insufficiently exploited, suggesting that governments need to play a more active role in reshaping innovation policy towards an explicit focus on services innovation.

D. IS THERE A ROLE FOR POLICY IN PROMOTING INNOVATION IN SERVICES?

The experience of the advanced economies

The specific properties of service innovation broaden the scope of policy intervention and pose a challenge to the shaping of innovation policy. Owing to the heterogeneity of services in relation to market structures, rivalry and regulatory environments, individual service sectors face distinct market and system failures that appear more significant than in manufacturing. Both market and system failures result in under-investment in R&D and innovation activities in services. This calls for stronger policy support through direct R&D and innovation policies as well as through indirect policies including competition policies, education policies, labour market and training policies (Rubalcaba et al., 2010). The experience of developed countries indicates that innovation in services was, until very recently, rarely the target of government support to innovation (Green, Howells, Miles, 2001). Nevertheless, the dominant role of services in national economies on the one hand, and a largely untapped potential for service innovation to contribute to improved competitiveness

---

[22] When referring to such changes, the entrepreneurs in Slovenia do not talk about service innovation, but rather about process changes, new business models or at best about non-technological innovation. It is our educated guess that similar problems and confusion about the terminology probably appears also in other transition economies. Further, cases of good practices in service innovation are usually communicated to a fairly limited audience.

on the other, have led to greater recognition that stimulation of services innovation is necessary and could be done in various fields (e.g. investment in ICT, human resource development, a more conducive entrepreneurial environment) (Van Ark, 2003, Howells, Tether, 2004). Moreover, it is acknowledged that the linkages between services and manufacturing need to be taken account of in the shaping of innovation policy, a fact which is already reflected in some developed countries (Rubalcaba, 2006)[23].

The European Commission (EC) supports activities that contribute to improved understanding of the specific nature of innovation in services, and to the shaping of related policy and accompanying instruments (Fostering Innovation in Services, 2007, CEC, 2007, CEC, 2009). New policy initiatives in support of services innovation extend horizontal framework policies and propose specific policy agendas for the service sectors. In terms of extending horizontal framework policies, a set of policy mechanisms are proposed associated with services innovation in the following areas: legal and regulatory frameworks, the knowledge base, entrepreneurship and finance and demand, including public procurement. Specific measures introduced by individual countries range from supporting R&D in the service sectors, fostering innovation in ICT, tourism, healthcare, logistics or in service clusters, through to innovation awards with a specific category for service innovation[24]. Some EU15 countries, most notably Sweden, the United Kingdom, Denmark, Finland and the Netherlands have developed good practices in promoting services innovation. Recently, there has been a strong trend towards introducing innovation voucher schemes to enhance service innovation, mostly via support to market studies, innovation management and business process engineering[25]. The existing policies and instruments in support of service innovation in EU countries indicate the direction of travel for potential policy actions, although it is for each country to adopt measures that best address its specific innovation gaps in services.

Scope for policy learning in transition economies

It seems evident that transition economies need to advance service innovation through a more explicitly supportive policy framework, and design appropriate policy measures reflecting the specificities of services innovation. What are their experiences in this respect so far? INNO-Policy Trendchart[26] reveals that NMS and candidate countries have launched a number of horizontal initiatives that could in the longer term encourage service innovation. There are, however, a very limited number of measures explicitly addressing service innovation. The most commonplace horizontal measures refer to human resources development, innovation awareness raising, upgrading skills in innovation management, promotion of ICT use in businesses, the introduction of clusters, linking manufacturing and service firms and entrepreneurship support, in particular to assist small enterprises in the start-up phase. On the one hand, support measures focus on direct support to R&D and innovation activity in enterprises by offering subsidies for R&D and innovation costs. Here, the problem appears to

---

[23] Such a case is the programme of the German government from 2006 – Innovation with services – that served as the basis for the introduction of instruments aimed at encouraging innovation in services, irrespective of activity in which companies are engaged (Rubalcaba, 2006).

[24] For a detailed description of measures see Challenges for EU support to innovation in services (CEC, 2009).

[25] Availability and Focus on Innovation Voucher Schemes in European Regions (EC, 2009) http://www.europe-innova.eu/c/document_library/get_file?folderId=122731&name=DLFE-6403.pdf

[26] For a full set of new measures in innovation policies in NMS, see INNO Policy Trendchart: policy measures site.

be that, while the measure is in itself sector neutral[27], the evaluation processes of the applications/projects received often remain biased towards technological innovation. The second set of measures support intermediate institutions including technology parks, incubators, design centres, advisory services in the area of different managerial skills and the application of contemporary ICT solutions for more efficient business management, as well as stimulating provision of start-up capital by establishing various public-private venture funds[28]. By and large, policy orientation and accompanying support measures concentrate on the supply side of innovation capability, while the demand side remains poorly addressed. As paraphrased by Edler, The Central and East European countries have one limping leg when walking the innovation path, since the efforts to articulate and support demand for innovations do not keep pace with attempts to boost supply (Edler, 2009).

To further illustrate some of the deficiencies in innovation policy design as it pertains to service innovation, we summarize the findings of a Service Innovation policy mapping exercise in Slovenia[29] (Stare, Bučar, 2007). The instruments of innovation policy were found to be largely generic in nature, and could be applied to all enterprises, irrespective of their sector. Yet their focus remains supporting the R&D that is linked primarily to technological innovation in manufacturing. Whereas various policy documents support broadly defined innovation that explicitly incorporates innovation in services, this is frequently forgotten when it comes to the practical design of policy instruments and mechanisms. The survey of existing measures and instruments in Slovenia to promote innovation reveals that they neither explicitly discouraged nor encouraged innovation in services[30]. In fact, a number of infrastructure support measures and networking mechanisms were introduced that have some potential and could facilitate service innovation. They were, however, poorly utilized due to modest awareness about service innovation or due to the fact that, in the implementation phase, these measures were revealed to be inappropriate for encouraging innovation in service firms or in service functions. The assessment criteria for the selection of beneficiaries of different programmes and mechanisms were not suited to service firms or to the specificities of service innovation, which revolves around intangible assets, non-technological innovation, methods and models[31].

---

[27] Description of the measure usually refers to « new product, process or service«, which is to be the result of R&D and innovation efforts.

[28] These measures, while not directed specifically to innovation in services, by themselves often support the development of knowledge-intensive services and their more intensive use in enterprises.

[29] The Service innovation policy mapping study on Slovenia was a part of Innovation Policy Project in Services (IPPS) carried out by Tekes, the Finnish Funding Agency for Technology and Innovation. http://www.proinno-europe.eu/page/publications-2

[30] Similar findings are confirmed in Service Innovation policy mapping document for the Czech Republic.

[31] In 2009, Slovenia introduced pilot innovation voucher with the aim to encourage cooperation and transfer of knowledge from research institutions to small firms. The instrument provides for co-financing of the costs of industrial research services needed by small firms in developing an innovative project. While in principle every small firm could apply for the innovation voucher, assessment criteria for the application make the instrument inappropriate for most service firms. The call stipulates that the beneficiary of the innovation voucher has to submit a patent application at the national patent office as a final result of the cooperation with the research institution. Acknowledging the gap, the voucher system was revised in 2010 so as to encourage also the innovation in firms that aim to introduce new models or trademarks as a result of their cooperation with research institutions.

In addition, the institutional organization to support innovation in transition economies favours traditional (linear) models of innovation, which are essentially technology and R&D related, and focus upon supply. Policies still focus on supporting high-tech, science based industries and, more recently, on promoting the linkages between research institutions and companies to foster technology uptake (Radoševic, 2004). Such an approach neglects an important shift from producers (supply) to users (demand) and related drivers of innovation.

It has been revealed that user-driven innovation, which is of particular significance for service innovation, makes little use of R&D activities, but relies more on the skills of engineers, managers and marketing staff. Furthermore, users (from the business or consumer market), could provide valuable signals to suppliers as to the characteristics of the products and services they prefer. In a number of activities, users can become co-creators of new products and services. The user-centric approach also creates a new business opportunity in service activities. These changes necessitate a different form of innovation policy support - one possibly focusing on capability development (Flowers et al., 2009) and user needs. The mix of skills needed for empowering innovation capacity include technical, but also non-technical skills, such as management, communication, marketing, creativity and collaboration among actors involved in the innovation processes.

Owing to the complex nature of service innovation, its multi-dimensionality and the number of stakeholders involved, it is clear that no single policy could contribute to rapid and substantial progress in service innovation. Transition economies need to adopt both horizontal and vertical (service sector specific) approaches in shaping policies to support service innovation. This calls for careful design and coordination among policies and measures in different fields to create synergies in the policy mix. In addition, policymakers should resist straightforward, non-critical imitation of supporting policy instruments applied in other countries, but rather learn from good practices and adapt them to the local capabilities and absorption capacity. Experience shows that, after the introduction of transition reforms and related institutional changes, the policymakers in transition economies have paid insufficient attention to their own socio-economic framework in transferring policy instruments from countries with a more advanced economic and institutional setting (Bučar, Stare, 2010).

The shaping of a services inclusive innovation policy and supporting instruments will differ among transition economies. However, some key elements and steps should not be overlooked. What follows is an indication of a non-exhaustive set of steps that could help transition economies in designing supportive policies for services innovation:

- Awareness raising among all stakeholders regarding the distinguishing features of service innovation and its benefits[32]. It needs to be recognized that innovation is taking place not only in service sectors, but also in service activities throughout the economy and society;

---

[32] Civil society organizations and professional organizations could play an important role in raising the awareness on different dimensions of innovation in broad public, such as for example the InnoAwareness programme, Estonia: http://proinno.intrasoft.be/index.cfm?fuseaction=wiw.measures&page=detail&ID=8178; Innovation communication movement, Slovenia: http://www.incomovement.si/foundations-of-the-inco-movement; and Innovation journalism http://injo.stanford.edu/node/35

- Identification of good local practices of service innovation by firms, institutions or the public sector, together with wide dissemination to foster take up and learning by businesses and policymakers;
- Introduction of innovation awards that target service innovation;
- Identification of the most important barriers to service innovation before shaping policy instruments to address these;
- Accommodation of existing support measures for innovation to better suit service innovation properties (in particular, specific tailoring of the eligibility criteria to be fulfilled by service innovators);
- Enhanced measures that target demand/user driven innovation (e.g. public procurement) to complement supply side innovation policies;
- Strengthened research, education and training in the field of humanities and social science related to service innovation (for instance in innovation management, user- and employee-driven innovation, consumer behaviour, marketing, new business models, cultural understanding, and communication). These areas of research and their respective skills have been neglected in transition economies compared to the more technological aspects of innovation research and education;
- Promotion of interdisciplinary education and skills, as service innovation is about problem solving, which needs to be addressed from various disciplines;
- Set-up of ICT-supported innovation platforms that enable networking and cooperation among stakeholders based on open innovation principles; and
- Small and local projects, where focusing on local user needs and learning to cooperate among actors might be less problematic than for the traditional "big projects" at the national level.

E. CONCLUDING REMARKS

The main conclusions of our analysis are based on the experience of new member states (NMS) with service innovation. They reflect the shortcomings of service markets' development, bias to supply side orientation and insufficient understanding of the complexity of the service innovation processes. These deficiencies are, however, even more pronounced for other transition economies, where structural and institutional reforms are not as advanced as in the NMS. It comes as no surprise that transition economies need to reinforce efforts to make best use of all assets for upgrading the innovation outcome of their economies. While increased expenditure on R&D is considered a prerequisite to launching new products and technologies, the analysis suggests that technological innovations per se cannot resolve the problem of insufficient competitiveness, let alone alleviate broader societal problems.

Transition economies need to establish new levers to promote growth, competitiveness and welfare improvement, and this is an area where service innovation could pave the way ahead. It is important to bear in mind that, alongside generating new services, service innovation is a key driver for the restructuring of manufacturing, and for modernization in the public sector. To date, public services in transition economies failed to evolve in line with new innovation concepts, hence the imperative to innovate is strong not only in terms of increasing efficiency, but also with regard to improved transparency and responsiveness to user needs. Finally, service innovation, which by definition builds on interactions among different actors, could provide new solutions for transition economies in coping with the great societal challenges of the day, such as environment, climate change, health, food and water security.

There is ample space for horizontal and vertical policy measures in promoting services innovation. The former would create supportive framework conditions (business and entrepreneurship-friendly environments, availability of a range of financial mechanisms, skills and education), and the latter would require the design of concrete policy mechanisms to support service innovations. The major challenge remains, however, how to translate the 'soft' side of service innovation into innovation policy measures in different fields that would constitute a coherent policy mix. Whereas the tangible economic benefits of service innovation may be expected to emerge only in the longer run, delays in providing support to service innovation now may impede growth and the 'catch-up' process in transition economies.

REFERENCES

Bučar, M. and Stare, M. (2002), "Slovenian Innovation Policy: Unexploited Potential for Growth", *Journal of International Relations and Development*, Vol.5, No.4, pp. 427-448.

Bučar, M. and Stare, M. (2010), "From Policy Imitation to Policy Learning: governance of innovation policy in the new EU member states", GARNET Policy brief, No.12, March 2010. http://www.garnet-eu.org/

Drejer, I. (2004), "Identifying innovation in surveys of services: a Schumpeterian perspective", *Research Policy*, no. 33, pp. 551-562.

Edler, J. (2009), "Demand Policies for Innovation in CEE EU Countries", *Manchester Business School Research Paper No. 579.*

Europe INNOVA (2007), "Fostering Innovation in Services: a Report of the Expert Group on Innovation in Services". http://www.europe-innova.org/index.jsp?type=page&lg=en&cid=7552

European Commission DG Enterprise & Industry (2007), "Towards a European Strategy in Support of Innovation in Services: Challenges and Key Issues for Future Actions", Commission Staff working document, SEC (2007) 1059.

European Commission DG Enterprise & Industry (2009), "Challenges to EU support to innovation in services - Fostering new markets and jobs through innovation", Commission Staff working document, SEC (2009) 1195.

European Commission DG Enterprise & Industry (2009), "Availability and Focus on Innovation Voucher Schemes in European Regions", http://www.europe-innova.eu/c/document_library/get_file?folderId=122731&name=DLFE-6403.pdf

European Commission DG Enterprise & Industry (2009), "Reinvent Europe through innovation: from a knowledge society to an innovation society", Recommendations by a Business panel on future EU innovation policy:
http://ec.europa.eu/enterprise/policies/innovation/files/panel_report_en.pdf

European Commission: Information Society and Media Service (2010), *Innovation, Yearbook 2009-2010*, http://elivinglab.org/ServiceInnovationYearbook_2009-2010.pdf

Eurostat (2004), "Innovation Output and Barriers to Innovation", *Statistics in Focus*, Theme 9, No. 1, Eurostat.

Eurostat (2009), "Quality in the focus of Innovation, Science and Technology", *Statistics in Focus*, No.33, 2009, Eurostat.

Eurostat, CIS 5 database:
http://epp.eurostat.ec.europa.eu/portal/page/portal/statistics/search_database

Gallouj, F. (2002), *Innovations in the Service Economy - The New Wealth of Nations*, Cheltenham: Edward Ellgar Publishing.

Green, L., Howells, J. and Miles, I. (2001), "Services and Innovation: Dynamics of Service Innovation in the European Union", Annex G to the *Report on Research and Development*, Economic Policy Committee.

Howells, J. and Tether, B. (2004), *Innovations in Services: Issues at Stake and Trends*, Final report, INNO-Studies 2001: Lot 3 (ENTRC/2001).

Kanerva, M., Hollanders, H and Arundel A. (2006), 2006 *TrendChart report: Can we measure and compare innovation in services?* Maastricht Economic Research Institute on Innovation   and   Technology,   www.proinno-europe.eu/.../eis_2006_innovation_in_services.pdf.

Kuusisto, J. and Meyer, M. (2003), "Insights into Services and Innovation in the Knowledge-intensive Economy", *Technology Review*, No. 134, TEKES.

Mickiewicz, T. and Radošević, S. (2001), "Innovation capabilities of the six EU candidate countries: comparative data based analysis", London: School of Slavonic and East European Studies for Community Research and Development Information Service (CORDIS).

Miles, I. (2001), "Services Innovation: A Reconfiguration of Innovation Studies", *Discussion Paper Series*, PREST, University of Manchester.

Muller, E. and Zenker, A. (2001), "Business services as actors of knowledge transformation: the role of KIBS in regional and national innovation systems", *Research Policy*, no. 30, pp.1501-1516.

OECD (2005), *Oslo Manual: Guidelines for Collecting and Interpreting Innovation Data*, 3rd Edition.

OECD (2010), OECD *Innovation Strategy: Getting a Head Start Tomorrow*, http://www.oecd.org/document/15/0,3343,en_2649_34273_45154895_1_1_1_1,00.html

Preissl, B. (1998), "Barriers to Innovation in Services", *Project SI4S*, topical paper no. 2, STEP Group.

Pro INNO Europe, *INNO-Policy Trendchart Policy Measures* http://www.proinno-europe.eu/index.cfm?fuseaction=page.display&topicID=262&parentID=52

Radosevic, S. (2004), "The Innovation Capacities of the CEEC in the Enlarged EU", *Journal of Common Market Studies*, vol. 42, no.3, pp. 641-666.

Regional KIS (2010), EUROPE INNOVA, http://www.europe-innova.eu/web/guest/home/-/journal_content/56/10136/201592

Rubalcaba, L. (2006), "Which Policy for Innovation in Services? Science and Public Policy", vol.33, No.10, pp.475-756.

Rubalcaba, L., Gallego J., Di Meglio, G. and Pim den Hertog (2010), "The Case for Market and System Failures in Service Innovation", *The Service Industries Journal*, Vol 30, Issue 4, April 2010, pp.549-566.

Schumpeter, J. (1934), *The Theory of Economic Development*, Harvard Economic Studies Series, Harvard: Harvard University Press.

Statistical Office of the Republic of Slovenia (SORS) (2010), Innovation activity in manufacturing and selected services, Slovenia, 2006-2008 - provisional data, downloaded 27.5.2010 from http://www.stat.si/eng/novica_prikazi.aspx?id=3163.

Stare, M. (2007), "Service Development in Transition Economies: Achievements and Missing Links", in J. Bryson, P. Daniels (eds.), *The Handbook of Service Industries*, Edward Elgar.

Stare, M. and Bučar, M. (2007), "Service Innovation Policy Mapping Study: Slovenia", INNO-NETS Project, http://www.proinno-europe.eu/doc/slovenia.pdf

Sundbo, J. (2001), *The Strategic Management of Innovation: a Sociological and Economic Theory*, Cheltenham: Edward Elgar.

Van Ark, Bart, Broersma, Jourens in Hertog den Pim (2003), *Services Innovation, Performance and Policy: A Review*, Synthesis Report, Ministry of Economic Affairs.

Von Hippel, E (1988), *The Sources of Innovation*, Oxford: Oxford University Press.

Von Hippel, E (2005), *Democratizing Innovation*, Cambridge, MA: MIT Press.

3. THE KEY ROLE OF THE CROSS-POLLINATION SPACE FOR INNOVATION IN SERVICES

Michel Léonard and Anastasiya Yurchyshyna, University of Geneva, Switzerland

A. GENESIS AND THE MOTIVATION FOR SUPPORTING INNOVATION IN SERVICES

Over recent decades, the development of the world economy has been largely driven by the evolution of information and communication technologies (ICT), which has accompanied an exponential growth in innovation in all spheres of human activity. Such innovations are often the means to simplify the implementation and use of traditional services in different sectors of the economy (e.g. supporting services in transport, education, health care sectors), and are the driving factor behind the creation of conceptually new ranges of information-based services (e.g. Internet providers, mobile communications, etc.). Our society can thus be viewed as a services-oriented society that relies on the interactive exchange and functioning of interoperable services (Demirkan et al, 2008). In this context, it becomes apparent that the general development of society is largely defined by progress in services, and that innovations in the services sector are crucial for the structured and coherent development of the world economy.

In this paper, we seek to address the following issues: why the "old" concept of innovation remains crucial today, and what are the challenges in our society that throw into sharp relief the importance of innovations in the economy, in general, and the services-based economy, in particular.

A new society: the services - and knowledge-based society

Due to the development of the role of services in contemporary life, both from scientific and practical business-related points of view, it has recently become clear that a new model of society – *the services-oriented society* – has appeared.

Generally speaking, the notion of services science or, more precisely, Service Science, Management and Engineering (SSME), is a term used to describe an interdisciplinary approach to the study, design and the implementation of services systems. SSME includes three strands: Science, Management and Engineering (Spohrer et al, 2007), and is, in fact, the science seeking to resolve the complex interdependences between them.

In its complexity, such service orientation is introduced at different levels of services science from traditional project management dimensions (e.g., scheduling, quality management, service marketing, etc.) to unique topics that are specific for idea development and management (Bakker et al, 2006). Services are incorporated in to the core of all economic processes and, in addition to this, are widely used in the paradigms of conceptual modeling and technical implementation. As a result, it becomes possible to conduct a multi-dimensional analysis of innovation activities, incorporating their economic, business, social and IT aspects, so that timely, user friendly, proactive services are sought to enhance future business or economic growth on the one hand, and on the other, to ensure dynamic adaptability to current conditions.

Our society thus becomes a services-oriented society, with services viewed as utilizations of specific competences such as the knowledge, skills and technologies of one economic entity for the benefit of another (Le Dinh & Léonard, 2009). In such a case, value creation occurs when a resource is transformed into a specific benefit. This activity, the *resourcing*, is performed by a *service system*. Consequently, the traditional supply chain is re-conceptualized as a network of service systems, called *a service value creation network* (Lusch et al, 2008).

Services are characterized by four main factors (Le Dinh & Léonard, 2009), (Tien & Berg, 2003) that can consequently be seen as characterizing a services-oriented society. They are as follows:

- Information is the core element of the design, production and management of services, so services are *information-driven*;
- Customers are co-producers of services; they may require the adaptation or customization of services, so services are *customer-centric*;
- A *digital orientation* of services is explained by the achievements in information and communication technologies, the (semi)automation of the main services-oriented activities and the creation of new domains: e.g. e-commerce, e-business, e-collaboration, e-government, e-environment; and
- Services are driven by performance criteria and are, as such, *productivity-focused*.

Guided by the current experiences in developing economies and the evolution of the underlying technologies, our society is based on information and knowledge that become the main sources of value creation. In this case, it is appropriate to define it as a *knowledge society*, where information and knowledge form a major component of all human activity, which is guided by creation, distribution, diffusion, use, integration and manipulation of information and knowledge (Webster, 2002).

Generally speaking, the phenomenon of services innovation mirrors the requirements of the knowledge society, where knowledge is both the primary production resource and the tool of value (co)creation, with information lying at the heart of services creation and functioning. We point to the practical importance of informatics in implementing this phenomenon: it supplies not only the tool for IT development, but also guarantees the consistency of the sustainable co-creation of its fundamental concepts (Leonard & Yurchyshyna, 2010).

The role of information and knowledge in innovation

The challenges of the services-based society are largely defined by its keystones: *information* and *knowledge*. Information and knowledge play roles as the key value added instruments leading to value creation. In this context, the increasing importance is achieving the complex analysis of the phenomena of information and knowledge, and the problem of their modeling and management.

Such a knowledge society becomes rapidly self-sustaining (Harrison, 2009) by reflecting current needs and the corresponding ICT infrastructure, which can meet these needs, as well as the role of actionable knowledge (Argyris, 1996) in its evolution for different contexts. Actionable knowledge implements the external validity (relevance) in the world (Argyris, 1996), in order to achieve the defined objectives in a more efficient way. More precisely, it represents the information resulting from the identification, capitalization, personalization and consumption of content (Cencioni & Bertolo, 2006) by services and information systems, which can be used for further improvement and adaptation of services and information systems.

In this context, a new dimension of the problem of innovation in services is introduced. It is the possibility to identify and study the parallel between the actionable knowledge and innovations in the context of the knowledge society. In other words, the problem of services innovation represents, in fact, one of the key elements defining the evolution of the knowledge society, which is based on advances such as artificial intelligence-oriented robotics, knowledge discovery, representation, interpretation and model- or expert-based reasoning.

In this context, an interesting solution can be found by applying the methods and technologies of the artificial intelligence (AI), particularly aimed at increasing the semantics of the described knowledge. Indeed, traditionally viewed as "the science and engineering of making intelligent machines, especially intelligent computer programs" (McCarthy, 2007), AI offers computational abilities to achieve modeling goals through application of the range of its disciplines. For example, for knowledge modeling of creativity-related issues, the emphasis is put on the ontology, defined as "the study of the kinds of things that exist", the epistemology, defined as "the study of the kinds of knowledge that are required for solving problems", and systems for common sense knowledge and reasoning, to mention but a few. A variety of studies on the ontological modeling of knowledge have recently been successfully fulfilled, including the aspects on computational creativity (Colton, 2009).

Richness in diversity - the one thing we have in common

Among the various challenges facing our society today, particular emphasis should be placed upon diversity – in its broadest sense. This concerns the expansive range of human activities, the multitude of actors, both experts in specific domains and non-professionals that are involved in creating, consuming and transforming information and knowledge (in social networks, for example), the trans-disciplinary nature of topics and situations of innovation, the cultural diversity and independence of geographical boundaries, etc. Thus, it has become current practice to assemble a team of international experts, each a professional in their respective, highly specialized domain, who collaboratively work on a complex problem requiring the processing and transformation of information and knowledge. This diversity often leads to the identification of new, innovative approaches for a traditional task that benefit from the dissemination and sharing of knowledge across actors.

Paradoxical as it may seem, this diversity may be the one thing we have in common. The need to nurture diversity is thus not only the requirement for services innovation, but also a necessary tool that enables it. Moreover, innovations in this context are often viewed as the "creation of something new", and interdependence between the two phenomena of innovation and creation are naturally established. By stating this it is, however, important to draw a clear distinction between these key conceptions of the domain of innovation in services, which will be discussed in the next section.

General discussion of the possibility to support innovations from the point of view of creation can thus be characterized as *trans-disciplinary*: From the management-oriented vision of (Nonaka et al, 2000), which perceives creation (and, consequently, innovation with respect to semantic correspondences between these notions), as a dynamic process in which an organization creates, maintains and exploits different kinds of knowledge, to the generic quality-based models of creative thinking, summarized in (Plsek, 1997).

As generally recognized, innovation is characterized by significant collaboration between different actors (people and machines), and requires a certain level of *collective intelligence*. This comparatively recent field is rapidly developing, in line with the demands of modern applied research tasks which, in turn, contribute to the conceptual definition and key characteristics of the phenomenon.

Schematically, the working definition (MIT CCI, 2010) of collective intelligence is described by the following aspects:

- It is the ability to learn, understand and reason;
- Exercised by a group of individuals doing things collectively in an intelligent fashion;
- Which addresses new or trying situations; and
- That applies knowledge to adapt to a changing environment.

This capacity for human communities to evolve towards higher order complexity and harmony can be achieved through various innovation mechanisms: e.g., variation-feedback-selection, differentiation-integration-transformation, and competition-cooperation-collaboration, and other mechanisms.

In its complexity, collective intelligence facilitates the acquisition and integration of innovative ideas from a group of experts while adapting them to fit a changing environment, which turns out to be one of the key prerequisites for innovation in services.

**The phenomena of innovation, creativity and idea development:
from contradiction to complexity**

It is notable that current debates around innovation in services combine different key concepts: innovation, creativity and idea development - the semantics of which may lead to confusion.

In the literature, these notions are sometimes used in contexts that may create certain semantic inconsistencies. In the scope of this research, creativity is viewed as the mental and social process involving the generation of new ideas or concepts, or new associations of the creative mind between existing ideas or concepts (Boden, 2004), while the idea development process is defined as the realization of the ability of creativity. It is, to some extent, the moment at which there is the spark of creativity. Innovation in its turn is seen as a process from the origination of an idea to its transformation into something useful, with subsequent implementation. Consequently, innovation in services is seen as a process aiming to increase the efficiency of existing services delivery, to improve service quality, and to produce product innovations through the generation of new types of services (Barras, 1984). Supporting innovation and the creation process has been recently studied by various scientists from economics, psychology, IT, as well as practitioners in innovation and business consultancy. For example, multiple innovation models were described and/or proposed in (Dubberly, 2010), (Tidd et al, 2005), and the evolution of different viewpoints on modeling the creation process was thoroughly discussed in (Plsek, 1997).

From the point of view of *engineering design*, an interesting insight to creativity and innovation is given in (Pahl et al, 2007). By defining two key concepts of their approach, "creativity" and "innovation", the authors envisage their modeling design context as the interdependence of "conflicting technical, economical, organizational and social demands". The proposed approach is generic and, on the one hand, is based on psychological and educational theories of creativity and innovation. On the other hand, the theoretical consistency of their approach is practically enforced by evaluation using 100 commercially available tools to enhance creativity and innovation. They are used for defining a so-called Taxonomy of Tools aiming to clarify the creative aspects of engineering design. This is partially based upon contradictory input data that become novel outcomes in "creative processes" that generate the knowledge co-evolution on both sides of a problem-solution equation. Thanks to algorithmically defined steps, this approach may be viewed as well defined and coordinated, according to the coincidence of the starting point of all actors/stakeholders.

One of the central themes in the discussion of creativity is the notion of *creative potential*. It is developed, for example, in the works of (Kristensson et al, 2004) on identifying and harnessing creative potential. It was noticed, for example, that professional developers and advanced users created more easily realizable ideas, and ordinary users created the most valuable ideas. These ideas were then discussed from the standpoint of divergent thinking, facilitated through the opportunity to combine different information elements that appeared distinct at the outset.

Within the scope of user-based creativity, it is also interesting to study the related processes that concretise the phenomenon of the creativity process: idea generation from users (or more specifically, the leader of idea generation process), the so called "lead user process" (Lilien et al, 2002) who demonstrate creative thinking (Balzac, 2006) and collaborative communities motivating competition in ideas (Piller & Walcher, 2006). In both cases, however, the accent is placed upon "divergent thinking" which is seen as "a critical element of creativity" (Balzac, 2006). This variety and multi-disciplinarity of ideas may also be viewed as a resource for the generation of ideas, and a certain level of sharing between their semantics is required, in order to extract the full benefit of their complexity.

An alternative vision of creativity is based on the belief that it is largely defined by *lead users* (or the main actors in an applied domain). The main idea of modeling the "lead user process" is to acquire information about both needs and solutions from users at the leading edges of the target market, as well as from users in other markets that face similar problems in a more pronounced form (Von Hippel, 1986). The idea-generation paradigm assumes thus that key elements of the desired creative idea already exist among leading-edge users. In other words, information regarding needs and solutions is acquired from semantically close contexts, with the challenge being to find this information, and develop its potential. This also means that the problem of modeling idea-generation is substituted by the problem of idea search in semantically close, usage-based contexts.

In contrast, the other source of idea development in an open innovation community is believed to be in collaborative communities that allow the access of innovative ideas and solutions from users. In (Piller & Walcher, 2006) this is proposed to be done with the support of internet-based toolkits for idea competitions in the context of an open innovation process. The ideas are acquired from non-expert users and are then evaluated by an expert panel, according to the consensual assessment technique. Such type of "crowd sourcing" (Ebner et al, 2008) aims thus to find and use the potential of the "collective brain". In their research, the authors draw upon a model of innovation after (Tidd et al, 2005) to underline the interdependence between innovations and communities that allow for "harvesting the wisdom of crowds in selecting the best ideas". It is remarkable that the same principles for open innovation are applied not only for problem solving in fundamental science, but also for industry-oriented R&D. (Lakhani and Boudreau, 2009). Note, for example, that communities are particularly useful when an innovation problem involves cumulative knowledge, continually building on past advances. In other words, communities are oriented toward the intrinsic motivations of external innovators, and thus to their collective creativity.

One of the most prominent ideas that defines the research on creativity is the existence of creative cognition introduced by (Ward et al, 1999) and developed in his later works. According to his approach, the result of creativity – creative ideas – are viewed "as being the natural result of applying basic mental operations to existing knowledge structures". In this series of work, Ward also gives a semi-formal definition of the originality of an idea as the balance between its novelty and familiarity that will be determined by the processes employed and the way in which existing knowledge is accessed. Of these, the main processes are conceptual combination, analogy, and initial problem formulation.

It is clear that study of the phenomena of innovation, creation and idea development is tightly interconnected with a series of works on means of supporting these phenomena, and/or modeling their progression. In the next section, we discuss in more detail some perspectives that, in our view, represent the main approaches towards providing such support, and that serve as keystones for the elaboration of our ontology-based and services-enabled approach to conceptualizing creativity.

B. THE PROCESS OF DECISION CONSTRUCTING

To some extent, this will always be based upon a shared understanding, a mutually accepted decision regarding the right way to construct the future. In other words, *innovation in services* represents, in fact, the result of collaborative decision-making, the *process of constructing a decision* for a commonly recognized problem, which is based on *highly competitive technologies and corresponds to the ever-changing conditions of the environment.*

Innovation: Why decision making is not sufficient any more?

Nowadays, the role of innovations in scientific and entrepreneurial practices can hardly be underestimated. Innovations are viewed as serious improvements in existing practices, and a source of added value for existing products and services. They are drawn upon to address the weaknesses of current products, in order to make them as close to an "ideal product" as possible. Nevertheless, let us examine whether this vision is truly innovative.

Indeed, by trying to *improve* something, we aim to create something whose criteria for success are to overcome the existing specifications of a product. For example, innovations are motivated by increasing the speed of a car, or the time-effectiveness of an IT-service, or by seeking to combine two functions in one product in the case of an online calendar with automatic mailing, according to current events. In this case, innovations are in fact aimed at optimizing the different characteristics of a product, which are predefined before the innovation process begins. We may broadly say that innovations result in effective decision-making regarding how to optimize existing outcomes.

This is, however, not sufficient to *create* new characteristics of a product, which are not made explicit, *a priori*. For example, introducing internet access to a mobile phone does not constitute the optimization of the characteristics of a traditional telephone, because this functionality was not predefined – or even conceived of – in classical usage, but was a product of the innovation process. In other words, the decision on innovation must not only be *made*, it must be *constructed*.

Innovation: Why decision constructing?

This straightforward example illustrates, however, an important reality. Innovations in services are more significant when they do not result from the optimization of existing characteristics, but are co-created during a collaborative decision-making process. One possible solution to support a collaborative decision-making process is the cross-pollination space (CPS), a platform for enabling the creation of new domain services. The CPS represents a collaborative space that brings together experts and non professional users from different domains that work collaboratively on the co-creation process. As a result, we move from the task of decision-making to the process of constructing the future by conceptually creating innovative services (cf. Figure I.3.1).

Figure I.3.1. Conceptual schematic for decision constructing

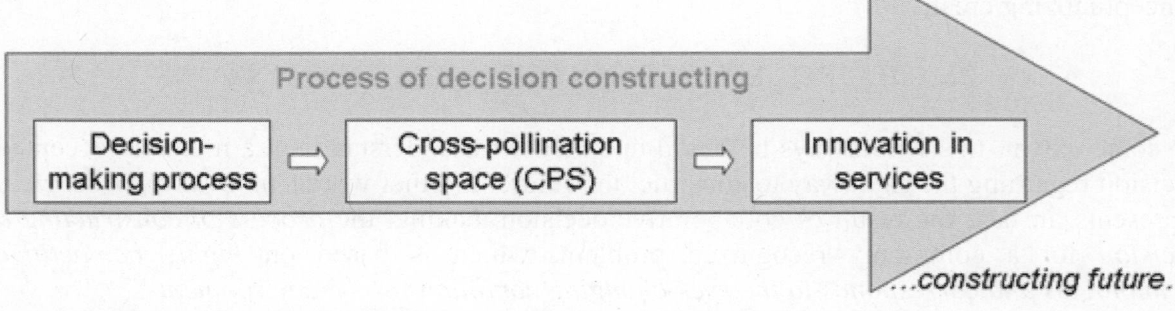

Services as tools and environment for co-creation

This section discusses the interdependence of the knowledge society and services-oriented economics, which are both driven by information systems. Generally speaking, information systems are not only tools for co-creation (Yurchyshyna et al, 2010), but also contribute to creating the environment that is conducive to sustainable development (Léonard & Yurchyshyna, 2010).

In particular, we highlight the practical importance of services for a sustainable development that contributes to both the development and implementation of information systems, while guaranteeing the coherent ·co-creation of its fundamental concepts. The result is the sustainable development, in its complexity, of the design principles of the knowledge society. We argue that services become the key element of knowledge value creation that is achieved by actioning the knowledge related to corresponding domain ontologies. We claim that it is the actionable knowledge (Argyris, 1996) that forms the basis for the cognitive information.

Our methodology for actioning knowledge in the knowledge creation process is schematically described at Figure I.3.2, and is viewed in the context of the sustainable development of the knowledge society.

Figure I.3.2. Co-creation of cognitive information by actioning knowledge

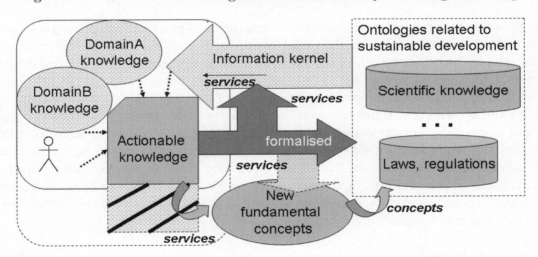

First, we specify a set of related ontologies as sustainable development ontologies: the scientific knowledge, the corresponding laws and regulations defining the principles of sustainable development, etc. Secondly, we clarify the role of services in the process of knowledge co-creation that is enabled by information systems. Services are used for the following main purposes:

- Acquiring the concepts, which characterise sustainable development ontologies;
- Evaluating the semantic coherence of the acquired concepts;
- Evaluating the impact of different domains upon sustainability;

- Capitalising upon the knowledge acquired from the use of this information (e.g. from the ecological, economic, construction domains, etc.);
- Identifying new fundamental concepts and integrating them into the information kernel; and
- Integrating new concepts into sustainable development ontologies.

This methodology leads us to an important conclusion: services are used not only as a tool for sustainable development, but they also become the key elements of the environment, driving as well as being driven by its fundamental characteristics ("co-creation"). In other words, this environment is dynamically created and semantically coherent to both initial sustainable development ontologies and the knowledge defining the usage of the related cognitive systems and/or services. As a result, it may be viewed as a self-perpetuating and self-regulating environment, which is the main characteristic of its sustainable development.

C. TOWARDS CO-CONSTRUCTING THE FUTURE: THE INNOVATIVE SERVICES CROSS-POLLINATION SPACE

According to our approach for supporting innovations in services, we claim that they are most effective when they are co-created as the result of a collaborative decision process (cf. Figure I.3.2). One potential tool to support this process is the cross-pollination space (CPS), a generic platform for enabling the creation of new domain services.

Our methodological approach towards service innovation is based on two principal keystones: the decisional construction on the one hand, and the support of co-creative and transdisciplinary work on the other. Indeed, we envisage decisions as being those that play a prominent role in innovation, as far as right of initiative in the development of informational services is supported. When supporting the process of decision-making with opening up the "decision ability" and/or "decision power", every actor is empowered to initiate, to decide upon and, thence, to co-create new informational services. Due to the transdisciplinarity previously discussed, the questions and results of diverse disciplines can be intertwined and combined with one another, so that from difference (and sometimes even from polar difference), can emerge innovation. Consequently, service innovation can be seen as a process that is identified and guided by decisions, as well as the collaborative work supporting their formulation and management.

This approach represents a generalization of our services-based method for governing initiatives in the context of e-Government services innovation, whose details are described in (Opprecht et al, 2010).

One of the most important stages in the process of decision construction is the content-based analysis of a problem that arises and requires solution. Its objectives are to identify the semantics of this problem and to create the necessary relationships (i.e., "related to", "is defined by", etc.) with the corresponding categories and/or other problems. For instance, a decision to allocate supplementary parking places for disabled people within the City of Geneva may be semantically associated with several non-correlated domains, such as "parking places", "disabled people", "City of Geneva", and as such – may be classified in various ways in the repository of initiatives.

The content-based analysis allows one to identify the main semantics of an arising problem, and to define its information kernel. Generally speaking, the information kernel can be viewed as a conceptual model of the knowledge that is exchanged. The development of the information kernel of a problem requiring resolution is based on our previous research on the generic, services-based information kernel, whose detailed description is provided in (Yurchyshyna & Léonard, 2009). As a result, the constructed decision might trigger the proposition of an initiative (in the meaning of Opprecht et al, 2010), which will be implemented as a new service.

To develop the information kernel of services, we propose a three-level, ontology-based model (cf. Figure I.3.3). The upper level is ontological: it corresponds to initial knowledge bases, expert knowledge, regulations and law repositories, etc. The lower level corresponds to the implementation of a strategy of services management, as well as its use in different contexts. The middle level is the information kernel itself, which is at the heart of our approach (Yurchyshyna et al, 2010), (Opprecht et al, 2010): it represents the knowledge required to define and implement services, which is shared by the main stakeholders and participants in the process of decision construction.

Figure I.3.3. The information kernel (generic view)

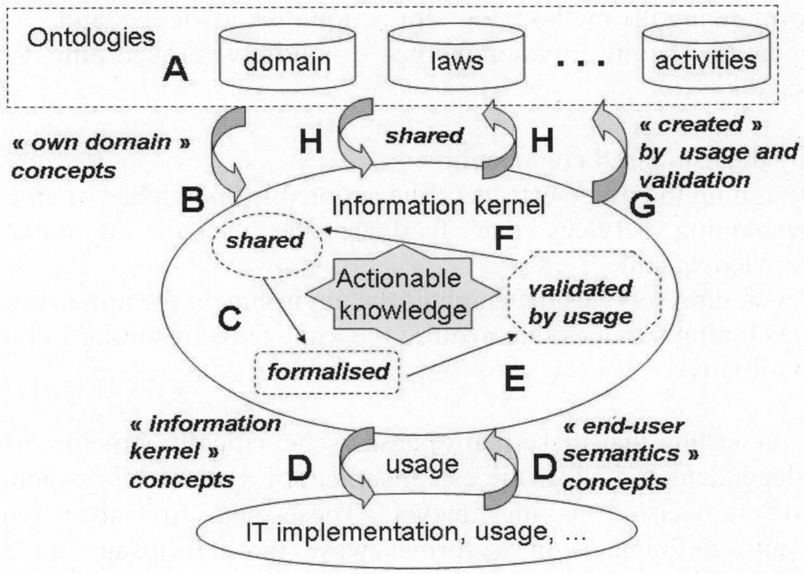

The development of the information kernel is based on the process of actionable knowledge (Argyris, 1996), which we enrich and adapt for the purpose of initiatives management. The information kernel of initiatives is defined as: (i) a conceptual information model that describes the correspondent domains in terms of concepts, facts and business rules; (ii) its concepts, properties, constraints and rules are defined with the help of ontologies, allowing the formal representation of the mandatory knowledge for determining the initiatives' content; (iii) the conceptual knowledge of the information kernel is non contradictory and is shared by all actors in the process of initiatives management; and (iv) this knowledge cannot be doubted during the decision process. In other words, this knowledge is valid during the whole lifecycle of decision construction.

Our approach for actioning "initiatives knowledge" corresponds to the three-level ontological model of the information kernel, which can be briefly described as follows:

- Firstly, by the ontological component:
  - Identifying the initiative's context by applying the content-based analysis;
  - Positioning this initiative in the repository of initiatives and establishing the necessary correspondences and/or relationships with other initiatives;
  - Positioning this initiative in the repository of the regulation base and establishing the necessary correspondences and/or relationships with other regulatory texts; and
  - Updating initial knowledge bases with the shared knowledge of the information kernel, as validated by usage.

- Secondly, by the information kernel component:
  - Identifying the information kernel of an initiative;
  - Evaluating the "action perspective" of the non-actioned knowledge of this initiative;
  - Defining the scope of the knowledge to be actioned and the ontological rules for actioning this knowledge;
  - Formalizing the methodology for actioning knowledge; and
  - Updating the information kernel of initiatives, according to their practical usage.

- Thirdly, by the use-based component:
  - Designing the usage effects of the actionable knowledge of an initiative;
  - Developing services that facilitate the use of an initiative's actioned knowledge; and
  - Developing services that support the environment for initiatives management;
  - Developing services that acquire the knowledge resulting in practical usage of an initiative.

It is important to underline that these main phases schematically structured by three groups are, in fact, interdependent and allow the establishment of dynamic correspondences between different phases of the decision-making lifecycle. These range from identifying the need for problem-solving and defining it in a formal way, through discussion and sharing to implementation and validation through practical use, with coherent updating of the initial knowledge bases following at the end.

Within the scope of this paper, we do not detail any technological characteristics of the CPS architecture. The interested reader is welcome to consult (Léonard and Yurchyshyna, 2010), (Yurchyshyna and Opprecht, 2010) for further details.

D. INNOVATION POLICIES IN SERVICES: SOME CONCRETE MECHANISMS FOR INTERVENTION

Following development of the theoretical background for an innovative approach to decision construction, our ongoing work becomes more concrete, with several practical implementations. These are oriented mainly towards development of the specialized CPS for a specific applied task, and promoting this approach through establishing an Executive Masters programme in innovative services.

The CPS: implementation in practice

The discussed conceptual approach and the general framework of CPS can be and already are modified, according to specific, applied tasks. Currently, we focus on the following:

- Developing the CPS for governing initiatives to encourage innovation in e-government services (Opprecht et al, 2010);
- Developing the CPS to formulate a richer vision of the complex principles of sustainable development (Léonard and Yurchyshyna, 2010); and
- Adapting the CPS for supporting creativity processes by integrating arts-oriented aspects into the Intelligent Negotiation table (Yurchyshyna et al, 2010).

The complexity of the conceptual approach therefore allows its adaptation to various practical cases, by developing the corresponding ontologies and establishing a coherent information kernel for different groups of experts and non-professional users.

We envisage this approach as being rather efficient, not least due to its generic character, which allows it to be tailored to any applied task with (comparative) ease. Its other important characteristics include the service oriented nature of its structure: the CPS allows its participants to identify, share and highlight the implicit (as opposed to predefined), requirements of the decision to be constructed, to identify new services, bringing additional value to this decision, and to integrate these seamlessly into the decision during the process of its creation.

The educational component of promoting innovative services

Services science creates a cognitive space, where results from various disciplines converge to create services belonging not only to one discipline, but creating a new platform where all disciplines contribute substantial inputs, and are enriched in turn. Services science must be thus presented from different perspectives depending on the skills and responsibilities of those involved. This challenge was made an integral part of the objectives of an International Executive Master programme EMISS[33], which was co-created and supported by several leading European universities:

- University of Geneva (UNIGE, www.unige.ch)
- University of Porto, Faculty of Engineering (FEUP, www.fe.up.pt)

---

[33] http://iess.unige.ch/emiss

- Masaryk University, Faculty of Informatics (FIMU, www.fi.muni.cz)
- Universitat Politècnica de Catalunya (Barcelona Tech, www.upc.edu)
- University of Amsterdam (VUA, www.cs.vu.nl).

The Executive Masters in Innovative Services Systems (EMISS) is a lifelong learning programme that offers various learning trajectories for business managers, IT (information technology) specialists, knowledge workers and services managers. It comprises 60 ECTS credits, and is divided into four certificates, each of 10 ECTS credits and an Executive Masters thesis of 20 ECTS credits.

Thanks to the wide range of themes which constitute the EMISS domain, and the large number of specialists coming from academic institutions and enterprises in different countries, the EMISS programme takes place in various European locations in the vicinity of the partner universities.

Figure I.3.4. EMISS masters framework

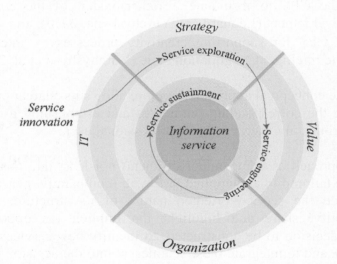

The EMISS programme consists of 4 EMISS certificates, which correspond to the main services-related activities (cf. Figure I.3.4):

- 1st EMISS Certificate - Innovative service innovation – setting up the roadmap for value creation;
- 2nd EMISS Certificate - Innovative service exploration - discovering new territories;
- 3rd EMISS Certificate - Innovative service engineering - putting innovation into action; and
- 4th EMISS Certificate - Innovative service sustenance - pursuing sustainability.

Each EMISS certificate lasts one and a half weeks; the total duration of the EMISS Master courses is six weeks. These weeks are distributed over the whole year. In addition, the EMISS Masters thesis lasts for six months. In all, the whole EMISS programme is thus spread over a period of eighteen months.

The objectives of the EMISS programme are to support services within the services-based society. In the first instance, the services economy (with management, marketing, risk, continuity, etc.), was developed before the emergence of ICT, and differs markedly from the product or manufacturing-based economy. Of course, the efficient delivery of such services is enhanced greatly by the support of ICT. In the next stage, ICT and, in particular, internet technologies, created a huge range of new opportunities in the services sector. These services can be embedded in any process, supply chain or company. This may even be in the processes of creation or innovation of new products, new services and new activities. They constitute a major component of the development of the company.

Such a development demands the competencies of *talented* persons. But these talented persons cannot be effective without being surrounded and supported by *skilled* persons.

The skilled persons will disseminate the collective culture of the services in the company, realize and set up services, motivate the relevant persons to collaborate in the conception and realization of services, and elevate the services initiatives taken by the enterprise.

The talented persons play a crucial role. They are responsible for taking care of the diffusion of innovation inside the enterprise through the services and, in particular, for recognizing and supporting the activities of the skilled persons.

Thus, the majority of enterprises face a transition phase to assure their own developments by the means of services with maturity. This transition brings new and exciting challenges for the enterprise itself, and for persons inside the enterprise.

The EMISS programme will thus instil in its participants a culture of services. They will be equipped to disseminate this within their own enterprises. This is vital for their enterprises, to lead to more and better jobs, to obtain greater cognitive cohesion – absolutely essential to developing services – and to bring new challenges to the development of enterprise and, in particular, of human resources.

E. CONCLUSION

The concept of innovation, already recognized as one of the key challenges of contemporary economic life, is particularly important today.

The previous analysis of course justifies the increasing attention paid to this matter. The new characteristics of modern society, the major tools for development, as well as success in ICT technologies are among obvious reasons for supporting innovation.

This work presents one of multiple attempts to answer a simple, but extremely important question: why the "old" concept of innovation is so important today. While recognizing the existence of a range of answers, we nonetheless point to the importance of innovations in the context of participative co-creativity, enforced by the new IT technologies and the phenomena of social networking and collective intelligence.

To contribute to innovation in services, we thus propose a means that supports their conception and development as the fruits of a collaborative decision process: the cross-pollination space (CPS), a generic platform for enabling the creation of new domain services by creating the collaborative environment for experts from different domains to support the decision process.

In conclusion, let us highlight once more the major contributions of the CPS to the development of innovative services. First, it allows the identification and co-creation of new services. Second, this platform benefits from the rich variety of knowledge coming from different domains for a specific applied task. Third, a shared understanding of a problem and its solutions are created between the groups of actors involved and, as a result, a better understanding is achieved across the involved – often highly heterogeneous – domains. And finally, decision construction supported by the CPS allows and motivates not only innovation, but discovery in services and, as such, contributes to the process of collective co-creation.

REFERENCES

Argyris, C. (1996), "Actionable knowledge: Design causality in the service of consequential theory", *Journal of Applied Behavioral Science*, vol. 32, no 4, pp. 390-406.

Bakker, H., Boersma, K. and Oreel, S. (2006). "Creativity (Ideas) Management in Industrial R&D Organizations: A Crea-Political Process Model and an Empirical Illustration of Corus RD&T", *Creativity and Innovation Management*, Vol. 15, No. 3, pp. 296-309.

Balzac, F. (2006). "Exploring the Brain's Role in Creativity", *NeuroPsychiatry Reviews* 7 (5): 1, pp.19–20, http://www.neuropsychiatryreviews.com/may06/einstein.html, accessed 10/03/2010.

Barras, R. (1984), "Towards a theory of innovation in services", *Research Policy* 15: pp.161-73.

Boden, M. A. (2004), *The creative mind: Myths and mechanism* (2nd ed.), London and New York, Routledge.

Cencioni, R. and Bertolo, S. (2006). "From Intelligent Content to Actionable Knowledge: Research Directions and Opportunities under Framework Programme 7, 2007-2013", *Lecture Notes in Computer Science*, Springer Berlin / Heidelberg, Volume 4276/ 2006, pp.1125-1131.

Colton, S., Lopez de Mantaras, R. and Stock, O. (2009). "Computational Creativity: Coming of Age". In *AI Magazine*, Vol 30(3), pp.11-14.

Demirkan, H., Kauffman, R., Vayghan, J., Fill, H., Karagiannis, D. and Maglio, P. (2008). "Service-oriented technology and management: Perspectives on research and practice for the coming decade", *Electronic Commerce Research and Applications* 7(4), pp.356-376.

Dubberly, H. (2010). "Creating Concept Maps", Dubberly Design Office, March 26, 2010. http://www.dubberly.com/wp-content/uploads/2010/03/ddo_creating_concept_maps.pdf, last accessed 29/06/2010.

Ebner, W., Leimeister, M., Bretschneider, U. and Krcmar, H. (2008). "Leveraging the Wisdom of Crowds: Designing an IT-supported Ideas Competition for an ERP Software Company",*Proc. of the 41st Hawaii International Conference on System Sciences* – 2008 (HICSS 2008), ISBN: 0-7695-3075-3. See: http://www.computer.org/plugins/dl/pdf/proceedings/hicss/2008/3075/00/30750417.pdf?temp late=1&loginState=1&userData=anonymous-IP%253A%253A129.194.8.73, last accessed 30/03/2010

Harrison, C. G. (2005). "Enabling ICT Adoption in Developing Knowledge Societies", *Education and the Knowledge Society*, Springer Boston.

von Hippel, E. (1986), "Lead Users: A Source of Novel Product Concepts", *Management Science* 32(7): pp.791–806.

Kristensson, P., Gustafsson, A. and Archer, T. (2004), "Harnessing the Creative Potential among Users", *Journal of Product innovation Management* 21 pp.4 – 14, see: http://userinnovation.mit.edu/papers/Kristensson.pdf, last accessed 29/03/2010

Lakhani, K. R. and Boudreau, K. J. (2009). "How to Manage Outside Innovation", *MIT Sloan Management Review* 50, no. 4 (summer 2009).

Le-Dinh, T. and Léonard, M. (2009). "A Conceptual Framework for Modelling Service Value Creation Networks", *1st International Workshop on Information Technology for Innovative Services* (ITIS-2009), IEEE 12th International Conference on Network-Based Information Systems (NBiS-2009), August 2009, Indianapolis, Indiana, USA.

Léonard, M. and Yurchyshyna, A. (2010), "Impact of Services on Sustainable Development of Creative Society", *Proc. Sixth International Conference "Technology, Knowledge and Society"*, 15-17 January 2010, Berlin, Germany.

Lilien, G. L., Morrison, P. D., Searls, K., Sonnack, M. and von Hippel, E. (2002), "Performance Assessment of the Lead User Idea-Generation Process for New Product Development", *Management Science*, Vol. 48, No. 8, pp. 1042–1059.

Lusch, R. F., Vargo, S. L. and Wessels, G. (2008), "Towards a conceptual foundation for service science: Contributions from service-dominant logic", *IBM Systems Journal*, Vol. 47, No. 1.

McCarthy, J. (2007). "What is artificial intelligence?", see http://www-formal.stanford.edu/jmc/whatisai/whatisai.html, last accessed 07/06/2010

Malone, T. W. and Crowston, K. (1990), "What is coordination theory and how can it help design cooperative work systems?", *CSCW '90: Proceedings of the 1990 ACM conference on Computer-supported cooperative work*, New York, NY, USA: ACM, p. 357–370.

Managing innovation website, http://www.managing-innovation.com/, last accessed 07/06/2010.

MIT Center for Collective Intelligence, Handbook of Collective Intelligence, available online at http://scripts.mit.edu/~cci/HCI/index.php?title=What_is_collective_intelligence%3F, last accessed 07/06/2010.

Nonaka, I., Toyama, R. and Konno, N. (2000), "SECI, Ba and Leadership: a Unified Model of Dynamic Knowledge Creation", *Long Range Planning*, vol. 33, Issue 1, pp. 5-34

Opprecht, W., Yurchyshyna, A., Khadraoui, A. and Léonard, M. (2010), "Governance of initiatives for e-government services innovation". Accepted and to be published in *Proc. EGOV2010, IFIP e-Government conference 2010*, 29 August – 2 September 2010, Lausanne, Switzerland.

Pahl, A.-K., Newnes, L. and McMahon, C. (2007), "A generic model for creativity and innovation: overview for early phases of engineering design", *Journal of Design Research* 2007, Vol. 6, No.1/2 pp.5 – 44.

Piller, F. T. and Walcher, D. (2006), "Toolkits for idea competitions: a novel method to integrate users in new product development", *R&D Management*, Vol. 36, No. 3, pp. 307-318.

Plsek, P. (1997). "Creativity, Innovation and Quality". Milwaukee, WI: ASQ Quality Press.

Spohrer, J., Maglio, P. P., Bailey, J. and Gruhl, D. (2007), "Steps Towards a Science of Service Systems", *IEEE Computer*, No. 1, pp.71-77.

Tidd, J., Bessant, J. R. and Pavitt, K. (2005), *Managing innovation: integrating technological, market and organizational change*, (3 ed.). Chichester, Wiley.

Tien, J. M. and Berg, D. (2003), "A case for service systems engineering", *Journal of Systems Science and Systems Engineering*, Vol. 12, No. 1, pp. 13-38.

Ward, T. B., Smith, S. M. and Finke, R. A. (1999), "Creative cognition". In R. Sternberg (Ed.) *Handbook of Creativity*, New York: NY, Cambridge University Press.

Webster, F. (2002), "Theories of the Information Society", Cambridge: Routledge.

Yurchyshyna, A. and Leonard, M. (2009), "Bridging Ontological Vision and Service-oriented Approach for Development of Cognitive Information Systems". In: *Cognitive, Computation World 2009*, 15-20 November, 2009, Athens, Greece.

Yurchyshyna, A., Leonard, M. and Brough-Heinzman, P., (2010), "Towards a Services-based Approach for Supporting Idea Development Process". In *Fifth International Conference on Internet and Web Applications and Services*, pp.321 – 326.

Yurchyshyna, A. and Opprecht, W. (2010), "Towards an Ontology-based Approach for Creating Sustainable Services". In: *Proc. First International Conference on Exploring Services Sciences (IESS 1.0)*, 17-19 February 2010, Geneva, Switzerland.

4. MEASURING INNOVATION INVESTMENT IN SERVICES AND POLICY IMPLICATIONS[34]

Michael P. Gallaher, RTI International, North Carolina, United States of America

A. INTRODUCTION

The service sector is the largest and fastest growing sector in the United States (US) economy, accounting for an increasingly significant share of US gross domestic product. However, the service sector has historically been viewed as having little or no productivity growth and being devoid of an ability to innovate, when, in fact, service-sector firms are on average active in all aspects of research and development (R&D) and innovation. The issue is the lack of ability to accurately identify and measure R&D expenditures and innovation activities in the service sector. This inability is a problem because measurement is key to the success of public policies targeted at stimulating research and innovation. For example, tax credits and other incentives rely on strict definitions and measurement of R&D to determine which activities are eligible. The applicability of definitions and the difficulties in identifying and measuring service-sector R&D has implications for the effectiveness of current innovation policies.

B. KEY CONCEPTS: INNOVATION IN THE SERVICE SECTOR

The service sector is the largest sector in the US economy and accounts for an increasingly significant share of US gross domestic product (GDP). Figure I.4.1 presents US GDP in billions of current dollars for the years 2000 through 2009, and it shows value added by industry for the government (federal, state and local), the private-goods producing industries and the private service-producing industries. In 2009, the service sector accounted for about 50% of US GDP. If government services are included with service-producing industries, this contribution by the more broadly defined service sector exceeds 75%.

However, the service sector has historically been viewed as having little or no productivity growth and being devoid of an ability to innovate (Tether, Hipp and Miles, 2001; Miles and Dachs, 2005). The sector has also been characterized as having low-paying jobs, low levels of technological dependence and a relatively undeveloped level of institutional organization. In contrast, the manufacturing sector, which collectively dominates all other private goods-producing industries, was seen as the source of most innovations and thus the engine of economic growth.

---

[34] This paper draws directly from Gallaher, Link, and Petrusa (2006).

Figure I.4.1. US Gross Domestic Product and value added by industry, 1999–2004 (US$ billions)

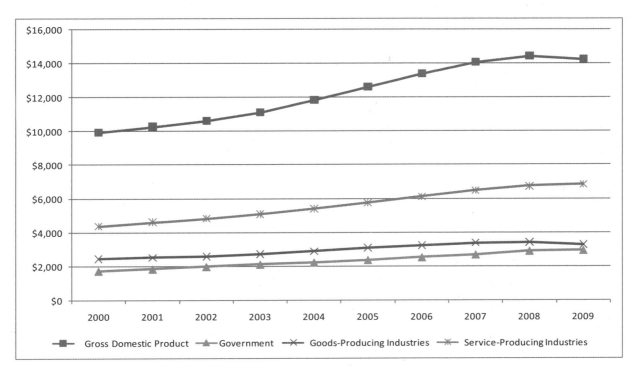

There are key differences between the service sector and the manufacturing sector in terms of their innovation-related characteristics. These include the following[35]:

- Intellectual property rights are weak in services and strong in manufacturing;
- Service-sector firms pull in new technologies in-house, whereas manufacturing-sector firms develop new technologies and push them into the market;
- Traditionally defined R&D occurs in-house in manufacturing firms. Service-sector firms outsource their research and innovation activity;
- Innovation cycles are short in manufacturing and long in services;
- Products produced by service-sector firms are relatively intangible compared to the tangible nature of manufacturing products; and
- Many manufacturing-sector firms operate on a national or global scale, whereas service-sector firms are more regional, or perhaps national, in spatial scale.

These innovation-characteristic differences are due in large part to the nature of R&D that occurs in services. Service-sector firms are, on average, active in all aspects of R&D, contrary to the stereotypical description of that sector's innovative activities. In 2001, according to the National Science Foundation (NSF) data, nearly 45% of all industrial basic research was performed in the service sector. This included over 36% of all applied research, and nearly 41% of all development research.

---

[35] Adapted from Howells (2000) and NIST (2005).

In recent years, the service sector has come to be viewed, both in the United States and in other industrialized nations, as a dynamic component of economic activity and growth. The observable growth in Internet and Web-based services and high-technology environmental services has brought attention to the service sector— in particular, knowledge-intensive services—as a significant contributor to economic growth (Howells, 2000). However, as pervasive and economically important as the service sector is, innovative activity in service-sector firms remains somewhat enigmatic and is not well understood.

The remainder of this paper investigates innovation investment in the service sector, with a focus on the ability to measure service-sector innovation activities and the implications this has for public policy. We begin with a general discussion of technology and innovation policy in the United States and then an investigation of issues related to defining and measuring service-sector innovations and R&D. Implications are illustrated using the US R&E Tax Credit as an example. We conclude with summary remarks and policy implications.

C. TECHNOLOGY AND INNOVATION POLICY IN THE UNITED STATES

The US Government has historically had an important partnership role with the private sector in fostering innovation. This relationship stems from the following logic: innovation leads to technology; technology is the prime driver of economic growth; in the absence of government intervention, firms in all sectors will under-invest in the innovation process (especially in R&D), due to knowledge spillovers and appropriability issues; and government has a responsibility to address this under-investment by providing incentives for the continued conduct of, or perhaps increase in, R&D.

However, it was under the Clinton administration that an innovation and technology policy was first formally articulated in the United States:

"The goal of technology policy is not to substitute the government's judgment for that of private industry in deciding which potential 'winners' to back. Rather, the point is to correct market failures." (1994 Economic Report of the President)

Market failure, in particular technological or innovation market failure, results from conditions that prevent organizations from fully realizing or appropriating the benefits created by their investments. Market failure is typically attributed to market power, imperfect information, externalities and public goods.

R&D and innovation policy in the United States has historically been related to three major categories:

- Market structure policies (such as patents) that affect firms' abilities to appropriate returns;
- Government support for basic R&D and infra-technologies that increase the efficiency of private-sector R&D; and
- Direct funding to firms to lower the private cost of R&D in the form of grants, R&D tax credits, or other incentives.

Each of these policy initiatives provided incentives to private-sector firms to increase the level of their R&D spending. The patent system is targeted at addressing appropriability issues associated with innovation. By granting what is in effect a temporary monopoly, patents provide innovators the opportunity to generate the revenue needed to offset their R&D investments. For service-sector R&D, however, patents frequently are less effective. Much of service-sector R&D is related to process innovation (also referred to as business methods), for which it is inherently more difficult to obtain and enforce patents. In addition, it is more difficult for process innovations to demonstrate that they are clearly distinct from all other processes (prior art).

Government also supports private R&D through the funding of basic research and infra-technologies. Basic research funded through universities or research laboratories leads to the development of generic technologies for which technical risk and spillovers are greatest. For example, the Preeminence Act of 1991 created the Advanced Technology Program, with the mission to fund research to "accelerate the development of innovative technologies for broad national benefit through partnership with the private sector."

Infra-technologies, such as standards and measurement technologies, have a strong public goods nature that leads to under-investment by the private sector[36]. Infra-technologies, such as standards, are particularly important in supporting service-sector innovation. A large share of service-sector R&D is focused on integrating technologies and knowledge imported from the manufacturing sector. Systems integration and customization of information systems depends heavily on the evolution of IT standards (Gallaher and Rowe, 2006). Without well-defined standards and protocols, most of the innovations in the telecommunications, financial services and other IT-dependent industries would not be possible.

Over the past few decades, the United States has introduced a variety of public/private partnerships to overcome market failure. For example, the US R&E Tax Credit of 1981 and its subsequent renewals (which are discussed in Section E), the National Cooperative Research Act of 1984 (and subsequent amendments), and the American Technology Innovation-based policies that are designed to increase the level of R&D spending by removing relevant barriers that cause there to be an under-investment, are economically appropriate.

D. DEFINING INNOVATION AND R&D

The term "innovation" has frequently been used to encompass a wide range of processes that include both R&D and non-R&D activities. In a broad sense, innovation may be new products, new processes, or new organizational methods that are novel and add value to economic activity. Historically, innovation and technology policy has focused on R&D or, more specifically in the United States, on R&E[37].

R&D is distinguished from the broader category of innovative activities in that R&D is defined to include activities that systematically use research findings and expand the frontier

---

[36] See Tassey (2005) for a discussion of infratechnologies.
[37] The "E" stands for experimentation, but for the time being we will use the terms R&D and R&E interchangeably.

of knowledge. Based on this definition, many activities frequently included as innovation are excluded from R&D, such as market research and technology adoption/or imitation. Table I.4.1 provides an overview of what is included in the US definition of R&D and what is not.

The classical definitions of R&D are grounded in creating an artifact or physical product (Tether, Hipp and Miles, 2001) and therefore are harder to apply to intangible outputs of services, such as methods or organizational theory. For example, Sundbo and Gallouji (1999) identify four major categories of service innovation—product, process, organizational and market—not all of which are considered R&D. However, the difficult distinction in services between product and process, also referred to as coterminality, often makes it difficult to interpret what is R&D and non-R&D (Evangelista, 1999; Sirilli and Evangelista, 1998).

Table I.4.1. Items included and excluded from the definition of R&D

The following are included in the definition of R&D	The following are NOT included in the definition of R&D
Basic research: Pursuing new knowledge whether or not the search has reference to a specific application— limited to federal, university and non-profit organizations	Testing and evaluation once a prototype becomes a production model
Applied research: Applying existing knowledge to problems involved in creating a new product or process	Routine product testing or troubleshooting for breakdowns in production
Development: Applying existing knowledge to problems involved in improving an existing product or process	Consumer, market and opinion R&D; advertising new products or processes
	Management and organization R&D
	Social sciences, etc.: Any research in the social sciences, arts, or humanities

E. R&D VERSUS INNOVATION: GREY AREAS

Innovation surveys have found that R&D accounts for a much smaller share of activity and expertise as related to service-sector innovation compared to innovation in the manufacturing sector. For example, R&D typically accounts for about half of manufacturing innovation expenditures, whereas, on average, R&D accounts for only about one-quarter of service-sector innovation expenditures. The exceptions are telecommunications, computer services and engineering services where R&D accounts for over three-quarters of expenditures related to innovative activity.

Innovation inputs (elements) that are not classified as R&D include market research, training in innovation, adoption and adaptation of new technology, start-up activities, organizational changes and incremental impacts. Such inputs characterize key activity in service-sector firms. Because service activities are generally labor intensive, investment in human capital costs often represents a larger share of total innovation expenditures. For example, staff training for evolving computer systems or new product offerings is a continual process in service industries.

Customization is also a grey area for distinguishing between R&D and non R&D innovation activities. Service-producing industries commonly take products developed in the manufacturing sector and add value to them by assembling customized systems or networks. Frequently, a system is specifically tailored to an individual client and its assembly represents a unique product. However, it may be unclear if this is the development of a new and improved product—hence, to be included as R&D—or the reapplication of existing methods and processes in providing a service. It is possible that new knowledge and refined techniques are developed as part of most custom systems integration services that could be classified as R&D.

Acquisition and integration of technology may also be an important component of innovation that is frequently not included as R&D. These activities are of particular importance to service-sector firms because much of the R&D associated with services is embodied in products acquired from outside of the service sector. The issue becomes what share of acquisition and integration activities is R&D and what share is simply technology adoption or imitation that is not classified as R&D.

F. DEFINITIONS OF MANUFACTURING VERSUS SERVICE SECTOR

Over time, the once sizeable distinction between manufacturing industries and service-producing industries is narrowing. This broadening of scope is referred to as servicization, or the trend in manufacturing to encapsulate the physical product in a shell of services (i.e., finance, monitoring, maintenance and repurchase). The largest contribution to growth in the service sector is from a small subset of all services known as knowledge-intensive business services (KIBSs) (e.g., telecommunications, information technology, networking and organizational consultancy). However, a growing number of authors point to such firms as IBM and Siemens (both large mass-production service firms), as examples of traditional manufacturers who now have a dominant share of their business activities associated with the sale of services.

Business interactions and joint product development between the service-producing industries and manufacturing industries represent an increasing trend in product and service innovation. For example, American Airlines (AA) played a significant role in developing the design specifications for Boeing's 777 series. However, much of AA's activities were likely conducted by staff in market research divisions, and it is unclear what share of this work was or should have been counted as R&D expenditures. Similarly, telecommunications and financial service providers are integrally involved in specifying components that go into their systems.

G. MEASUREMENT ISSUES

Empirical evidence demonstrates that service-producing industries innovate and have been doing so increasingly over time (Sirilli and Evangelista, 1998). As national institutions began measuring innovation activities in the service sector, the original models and data collection instruments were based on an understanding of the technology innovation process as it applied to manufacturing firms. However, because of the intangible nature of the service sector's output, it is difficult to measure the productivity of R&D performed using the historical measures of innovation, such as new products or patents (Gallouj and Weinstein, 1997). The manufacturing sector adds value to inputs—R&D is an input in the innovation process—by continuously improving the materials and design of their products, whereas the service sector applies accumulated knowledge to build organizational models or systems, which is a more abstract output than in manufacturing (Jankowski, 2001). In the absence of such appropriate metrics, any resulting measure of innovative activity would, by definition, be limited.

Service innovations draw less directly on scientific breakthroughs and are often small or incremental in nature, this means that small changes can lead to new applications or reorganization of an existing technology or system (Pilat, 2001). Some large service-sector firms actually have an innovation department that promotes and collects ideas. However, this organizational design may be the exception rather than the rule. Service-sector innovations are typically based on both market-wide and consumer-specific needs.

Patenting in the service sector is at times more difficult because of high visibility or the inexcludability of the product or process. If a manufacturing firm develops an innovative process or product, it can keep the process or product a secret by not allowing anyone outside the firm to see it. Service-sector firms offering intangible products have much higher visibility, which makes it hard to contain trade secrets and easier for other firms to imitate the product or process.

Innovation in service-sector firms is generally not a systematic process and often consists of spontaneous ideas developed internally to meet the real-time needs of a specific client. In contrast, innovation in manufacturing firms is typically highly structured, with a systematic approach to developing new products following the product lifecycle. Although there is an attempt to systematically organize and account for innovation across all sectors, measuring innovation in the service sector is extremely subjective because of the intangible nature of its products (Pilat, 2001). Measuring innovation is further complicated in the service sector because it occurs throughout the organizational process.

In the service sector, activities that are of an R&D nature are often decentralized through different business units of a firm, making them difficult to measure. Often these activities occur in very small groups that, reasonably, cannot segment their time between traditionally defined R&D and other technical areas. In addition, the product/service development process in the service sector does not fit well with the fundamental R&D concepts of engineering design, prototype testing and manufacturing process design leading to mass production (concepts that emerged from the manufacturing sector).

H. PUBLIC POLICY ISSUES: EXAMPLE OF THE US R&E TAX CREDIT

The US R&E Tax Credit of 1981 is a good example of how shortcoming in definitions and measurement issues can hamper public policy from stimulating many forms of innovation activities. The US R&E Tax Credit definition uses the term "qualified research" to identify activities aimed at creating new information or products and new applications of existing knowledge as applied to existing products. As shown in Table I.4.2, the US R&E Tax Credit excludes several types of innovative activities, such as the customization, modification or adaptation of existing products to meet a client's needs.

Table I.4.2. Activities included and excluded from the US R&E tax credit

Included in the definition of R&D	Not included in the definition of R&D
Research that is undertaken to discover information that is technical in nature and holds applications useful in developing a new or improved business component of the taxpayer	Adaptation of existing business components to fit a particular customer's requirements
Research that seeks a new or improved function performance, reliability or quality	Research after commercial production of the business component
	Market research, testing or development (including advertising or promotions); routine data collection; efficiency surveys
	Routine or ordinary testing or inspection for quality control
	Scientific and technical information assistance
	Social sciences, etc.: Any research in the social sciences, arts or humanities
	Activity relating to management function or technique

Designed to stimulate significant advances in technology, as opposed to incremental improvements in products or processes, qualifying activities must be attempting to obtain knowledge that exceeds, expands or refines the common knowledge of skilled professionals. And the process must rely on principles of the physical or biological sciences, engineering or computer science.

From the perspective of the service sector, a key shortcoming of the US R&E Tax Credit is that 80% of research must be of an experimental nature: developing hypotheses, designing and conducting experiments and refining and discarding hypotheses. Other shortcomings of the US R&E Tax Credit include the following:

- The US R&E Tax Credit has been "temporary" for 25 years. It was recently renewed as part of the US stimulus package. This makes long-term investment planning difficult.
- The incremental nature of the US R&E Tax Credit (only R&E expenditures above a company's historical levels are eligible), results in limited impact on long-term business investment decisions and strategic planning.
- The "experimentation" focus of the US R&E Tax Credit (targeted at shifting the composition), excludes many important aspects of R&D, including much of innovation.
- Because credits cannot be banked, start-up companies (with negative profits), are not able to take advantage of the program.

The result is that researchers have found little evidence of the benefits of the US R&E Tax Credit on technology development and innovation (Tassey, 2007).

However, it should be noted that the US government engages in a wider range of technology policy initiatives. For example, the public sector has been successful in promoting the development of infra-technologies - which are very important to the service sector - through:

- Organizations, such as the National Institute of Standards and Technology (NIST), which are active in developing standards and protocols essential for "integration" activities;
- Government-led consortiums;
- Test beds for interoperability; and
- Certification and conformance testing.

I. SUMMARY REMARKS

R&D is a constant driver in both the manufacturing and a service sectors, although its purposes are sometimes very different. Certainly, the innovation process is markedly different between the two sectors. However, the categories of market failures and the policy approaches to address these failures are just as relevant for service-sector R&D investment as for manufacturing R&D investment. However, issues of defining and measuring service-sector R&D are different in many instances and need to be investigated.

Among manufacturing firms, in-house R&D is intended to develop proprietary technology that leverages productivity growth. Among service-sector firms, in-house R&D is intended to leverage the process of adopting and modifying purchased technology that also leverages productivity growth. Thus, innovation polices that stimulate R&D will enhance the productivity growth of firms in both sectors.

We recommend reviewing and potentially broadening the US definition of R&D for reporting purposes and for targeted innovation policy purposes. Being able to identify and measure service-sector R&D is critical, if accounting-based policies (such as tax credits), are to effectively stimulate R&D investment. In addition, there are uncertainties and inconsistencies in how process- and business-methods innovation fit into the definition of R&D and how they are covered under the current patent system.

Note that to address many of the measurement issues, the United States has engaged in a redesign of its R&D and Innovation Survey based largely on a National Academies' 2005 report, *Measuring Research and Development Expenditures in the US Economy*. The report recommended a redesign of the US Survey of Industrial Research and Development to benchmark it against best practices in other countries (Frascati Manual). Similar to the European Community Innovation Survey, several innovation activities were specifically recommended to be included in the new survey:

- The introduction of new products to the market;
- The development of new processes to produce or deliver new products for the market;
- The development of new markets;

- The finding of new sources of supply or raw materials; and
- Changes in the organization of the firms.

The result is the development of the new US Business R&D and Innovation Survey (BRDIS), which was developed by the US National Science Foundation (NSF) and US Census Bureau. BRDIS expands the range of data collection topic areas to include: (1) Measures related to R&D management strategy; (2) the share of R&D devoted to social science; (3) new business areas; and (4) measures related to intellectual property, technology transfer and innovation. This new information will greatly enhance the development and implementation of R&D and innovation policy in the United States.

REFERENCES

Evangelista, R. (1999), *Knowledge and Investment*, Northampton, MA: Edward Elgar Publishing, Inc.

Gallaher, M. P., Link, A. and Petrusa, J.E. (2006), *Innovation in the US service sector*, Abingdon, UK: Routledge Publishing.

Gallaher, M. P. and Rowe, B. R. (2006), „The costs and benefits of transferring technology infrastructures underlying complex standards: The case of IPv6", *Journal of Technology Transfer*, 31, pp.519–544.

Gallouj, F. and Weinstein, O. (1997), "Innovation in services", *Research Policy*, 26, pp.537-556.

Howells, J. (2000), "Services and systems of innovation". In B. Andersen (Ed.), *Knowledge and Innovation in the New Service Economy*. Northampton, MA: Edward Elgar Publishing Inc.

Jankowski, J. E. (2001), "Measurement and growth of R&D within the service economy", *Journal of Technology Transfer*, 26, pp.323–336.

Miles, I. and Dachs, B. (2005), *The future of R&D in services: Implications for E.U. research and innovation policy*, Report for the European Commission: Directorate-General Research.

National Institute of Standards and Technology (NIST) (2005), *Measuring service-sector research and development, planning report 05-1*, Gaithersburg, MD: National Institute of Standards and Technology.

National Research Council of the National Academies (2005), *Measuring research and development expenditures in the US economy*. Washington, DC: The National Academies Press.

Pilat, D. (2001), "Innovation and productivity in services: state of the art". In *Innovation and Productivity in Services*. Paris, France: Organisation for Economic Co-operation and Development.

Sirilli, G. and Evangelista, R. (1998), "Technological innovation in services and manufacturing: results from Italian surveys", *Research Policy*, 27, pp.881–899.

Sundbo, J. and Gallouji, F. (1999), *Innovation in services in seven European countries*, Report for the European Commission.

Tassey, G. (2005), "Underinvestment in public good technology", *Journal of Technology Transfer*, 30, pp.89-113.

Tassey, G. (2007), "Tax incentives for innovation: Time to restructure the R&E tax credit", *Journal of Technology Transfer*, 32, pp.605–615.

Tether, B., Hipp, C. and Miles, I. (2001), "Standardisation and specialisation in services: evidence from Germany", *Research Policy*, 30, pp.1115–1138.

5. ARE SPECIFIC POLICIES NEEDED TO STIMULATE INNOVATION IN SERVICES?

Adriana van Cruysen and Hugo Hollanders, UNU-MERIT, Maastricht University, the Netherlands

A. INTRODUCTION

The increased macroeconomic significance of the services sector has been well documented in terms of its contribution to employment, productivity, innovation and economic growth. However, productivity growth has not been uniform across all subsectors. KIBS (Knowledge-intensive Business Services), for example, differs from traditional service sectors, as it has shown not only productivity growth in its own right, but has also had a profound impact on productivity growth in other sectors. Nonetheless, innovation in the services sector has generally been characterized by low budgets for R&D. According to Gronroos (1990), there are a wide range of possible sources of innovation in services: not only the service concept (service as a product) innovation, but also service process innovation, service infrastructure innovation, customer process innovation, business model innovation, commercialization innovation (sales, marketing, delivery), hybrid innovation serving several user groups in different ways simultaneously and service productivity innovation. As a result of the different types of innovation that can take place in the sector, there is a lack of indicators and methodologies to measure services innovation, which makes it even more difficult to determine the need for and develop appropriate policies. While codification and standardization of services have scope to improve the sector's tradability, location remains important in the service sector and plays an important role in innovation activity, as services are often provided close to where consumers are located.

Policy in services innovation is considered to be underdeveloped when compared to policy in manufacturing innovation. The development of policies to support innovation in the service sector needs to take account of the sector's specificities, which have an impact on how the sector innovates. Most relevant sector specificities relate to the interactive nature of services (involvement of customers in the innovation process); the 'fuzzy' nature of services (making it difficult to differentiate among product, process and organizational innovation and their individual economic impacts); intangibility (appropriation regime difficulties); heterogeneity (variability); a relative absence of quality standards; and lack of market transparency (which creates the risk of dissatisfaction once the service is delivered) (Gallouj, 1997).

Moreover, the division between services and manufacturing is becoming increasingly blurred. Manufacturing firms increasingly provide services complementary to their products and consequently face the same kind of regulatory obstacles as service sector firms when trading. Innovation policies directed to the service sector also have an impact on the manufacturing sector when performing or consuming services activities, affecting manufacturing firms' competitiveness.

A recent study by Arundel et al. (2007) on Innovation Statistics for the European Service Sector demonstrated that relatively fewer firms in the services sector can be seen as technological innovators (new products and processes) than firms in the manufacturing sector. The exception were the firms in the Knowledge-intensive Business Services (KIBS) sector[38], which were more likely than the firms in the manufacturing sector to introduce either a product or process innovation. With regard to non-technological innovations (organizational and marketing innovations), there were no differences in the percentage of all industrial and service sector firms that introduced either an organizational or marketing innovation, although KIBS firms were far more likely to introduce each type of innovation.

These empirical results corroborate the idea that the services sector is highly heterogeneous, and consequently cannot be treated as one sector for policy purposes. KIBS tend to be more in line with the manufacturing sector when it comes to both technological (new products and processes) and non-technological (organizational and marketing) innovations, while firms from the rest of the service sector lag behind in terms of technological innovation, but have similar patterns to manufacturing firms when it comes to non-technological innovations.

Policymakers must take into account the heterogeneity and the multidimensional nature of innovation within the service sector when formulating and implementing policies. The increasing importance of the services sector and services activities in the economy in general and KIBS in particular calls for greater intelligence at the sector and subsector levels, which would greatly assist the policy making process.

B. MARKET AND SYSTEMIC FAILURES

This paper examines both market failure and systemic failure rationales to justify policy intervention, although they may lead to different types of policies. Much of the literature analyses such failures as they apply to innovation based on R&D activities. Here, we examine these concepts as they might apply to innovation in services, and in particular KIBS.

The market failure approach focuses on resources allocation to knowledge production and other innovative activity. Failure is associated with risk and uncertainties. On the other hand, the systemic failure approach focuses on units' interactions in knowledge exploration and exploitation. It recognizes that actors have different motivations when engaged in knowledge creation and diffusion. This approach is broader in nature. Nonetheless, the relations between the two are not always clear, and not always mutually exclusive. In certain senses, they may overlap. The main goal of both approaches is to facilitate innovation activity by creating incentives for those actors that are considered to be constrained. In terms of intervention, the market failure approach leads to more specific types of intervention, while the systemic approach leads to more generic ones.

---

[38] KIBS includes Computer and related activities (NACE K72), Research and development (NACE K73), Architectural and engineering activities and consultancy (NACE K74.2) and Technical testing and analysis (NACE K74.3).

Market failures - introduction

Market failures may lead to firms under-investing in innovation activity (e.g. R&D). For example, they may not be able to appropriate the full benefits of their investments, which may also benefit competitors who have not made the corresponding investment. On the other hand, society benefits from these spillovers (called externalities), as they have a wider positive impact on productivity. Price mechanisms may also incorrectly reflect the benefits of new technologies and innovations.

According to Gustafsson and Autio (2006), market failure in knowledge production relates to underinvestment in knowledge creation (notably R&D) due to (1) *uncertainties and risks* in innovation (R&D) efforts, (2) *insufficient appropriability* (leading to failure to appropriate return from innovation and new knowledge), (3) *information asymmetries*, (4) failure of markets to reflect *externalities* (impacting knowledge diffusion) and (5) undervaluation of *public good* technologies in firms' strategies. The first two types of market failures involve risk aversion, hampering innovation activity. Typically, SMEs would be most affected, due to their limited sources of funds. Larger companies would also be affected but to a lesser extent, as they can make use of their market, financial and negotiation power.

According to the authors, markets would under-invest in innovation activity due to the non-proprietary nature of knowledge (potential leaks), and the uncertainty in the exploration of new knowledge. Moreover, due to the public good nature of knowledge, economic actors would take advantage of the innovation activities of other actors. This would explain the second mover advantage, where firms wait for somebody else to make the investments that lead to knowledge creation and only then invest in the market, avoiding risks and high exploration costs.

Gustafsson and Autio (2006) suggested a few actions to correct these failures, including the implementation of appropriability regimes with IPR legislation, subsidies (tax breaks, direct funding and loans), and setting up R&D labs to facilitate access of firms to knowledge and support for university research. A more detailed discussion on policies will follow in section C.

Market failures in services innovation

Different types of market failures may have an impact on innovation activity in the services sector. We build upon the work of Kox and Rubalcaba (2007) to classify market failures in the services sector, even though the authors have concentrated on the business services subsector.

When an agent in a market gains market power, due to lack of adequate competition (imperfect competition), this may lead to inefficiencies.

Imperfect competition can take different forms, such as monopolies, monopsonies and cartels. In this case, intervention is necessary to control for entry barriers, monopolistic or strategic oligopolistic behaviour, which may result in suboptimal allocation of resources and/or high prices for consumers. Today's markets have seen a wave of mergers and acquisitions, resulting in an increasing number of larger firms in many industries. In imperfect competition markets, the consumer is denied the benefit of choice. Firms with market power may use their market position to hamper competition, restricting production, manipulating offers (which may lead to shortages), and setting higher prices. The lack of competition may lead to inertia in terms of innovation activity. Competition forces firms to constantly innovate, offering better quality, and lower prices.

Firms in the services sector that provide more standardized services (limited differentiation and relative role of price) can gain some economies of scales. These are often a reduced number of large international firms, who together have a significant market share (between 20 to 50% of the market), (Kox and Rubalcaba, 2007). The concentration of these sectors in the hands of a few large firms may lead to collusive behaviour, or oligopolistic strategies. On the other hand, firms that offer more standardized services have a certain degree of transparency, making it easier for authorities to detect collusive behaviour.

Markets for client-specific products, on the other hand, are fragmented. Firms in the services sector that provide client-specific business services are characterized by smaller firms, with smaller combined market shares when compared to those providing standardized services. In this case, markets are not transparent (either in terms of tariff structure or real quality of the services provided, at least before purchase and consumption), but segmented. Prices do not play a significant role in competition. Moreover, demand for client-specific business is not perfectly price-elastic; switching costs are relevant from the client's point of view, possibly leading to market failure. Firms in fragmented markets tend to compete in terms of specific knowledge-based inputs, which may result in localized monopolies. In addition the localised nature of much services activity can mean that markets in the service sector are more geographically fragmented than for manufacturing sectors.

Actions of agents can create economic "side effects" to an uninvolved third party, known as externalities.

There are two types of externalities: negative externality relates to a harmful side effect, which in most cases, constitutes an external cost, while positive externality relates to a beneficial side effect impacting an uninvolved third party. Intervention would be necessary to either correct negative externalities or to reinforce positive ones.

Negative externalities: In the case of KIBS markets, intervention is based on social externalities that are "attached" to these services. For example, in the case of accountancy, the aim is to safeguard reliable financial information that leads to trust in capital and financial markets. A possible negative externality would be fraud that could be reduced by an independent, reliable and accountable control and reporting system.

Moreover, slow productivity development seems to be a serious obstacle for the service sector in general. Because services have an impact on the economy, productivity problems in the sector can affect the whole economy and hamper economic growth. Low productivity in the services sectors is passed down as an intermediary input to other sectors through high prices. The negative externality (in the form of lack of competition, poor incentive to innovate and cost efficiency), "travels downstream" reducing competitiveness and innovation in other sectors.

Positive externalities: Growth in business services has proved to create positive externalities outside the sector. For example, business services contributes directly to technological innovation (in software and engineering), as well as to non-technological innovation (labour productivity), in client industries. Another relevant positive externality benefits SMEs, which can overcome scales limitations and setup costs by using external business services.

There are other areas where positive externalities may lead to under-provision. One of these areas relates to incentives for innovation whereby the benefits of an innovation are picked up by firms other than the innovating firm and the social returns from the investment in the innovation are higher than the private one. This argument has often been applied in the case of technological innovation, but may apply equally well to non-technological innovations. In addition, it is known that SMEs in particular, spend a small share of their revenues in innovation, even though innovation would be fundamental for the industry. More could be done in terms of incentives, institutional structures, bureaucratic procedures, fiscal climate and intellectual properties, although most of these issues relate to systemic failures and not market failures. Knowledge diffusion is hampered when knowledge assets become obsolete. This is particularly relevant in small firms, which dominate the business services sector, where employees are required to spend most of their time in daily activities, with little opportunity to acquire new knowledge and skills.

Markets can also fail due to the nature of certain goods, or the nature of their exchange. For example, goods can display attributes of public goods, while markets may have significant transactions costs, agency problems or informational asymmetry.

Public goods are goods and services provided by the government because a market failure has occurred. In many cases, provision of public goods and services (defined as economic products that are consumed collectively, like highways, schools, defence), may be beneficial, but in others, it would be preferable if markets could provide them.

Credence goods are related to many knowledge-intensive business services. It means that before or even just after purchasing them, the customer may not be able to assess their quality. According to Kox and Rubalcaba (2007), markets tend to correct this situation by using a firm's reputation, where the clients rely on a firm's past experience, trusting that the economic agent will behave in the same way as it did in the past. Reputable firms consequently earn a price premium, normally charging a higher price for their offerings. Moreover, firms with reputation have less incentive to reduce inefficiencies and to exploit scale economies to gain cost advantages. Building reputation requires time. It also functions as an entry barrier, leading to market segmentation. As a result, the premium segments of the market are "protected" by firms with a proven reputation. New entrants or SMEs are kept outside these premium segments.

Information asymmetry and non-transparencies happen when buyers and sellers are not well informed or when information is not equally distributed among participants. Without proper and timely information, uneducated decisions are made. This is particularly relevant for SMEs. The less-informed parties end up in disadvantage or they avoid taking risks to reduce exposure. The result of such behaviour is a reduction in the volume of transactions.

Due to certain characteristics of the services sector, including less tradability (services tend to be locally produced and consumed), intangibility (making it difficult to consumers to evaluate services quality before purchase and consumption), and the fact that SMEs are particular predominant in the sector, firms operating in the sector and their consumers are less informed about alternatives and choices. Information asymmetry has a negative impact on innovation activity as less-informed parties tend to avoid risk by reducing exposure, which would negatively impact innovation activity.

Resource immobility occurs when resources are not free to move from one industry to another or geographically.

The efficient allocation of resources requires that the factors of production (land, labour, entrepreneurs and capital), be free to move to wherever returns are the highest. Resource mobility is considered ideal in competitive market economies. Efficient allocation of resources in the services sector is more difficult due to the sector characteristics. Mobility of factors of production is impacted by more stringent regulations in the sector, resulting in more obstacles for services firms to cross borders. Internal regulations at member state level affect the services sector in terms of establishment, use of inputs, provision, promotion, distribution, sales and after sales activities. Other barriers include legal ones: protection leading to lack of transparency and imperfect competition, intellectual property appropriation and other restrictions to cross-border provision. Although barriers impeding the formation of an EU services market still abound, most of them could be removed through common regulations and setting of standards.

Moreover, culture and language are also important factors affecting mobility and efficient allocation of resources in the sector. Because resources cannot freely move along national borders, the service sector is less competitive when compared to the manufacturing one: lack of competition leads to inefficiency and increasing costs.

Across the EU, an obstacle to raise competitiveness in the service sector is the lack of a European common market for services or the existence of national markets' access restrictions at the nations' level within the EU. The reduction, if not elimination of such barriers would create incentives for firms to invest in innovation. When resources cannot move freely across borders, innovation activity is restricted to national borders; not being able to tap knowledge and skills developed elsewhere. Access to larger markets implies that EU firms would be able to make use of economies of scale, and recuperate investments in innovation activities in a shorter period of time. The opening of markets would create more competition, forcing firms to compete in terms of better quality and novel offerings, and consequently, they would have more incentives to innovate. According to the European Commission report "An Internal Market Strategy for Services" (2000), "If firms do not, or cannot, innovate by aggregating demand into larger geographical markets, the drive to compete on the basis of quality will be stopped dead in its tracks".

European consumers and firms would benefit from common ground rules regulating an EU services market. The opening of services markets to competition would result in increased productivity, and have a positive impact in terms of innovation, growth and creation of new jobs across borders.

Frequently, the underlying cause of market failure is a problem of property rights.

Firms engage less in innovation activity, if they cannot have control on innovation output because of a poor system of property rights. Even though firms in the service sector tend to invest less in R&D due to the nature of the sector, some subsectors have R&D investments that compare to the levels of investments in manufacturing firms. In these subsectors the use of property rights should not have many differences when comparing to manufacturing.

On the other hand, it is exactly the nature of the sector that opens up the need for property rights, and more specifically, trademarks. Many services are considered credence goods, meaning that it is not possible to evaluate the quality of the service before it has been purchased and consumed. There is a high risk involved when acquiring credence goods. One way to reduce the risk is to buy from reputable firms. Reputation takes time to build and involves brand recognition / brand awareness. Once consumers can make the link between credence goods and a brand name, they tend to repeat sales and reject alternative providers. In this case, the use of trademarks in the service sector functions as a differentiating factor.

Systemic failures - introduction

The review by Gustafsson and Autio (2006) of innovation system literature pointed out four types of failures: failures in evolutionary dynamics of innovation systems, lack of actor interactions and functions bridging knowledge production and use, suboptimal lock-ins by implementing actors and lack of supportive structures for innovation.

For the purpose of this paper, we group the different typologies of systemic failures under the general title "systemic failures," as there are many linkages between structures for innovation, systems and functional elements within systems.

The suboptimal adaptation of innovation structures may take place due to firms' inability to unlock from dominant externalities. Firms are locked into systems and find it difficult to break away from them and pursue new knowledge or to establish new collaborations. The failure to be to engage in new and better opportunities has been called "lock-in or path-dependency failure" by Smith (1997). Factors leading to failure to evolve from present systems may relate to institutional commitments and power relations (Walker, 2000). There is a tendency to strengthen both social and technological relations over time, making it difficult to break free (Weick and Roberts, 1993). The increasing rigidity of systems is due to uncertainties and financial risks. Consequently, systems tend to enforce exploitation rather than exploration. The actors and new technologies are hampered by both lack of legitimacy (Stinchcomb, 1965) and lack of interaction within the system (Carlsson et al., 2002).

Firms fail to react to discontinue technological change due to their path dependencies. If change is incremental, the tendency is towards structural inertia (Lundvall, 1988). Inertia creates a barrier for adaptation of new technologies. Firms may be able to overcome changes by establishing structures under the new technology regime. They can do that through standardization and new venture funding. If firms are not able to overcome changes brought about by radical or new technologies unrelated to their domains, they may not be able to establish structures under the new technology regime (Salter and Martin, 2001). Lack of standardization and market acceptance will increase users' risk to adopt new technologies and products. Moreover, in face of disruptive technological changes, deeply rooted path-dependent information processing mechanisms make adaptation difficult (Nelson and Winter, 1982).

Failures in structures for innovation, systems and functional elements within systems hamper innovation activity and consequently may require intervention.

Systemic failures in services innovation

Systemic failures refer to structural, institutional and regulatory deficiencies which lead to suboptimal investment in knowledge creation and other innovative activity. Actors not only perform at individual levels but they interact and exchange knowledge. Consequently, firms establish links with other firms, universities and government. If these interactions are poor, they will have a negative impact in the pace of innovation activity.

Moreover, systems interactions may be suboptimal, due to the system inability to function free from established externalities. Smith (1997) called it "lock-in or path-dependency" failure. Systems tend to evolve from more loose arrangements to more tight ones. Resources dependency limits action by individual actors, who tend to favour exploitation rather than exploration (Pfeffer and Salancik, 1978).

Gustafsson and Autio (2006) pointed out that systems tend to perform suboptimally specifically when profound technological changes are taking place. This is mainly due to lack of internal interactions and the high costs and risk involved in exploratory reconfigurations. When confronted with high uncertainty, systems tend towards inertia, and avoid taking the necessary measures to adapt to new circumstances. Government intervention is then necessary to help structural adaptation of innovation systems. Suggested measures to correct system failure include policies to enhance interaction, trust, and coordination (Lundvall, 1988). Other incentives to correct system failures include academic spin off schemes, science parks, venture capital, public procurement incentives in novel technologies (information, communications and health), (Gustafsson and Autio, 2006).

C. POLICY AREAS AND INTERVENTIONS

A common concern is that innovation policy is not adequately serving the needs of services firms. By comparing innovation indicators for firms in the service and manufacturing sectors one can examine whether firms' responses to questions related to their innovation behaviour support this concern or not. The 2007 INNO-Metrics thematic paper on "Innovation Statistics for the European Service Sector" has analyzed two different databases; the Community Innovation Survey (CIS) and Flash Barometer Survey (FBS), to look at differences between manufacturing and services firms in eight different policy areas. We first discuss the eight policy areas and related market failures in more detail, in particular as they might apply to KIBS, followed by a discussion of the policy areas and related systemic failures. Finally, we will discuss four types of broad policies which could be used to solve market and systemic failures. This is used as a basis for drawing conclusions and key messages for policymakers. A summary table is provided on services innovation policy areas and market failures, with selected examples of policy interventions.

Policy areas

1. *Intellectual property*

Approximately twice as many manufacturing than services firms applied for a patent and more manufacturing than services firms applied for a trademark (cf. Arundel et al., 2007). A much lower percentage of firms in KIBS apply for a patent than manufacturing firms (12% versus 20%) and KIBS firms are also less likely to apply for a trademark. The percentage of service and manufacturing firms that registered an industrial design is similar (16% versus 19%). Service sector firms are slightly more likely than manufacturing firms to claim copyright (6% versus 5%). However, this is almost entirely due to KIBS, where 13% of firms claim copyright. This is probably due to the use of copyright by computer software firms.

Two possible market failures may be present when innovation involves protecting intellectual property. The first one relates to externalities. It is commonly agreed that the services sector has a positive impact on other sectors. In specifically, certain services subsectors, such as business services, contribute directly to technological innovation (software and engineering), and impact other industries that make use of the subsector outputs.

Even though the sector, in general, has a lower participation in R&D investments, when compared to manufacturing, due to the sector heterogeneity, the degree of R&D investment and consequently, the use of intellectual property are unequal. Engineering and computer services, for example, score higher in R&D expenses when compared to retailing, wholesale, transport, and financial services.

When the services subsector involves technology, protecting intellectual property becomes relevant for firms investing in R&D to safeguard their findings, so as to recoup R&D costs. This would be particularly relevant for SMEs, due to their limited market power and financial constraints. Developing strong systems that would prevent appropriation of intellectual property would pave the way for increasing investments in the services subsectors that have an R&D (technology) component, with consequent positive impact in other sectors.

The second market failure relates to asymmetric information or lack of transparency. One possible way to avoid less informed parties ending up at a disadvantage or avoiding taking risk (and to innovate), is to protect innovation through intellectual property rights. Furthermore, as pointed out by Kox and Rubalcaba (2007), many knowledge-intensive business services are considered credence goods, where reputation is fundamental. The large gap between manufacturing and services firms for the use of trademarks suggests a lack of information or experience by service sector firms, since trademarks should be equally relevant to both industrial and service sector firms.

Encouraging service firms in general to make use of intellectual property (such as patents, design registration), would not be relevant considering the sector heterogeneity, but qualified policies, designed specifically for certain subsectors, which have an important component of R&D, for example, software, engineering and computer services, would not only create incentives for firms to take risks and invest in R&D, knowing that their innovations would be protected by intellectual property laws, but would also reduce relative disadvantages of less informed parties, specifically SMEs.

Moreover, there is no apparent reason for services firms not to make use of trademarks, considering the relevance of reputation (and consequently the need for brand recognition). The fact that the sector recurs less to trademarks when compared to the manufacturing sector, suggests the existence of information asymmetry, where firms that make use of trademarks have an advantage in terms of brand recognition and repeated sales.

In summary, policy might be able to correct externalities and asymmetric information, by designing qualified IPR policies for services firms involved in innovation activities; with specific incentives for SMEs due to their vulnerable position; and by creating the necessary incentives for firms to make use of trademarks and build awareness through brand recognition and the building of reputation.

2.   *Public procurement*

According to Arundel et al. (2007), a higher percentage of innovative manufacturing firms (14%) than service sector firms (11%) report a lack of demand as a problem, although there is little difference between KIBS and manufacturing firms. Government plays a role in demand, as a consumer of innovative products and services. The existence of a public procurement mechanism that is open, competitive and efficient would have a positive impact in innovation activity. Public procurement can stimulate the development of new services, as for example, e-government, e-health, e-education, etc.

The three market failures that would impact negatively on public procurement relate to asymmetric information/lack of transparency, market power and property rights. It is only through an open, competitive and efficient public procurement that the development of new services could take place. To be open, all participants should have access to information. To be competitive, markets cannot be dominated by monopolies or few large players. Market power should be spread, so more firms are able to participate.

In summary, public procurement if used well could be an important driver for those sectors where the public sector is a major client. In particular, public procurement could drive innovation by increasing competition and the number of companies active in a market.

3.   *Qualified personnel*

The CIS asks innovative firms about the importance of a 'lack of qualified personnel' as a factor hampering their ability to innovate. According to Arundel et al. (2007), more manufacturing than service sector firms report this factor as of high importance (12% versus 10%). There is little difference within the service subsectors, with equivalent percentages for KIBS and other service sectors. Moreover, according to the FBS survey, there is no difference between the two main sectors in terms of satisfaction with the qualifications of university graduates.

These findings suggest that there might be no reason to preferentially favour service sector firms over manufacturing firms in innovation programmes to improve the supply of trained personnel. On the other hand, the nature of the skills need for innovation in service sectors may differ from manufacturing and there are a few areas where policy could benefit the services sector: private household as employer and family policy measures (and their inter-relations), and special skills.

Family policy measures may improve the balance between family and work, which is specifically beneficial for women, and specifically mothers. These measures could have a positive impact in the number of highly skilled women joining the job market. Although family policy measures would benefit all economic sectors, they would have a significant impact in the service sector due to its nature and characteristics. Service sector allows for greater flexibility in terms of location (for example, the household has become an increasingly important field for new jobs), and time. Part-time arrangements are more common in the services sector than in manufacturing, due to greater flexibility in services in general. Related policies would include infrastructure of education (child care, day care centres, full-day schools), tax allowances for the cost of child care, encouraging mothers to take jobs, etc.

Services require not only highly qualified personnel, which are supplied by the tertiary sector, but due to the sector's heterogeneity, a wide range of skills, which can be acquired through vocational training and training on the job. To make the qualifications obtained in the dual system easily accepted elsewhere in Europe and increase mobility, foreign language skills and intercultural competences could be improved and more periods spent abroad included as part of any training.

In summary, policy on supplying qualified personnel, in particular, tertiary education would benefit the economy as a whole, but policy focus on promoting new services skills, vocational training, and training on the job, with a clear mobility component (training abroad, language and intercultural skills), would be specifically beneficial for the services sector and the formation of an EU common market for services. Policy intervention in the supply of qualified personnel and programs geared towards labour mobility (training abroad, languages and intercultural skills), would facilitate resource (labour) mobility.

4. *Access to public science*

Due to the complexity of modern science[39] and the need to combine knowledge in new ways, firms frequently source knowledge and capabilities from other firms and institutions. Of interest to policy is the function of the 'public science' sector (publicly funded universities or other higher education institutes plus government or public research institutes). National innovation policies may facilitate public science to transfer research results with potential commercial applications to the private sector. This system has focused largely on the manufacturing sector. The service sector, on the other hand, may be at a disadvantage.

The CIS contains several relevant questions, based on the percentage of firms that collaborate with public science and the percentage of firms that give a 'high' rating to the importance of public science as a source of information to their innovation activities. Results are available separately for universities and higher education institutes and for government and public

---

[39] Public science is used here in a broad sense to include engineering, humanities and the arts.

research institutes. The question on collaboration also asks respondents to indicate which collaboration partner was 'most valuable for their innovation activities?'

With the exception of KIBS, service sector firms are considerably less likely to collaborate with universities than manufacturing firms. One possible explanation could be that service sector firms, except for KIBS, could have little to gain from university research results, which are often far from the market. As suggested by Arundel et al. (2007), the fact that the gap between manufacturing and services declines for collaboration with government and public research institutes, which tend to focus on applied research, suggests that part of the lack of collaboration with universities is due to research results that are not of use to service sector firms.

According to the theory of market failures in resource mobility, the efficient allocation of resources requires that the factors of production are free to move to wherever returns are the highest. If the public science sector sees limitations for the service sector (except for KIBS) to find commercial applications for their research results (possibly due to the intangible nature of services), then resources for funding-applied research may not be allocated for the public research with possible service-oriented (intangible) output. In this case, innovation activity in the service sector would be hampered by lack of resources in the public sector for projects not involving tangible outputs. If this is correct, then policy is required to support research in the public science sector that would result in intangible outputs with commercial application in the services sector.

In summary, some re-orientation of policy intervention on links between public science and firms may benefit KIBS in particular, which is more likely to gain from collaborations with both universities and governments due to its knowledge component and for a broader incentive for the public science sector to invest in research with possible intangible results that could have commercial applications in the service sector.

5.   *Start-ups*

CIS firm-level data provides information about start-ups between the years 1998-2000. The data indicates that higher shares of firms in services than in manufacturing are start-ups and start-up formation is highest in KIBS, particularly among innovative firms. Even though these results suggest that there is no need to preferentially support start-ups in the service versus manufacturing sectors, considering that in general, start-up formation rates are higher in services, the same conclusions may not apply across all services subsectors. A more detailed analysis of start-up formation at subsector level would be relevant for designing policies.

Although SMEs have the potential to innovate, they tend to spend low shares of their revenues in innovation, negatively impacting innovation activity and productivity growth in their industry and in the economy in general. One of the reasons is that SMEs lack the necessary funds to both be established and to develop. One possible market failure at play would be related to resource mobility, in specific, lack of venture capital.

The establishment of attractive conditions for an internationally oriented venture capital market would facilitate the formation and development of new firms. In Germany, for example, one of the aims for creating new businesses is to increase the self-employment ratio (Annual Economic Report, 2006).

Although the presence of new and small businesses in an economy creates a series of positive externalities (such as employment), small businesses are mostly bounded to operate in domestic markets and in certain subsectors. For these reasons, policy at national level could be more effective. Even though SMEs tend to operate at national level, the formation and development of new firms would benefit from a common EU services market, with common regulations and standardization.

There may be other types of market failures at play, including the existence of market power in the hands of a few larger firms, creating entry barriers for new firms with innovative offerings; or the existence of information asymmetries, leading to the use of reputation by incumbents, which would be more difficult in the case of new and small firms, that have not had the time to build their own brands.

In summary, policy could benefit all economic sectors by creating an attractive venture capital market, with a particular positive impact on new and small firms. Considering that services firms face more barriers than manufacturing ones to operate outside national borders, and consequently have less opportunities to grow based on economies of scales created by larger markets, SMEs in the services sector would benefit from an increased access to available financing and from an increase in financing.

6.   *Support for innovation programmes*

Policy support for innovation is believed to favour industrial over service-sector firms. This could partly be due to higher levels of investment in innovation in manufacturing firms, or at least in activities such as R&D where public support is widely available. An evaluation of a possible bias in innovation support to industrial firms should be informed by the percentage of firms by sector that are eligible for receiving specific types of support.

The CIS data only permit an evaluation of the percentage of all innovative firms that receive public support. Data is available for firms that received any public support for innovation and such support from the European Union. A substantially higher percentage of manufacturing firms (29%) than service sector firms (16%) report any support (mostly from regional or national authorities), although KIBS firms (23%) perform almost as well as manufacturing firms. A higher percentage of manufacturing (5%) than services firms (4%) receive support from the European Union, although this percentage is inflated by the presence of KIBS firms, which reports an even higher percentage of firms receiving European support (7%).

The bias towards the manufacturing sector when compared to services (excluding KIBS) in receiving EU support may be related to the fact that there is already a well developed EU common market for goods, and consequently manufacturing firms have access to larger markets and can make use of economies of scale to recover investments in innovation. The lack of scale in the services sector in general, and the difficulties faced to develop a common European services market may explain the sectors' differences in support at EU level.

In summary, there may be a need to re-orientate innovation support programmes more towards the needs of service sector companies. This applies equally to EU programmes which can also then influence national and regional programmes, and may also play a role in fostering a common market in services.

7.   *Regulatory burden*

In the FBS, innovative SMEs that had introduced a product or service innovation in the previous two years were asked if the need to meet national regulations for their innovations placed their firm at a competitive disadvantage in respect to their competitors. The regulations were divided into four types: environmental, consumer protection, safety, and product design characteristics. Although a lower percentage of service-sector SMEs than industrial SMEs report that national regulations on product and process innovations placed them at a competitive disadvantage, with the exception of consumer protection rules affecting service sector, these results may not be applied to all services subsectors. In addition, service firms may be less affected than manufacturing firms by differing national regulations because services are less likely to be traded across national boundaries.

The services sector is seen as highly regulated. Due to its heterogeneity, regulatory burden needs to be explored at subsector level. Certain subsectors may require de-regulation while others may even require re-regulation. To add to the problem, the fragmented nature of the European markets leads to heterogeneity in regulation not only at subsector level but also at national level.

Negative impact of regulation at subsector level may be related to different types of market failures, including negative externalities, market power, asymmetric information and lack of resource mobility. These market failures may be present in different subsectors, at different intensities. Considering that regulation differs at subsector level, and national level, the creation of a European common services market would be influential in terms of common regulations at subsector level. Such policies should have the greatest impact in specific subsectors where excessive rules hamper cross-border provision of services, leading to diseconomies of scales and lack of incentives to innovate.

8.   *Access to finance*

According to CIS-4 data, a higher percentage of manufacturing than service-sector firms report problems with shortage of funds within the firm, which could be related to higher innovation costs. In terms of external financial sources, a higher percentage of manufacturing than service sector firms report difficulties. As for KIBS firms, considering that many of them are likely to be start-ups, there seems to be a lack of venture capital in general, rather than a bias in supply towards manufacturing.

Results indicate that firms in the services sector were less likely to report high innovation costs as a barrier for innovation compared with manufacturing firms, suggesting that innovation is less expensive in the service sector. However, both services and manufacturing responses indicate that there might be a problem of finance due to underdeveloped venture capital markets within Europe.

Efficient and sound financial markets are necessary to ensure a constant supply of capital for both formation and development of enterprises, regardless of the sector. Financial markets not only benefit established firms, but also provide venture capital for new firms and for firms to fund innovation programmes. Sound financial markets demand also a sound legal and regulatory system, which provides for the efficient functioning of the markets. Moreover, in order to attract funds from outside, EU financial markets must ensure that international standards are complied with and that markets are transparent. Consequently, sound financial markets demand a certain level of homogenization, transparency and supervisory systems in place. The existence of such markets would benefit all economic sectors. In this sense, possible market failures in this area would relate to negative externalities, market power (control of financial markets by large institutional investors, for example), asymmetric information and lack of mobility in terms of funds. There do not appear to be market failures that are specific to services firms.

Systemic failures and policies

Systemic failures may be related to several of the policy areas discussed in this paper. Considering that systems might be under-performing due to poor or lack of interactions among actors, the policy areas "Improve use and access to public sciences," and "Improve support of innovation programmes for service sector firms," would be relevant for intervention. Effective measures in both policy areas would lead to more coordination and incentives for services firms to invest in innovation activities leading to novel technologies. Such measures can help firms to break away from lock-in systems, and explore new configurations, involving new collaborations.

Other policy areas may be connected to systems failures. For example, policies can help building up trust, so firms will be motivated to engage in exploratory activities. One way to build trust is to ensure a regime of appropriability ("use of intellectual property") that would create incentives for firms to explore new configurations and exploit the results of their efforts. Another example relates to policies in "public procurement", which would also create incentives for firms to explore novel technologies or configurations.

Policies in the area of "support foundation of start-ups" (venture capital), and "financing" would help firms in terms of costs and risks involved in new exploration activities, such as these firms' new ventures or incumbents taking the risk of breaking free from rigid systems and looking for new alternatives.

Finally, systems failures may relate to policies to "reduce regulatory burden". As discussed, systems tend to evolve from loose arrangements to more tight and rigid ones, or from less bureaucratic ones to highly regulated, with little margin for change. The end result is that firms tend to favour exploitation instead of exploration. For innovation activity to take place, policy needs to assess the necessary level of regulation, so firms have a supportive environment to pursue new knowledge, and break away from inertia, which is characteristic of highly regulated systems.

In summary, systemic failures may be associated with most policy areas discussed in this paper, which may indicate the need for policy interventions.

Mapping policies

There are many different ways to map services innovation policies. Van Ark et al. (2003) suggested grouping them into four categories: horizontal, vertical, broadening and deepening policies. By using this structure, the authors emphasized the idea of convergence with manufacturing policies/cross-sector policies plus the reinforcement of synergies and complementarities between manufacturing and services sectors, avoiding contradictory effects between the two sectors. We adapted the authors' 4D structure to incorporate targeted policies, which we believe would be relevant for the services sector. Considering the sector's heterogeneity, and different needs at subsector level, we believe there is scope for targeted policies that would be developed to access specific needs at subsector level.

Horizontal policies

Horizontal policies are not directly related to innovation, but they are important in supporting innovation activity. Horizontal policies are cross sector, and consequently they lead to convergence with manufacturing-oriented policies. For example, human capital in terms of education, training, and mobility; cooperation among firms and between firms and research institutes. Another important area relates to demand as a driver for innovation and the need to deregulate markets to stimulate demand for new offerings, leading to an innovation culture.

Deepening of current innovation policies

The idea of deepening current innovation policies suggests that existing policies that have been developed for the manufacturing sector should be extended to the services sector and should focus more on non-technological aspects of innovation. The deepening of current innovation policies should also aim to create spill over effects, with clear benefits for all sectors.

Innovation policies in place tend to focus on technological aspects of innovation (R&D). The deepening of such policies would mean incorporating incentives for non-technical innovation (organizational and marketing innovation). Furthermore, the technological component of actual innovation policies should also be extended to both services firms and services functions and to promote an "innovation culture" in the service sector. Van Ark et al. (2003) suggested that current policies should promote links between services firms and public and private research organizations in areas of technical and non-technical innovations.

Broadening policies

Considering the links between the manufacturing and services sectors, the existence of services functions within manufacturing firms and the link between organizational innovation and ICT, it is clear that services and manufacturing are increasingly inter-connected. If this is true, then there will be less need to develop specific policies tailored to the services sector, as the lines between the two are becoming more and more blurred. Van Ark et al. (2003) suggested that in the future, when designing new innovation policies, they should be aimed at the services function in both services and manufacturing sectors. Broadening policies would be particular relevant for reinforcing synergies between the two sectors.

Targeted policies

Due to high heterogeneity within the services sector, there is scope for targeted policies. As discussed, KIBS has a significant role in services innovation. KIBS firms are more likely to introduce a technical innovation than other services firms, although less likely than industrial firms to apply for patents and trademarks. Moreover, KIBS firms rely more on public sciences than others in the services sectors, probably due to the technology component of its innovation activity. KIBS firms also collaborate more with universities than any other services subsector and are more likely to be start-ups than firms in other sectors or services subsectors. These results place KIBS firms in a different position when compared with other services subsectors. If KIBS occupies such a relevant position in the services sector, then policy directed for further development of KIBS could be relevant, considering positive spill-over in other areas of the economy.

But the relevance of KIBS in the services sector also points to the need to support other subsectors where innovation is non-technology oriented (organizational and marketing innovation), that lack adequate (financial) support. Moreover, there are a significant number of SMEs in the services sector, due to its more local oriented scope. SMEs require more support in terms of venture capital, financing and intellectual protection to engage in innovation activity. Furthermore, other areas may require target policies. For example, although policy related to education benefits the economy as a whole, there is a need to develop vocational training targeted to new skills demanded by the services sector. These are only a few examples that illustrate how targeted policies could benefit the sector and its subsectors.

Market failures and policies

Innovation in services faces a range of market failures and systemic failures that are similar to those that occur in the manufacturing sector. But for services innovation these failures differ in their nature and their degree as compared to manufacturing. The existence of these failures suggests that there is under-investment in services innovation. Governments could remedy the effects of these failures by either extending and/or adjusting already existing policies or by designing and implementing new polices. Based on the discussion in the previous sections, Table I.5.1 seeks to summarize the nature of the different market failures in the eight identified policy areas, and suggests which kind of policies could be used to correct these failures and lists several examples of national policies already implemented in some EU Member States[40].

D. CONCLUSIONS

Services are becoming increasingly important as an engine for economic growth. Innovation policies have for a long time focused on technological innovation, in particular on R&D-driven innovation. The Knowledge-intensive Business Services (KIBS) come closest to this concept of technological innovation. But in most services firms a significant share of innovation is of a non-technological nature; firms innovate by way of organizational and

---

[40] Annex D gives examples of countries' approaches to innovation policies in services. Annex E gives examples of specific policies at the national level.

marketing innovations. These firms face similar market and systemic failures as manufacturing firms relying on technological innovation. But for a long time innovation policies have been focused on correcting market failures in technological innovation. Nevertheless, there is a growing consensus that services innovation is in need of similar support mechanisms in order to raise investments in innovation towards a socially optimum level.

This report has tried to identify existing market failures in services innovation and to match them with eight policy areas where services innovation might be different from manufacturing innovation. An attempt has been made to identify relevant policy types for each of these failures and to suggest examples of already existing policies at the national level within the EU.

Market failures are most prevalent in the following policy areas: use of intellectual property, public procurement, start-ups, support of innovation programmes, reducing regulatory burden and improved (access to) financing. Systemic failures have been identified in the following policy areas: use of intellectual property, public procurement, use of and access to public science, start-ups, support of innovation programmes, reducing regulatory burden and improved (access to) financing. Government intervention could be called for to correct these failures, but more research is needed to identify the extent and impact of these failures so that the most appropriate policies can be implemented[41].

Some of the key messages resulting are:

- There is a need to increase competition in services to raise innovation. Competition could be stimulated e.g. by increasing cross-border tradability and by an increased use of public procurement aimed at incentivising creative solutions.
- Within services we observe that there is a relatively greater importance of intercultural and language skills. These could be supported by more (and targeted) training and mobility programmes.
- Non-technological innovation is much more prevalent in services than in manufacturing. Innovation support programmes are needed which support organizational and marketing innovations in the same way as R&D support programmes have supported technological innovation.
- Services firms need to be encouraged to make more use of existing intellectual property rights. IPRs may need to take further into account the specificities of services and services innovation such as their reliance on non-technological innovation and the fact that many services are credence goods where reputation plays a determining factor in achieving market success.

---

[41] It is necessary to first identify these market and systemic failures in detail as implementing policy interventions which do not precisely tackle these failures might lead to other market distortions.

Table I.5.1. Services innovation: policy areas, market failures, and examples of policy interventions

Policy area	Market failures/Systemic failures	Yes/No	Type of policy (horizontal/deepening/broadening/targeted)	Examples of (national) policies[42]
1.Encourage service sector firms to use intellectual property	Externalities (positive/negative)	Yes	**Deepening/Targeted** Attention to credence goods, where reputation is fundamental Brand awareness and trademark registrations Subsectors with R&D component SMEs	**Sweden**: Intellectual property rights to assess risks and future investments **Belgium:** Attention to legal issues (EU regulation on copyrights)
	Market power/distortion			
	Asymmetric information/Transparency	Yes		
	Resource mobility			
	Appropriability/Property rights	Yes		
	Systemic failures	Yes		
2. Public procurement (demand factor)	Externalities (positive/negative)		**Horizontal/Deepening** Indirect effects from policies in other areas: – Creating a financial market – availability of credit – Reduction of regulatory burden to create conditions for firms to tap foreign demand – Clear regulations and creation of standards (facilitating cross border operations) – Incentives for firms to compete/control of market power	**Estonia:** E-government (e-taxation; e-voting) **Sweden:** Public e-services (e-health) **Bulgaria:** E-government
	Market power/distortion	Yes		
	Asymmetric information/Transparency	Yes		
	Resource mobility			
	Appropriability/Property rights			
	Systemic failures	Yes		
3. Improve supply of qualified personnel	Externalities (positive/negative)		**Horizontal/Targeted** Private household as employer (tax benefits)/family policy measures (child care, flexible hours) supporting women's participation in the workforce Vocational training, training abroad, language, intercultural skills New services skills	**Finland:** Focus on education **Ireland:** Attention to education **Lithuania:** Innovation skills and culture
	Market power/distortion			
	Asymmetric information/Transparency			
	Resource mobility	Yes		
	Appropriability/Property rights			
	Systemic failures			
4. Improve use of and access to public science	Externalities (positive/negative)		**Horizontal/Deepening/Targeted** KIBS Incentives for Public Sciences sector to invest in research with intangible results, which could be commercialized by the services sector	
	Market power/distortion			
	Asymmetric information/Transparency			
	Resource mobility	Yes		
	Appropriability/Property rights			
	Systemic failures	Yes		

---

[42] Based on Cunningham (2007).

Policy area	Market failures/Systemic failures	Yes/ No	Type of policy (horizontal/deepening/broadening/targeted)	Examples of (national) policies[42]
5. Support foundation of start-ups	Externalities (positive/negative)	Yes	**Horizontal/Targeted** KIBS Internationally attractive conditions for venture capital Availability of financing for start-up formation, development and investment in innovation activities	**Portugal:** Financing and risk sharing **Croatia:** Facilitation of innovation-based start-ups (innovative services companies in IT) **Greece:** Entrepreneurship
	Market power/distortion	Yes		
	Asymmetric information/Transparency	Yes		
	Resource mobility	Yes		
	Appropriability/Property rights	Yes		
	Systemic failures	Yes		
6. Improve support of innovation programmes for service sector firms	Externalities (positive/negative)	Yes	**Horizontal/ Deepening/Broadening** Support in this policy area will require first the formation of an EU common services markets, so services firms will have the incentives to invest in innovation-gaining economies of scales due to larger markets Formation of an EU common market for services will require intervention in several areas, correcting negative externalities, market power, asymmetric information among agents, lack of resource mobility across borders and lack of a culture of property rights in the services sector	**Finland:** Support for research, innovation, development of partnerships between public and private actors, internationalization and linkage with export industry **Ireland:** Support for international traded services (financial services) Support for research in services Support for generation of critical mass **Czech Republic:** Improvement of innovation environment, including organizational and marketing innovation **Spain:** Support for R&D in services
	Market power/distortion	Yes		
	Asymmetric information/Transparency	Yes		
	Resource mobility	Yes		
	Appropriability/Property rights	Yes		
	Systemic failures	Yes		

Policy area	Market failures/Systemic failures	Yes/ No	Type of policy (horizontal/deepening/broadening/targeted)	Examples of (national) policies[42]
				Lithuania: R&D intensive services Facilitation of knowledge transfer among actors
				Luxembourg: Innovation policy in financial sector
7. Reduce regulatory burden	Externalities (positive/negative)	Yes	**Horizontal/Broadening** Need to look at subsector level, as regulation may be subsector specific At EU level, need for a common ground in terms of regulations and standards to allow for efficient cross border provision	**Sweden:** Deregulation of services markets
	Market power/distortion	Yes		
	Asymmetric information/Transparency	Yes		
	Resource mobility	Yes		
	Appropriability/Property rights			
	Systemic failures	Yes		
8. Improve financing	Externalities (positive/negative)	Yes	**Horizontal/Targeted** Policy would benefit all sectors, not necessarily services. Within services, KIBS due to numbers of start-ups in the subsector	**Portugal:** Improvement innovation financing services
	Market power/distortion	Yes		
	Asymmetric information/Transparency	Yes		
	Resource mobility	Yes		
	Appropriability/Property rights			
	Systemic failures	Yes		

REFERENCES

Annual Economic Report 2006 – Reforming, Investing, Shaping the Future – Policy for More Employment in Germany, Federal Ministry of Economics and Technology, 2006.

Ark, B., van, Broersma, L. and den Hertog, P. (2003), "Services Innovation, Performance and Policy: A Review", Synthesis Report in the Framework of the Project *Structurele Informatievoorziening in Diensten (SSID)* (Structural Information Provision on Innovation in Services).

Arundel, A., Kanerva, M., van Cruysen, A. and Hollanders, H. (2007), "Innovation Statistics for the European Service Sector", *INNO-Metrics 2007 Report*, Brussels: European Commission, DG Enterprise.

Carlsson, B., Jacobsson, S., Holmén, M. and Rickne, A. (2002), "Innovation systems: analytical and methodological issues", *Research Policy* (31: 2), pp.233-245.

Cunningham, P. (2007), "Innovation in Services", INNO-Policy Trendchart Thematic Report. http://www.proinno-europe.eu/admin/uploaded_documents/Thematic_Report_Innovation_Services_Nov_2007.pdf

European Commission (2000), "An Internal Market Strategy for Services", COM (2000)888.

Evertsen, J. (2006), "Services Innovation, A dedicated policy?" Presented at *Services and Innovation Conference*, 10-11 October 2006, Helsinki.

Gallouj, F. (1997), "Towards a neo-Schumpeterian theory of innovation in services", *Science and Public Policy*, Vol. 24 No.6, pp.405-20.

Gronroos, C. (1990), "Service Management and Marketing", D.C. Heath & Company, Lexington, MA, USA.

Gustafsson, R. and Autio, E. (2006), "Grounding for Innovation Policy: The Market, System and Social Cognitive Failure Rationales, Innovation Pressure – Rethinking Competitiveness, Policy and the Society in a Globalised Economy", *International ProACT conference*, Tampere, Finland, March 15-17, 2006.

Kekkonen, T. (2006), "Innovation Policy and Services – A brief summary of the parallel session", Confederation of Finnish Industries, October 2006.

Kox, H. and L. Rubalcaba (eds.) (2007), "Business Services in European Economic Growth", Palgrave Macmillan.

Lundvall, B.A. (1988), "Innovation as an Interactive Process: From User-Producer Interaction to the National System of Innovation". In Dosi, G., Freeman, C., Nelson, R., Silverberg G. and Soete, L. (eds.), *Technical Change and Economic Theory*, pp. 349-369. London: Pinter, 1988.

Ministry of Economy Trade and Industry Japan, "Present Status of Services Industries in Japan and its Innovation Policy".

Nelson, R.R. and Winter, S.G. (1982), "An Evolutionary Theory of Economic Change", Cambridge, Mass: Belknap Press.

Pfeffer, J. and Salancik, G.R. (1978), "The external control of organizations: A resource dependence perspective", New York: Harper & Row.

Smith, K. (1997), "Economic infrastructures and innovation systems". In C. Edquist (Ed.), *Systems of Innovation: Technologies, Institutions and Organizations*, pp.86-100. London: Pinter.

Stare, M. and Bucar, M. (2006), "Innovation in Services in New Member States", Faculty of Social Sciences, University of Ljubljana, October 2006.

Stinchcombe, A. L. (1965), "Social Structure and Organizations". In March, J.G. (ed.), *Handbook of Organizations*, Chicago: Rand McNally and Company, pp.142-193.

Tanninen-Ahonen, T., "Tekes' role in Fostering Innovation in Services", European Association for Research on Services (RESER) 14.9.2007.

Walker, W. (2000), "Entrapment in large technological systems: institutional commitment and power relations", *Research Policy*, 29: pp.833-846.

Weick, K. E., and Roberts, K. H. (1993), "Collective mind in organizations: heedful interrelating on flight decks", *Administrative Science Quarterly*, 38 (3), pp.357-381.

Zahn-Elliott, U. (2006), "Innovation and Services – a German approach to Research and Development in the Services Sector", Bundesministerium fur Bildung und Forschung, October 2006.

6. "STRUCTURALLY NON-PROGRESSIVE" SERVICE INDUSTRIES NEED NOT REMAIN SO FOR EVER: A CASE STUDY ON EDUCATION

Dominique Foray and Julio Raffo, Ecole Polytechnique Fédérale de Lausanne, Switzerland

A. INTRODUCTION

Many years ago, Baumol introduced an interesting distinction between the so-called "progressive" and "non-progressive" sectors within the economy. Non-progressive sectors are those in which productivity growth is limited, sporadic and much smaller in magnitude than those happening in the progressive part of the economy (Baumol and Bowen, 1965; Baumol, 1967).

The macroeconomic implications of the coexistence of these two sectors in the economy have come to be collectively referred to as "Baumol's disease" (or alternatively, the "cost disease"): Baumol assumed that wage growth in both sectors is driven by productivity growth in the progressive sector. As a result, the labour costs per unit of output in the non-progressive sector rise steadily and far more rapidly than the production costs in the economy as a whole. The implications for financing the non- progressive sector are clear cut: what is sufficient for today must be inadequate tomorrow; enough for tomorrow will be insufficient the day after (Baumol, 1993; Hartwig, 2008 and 2009). To quote Baumol, *"faster technical progress is no blessing for the laggards"*.

While Baumol's theory has delivered predictions consistent with reality and has been validated by numerous empirical tests (see for instance Nordhaus, 2008), the starting point of this chapter involves some slight modifications of Baumol's argument. Baumol explained that the difference between the progressive and the non-progressive parts of the economy is essentially due to what he referred to as the "technology structure" of each sector: in the progressive sectors, labour is primarily an instrument – *"an incidental requisite for the attainment of the final product"*- which is subject to rationalization and optimization. In other words, the essence of technical progress is labour saving. In the non-progressive sector, the labour is in itself the end product, and cannot be reduced through rationalization strategies and technical progress. As Baumol said: *"Mozart cannot be played quicker and you cannot reduce the number of actors necessary for a performance of Henry IV."* In this sector (live performance arts), there is some room for improvements in productivity (for example, the jet has increased the productivity per man hour of a Symphonic Orchestra), but the scope for such improvements is narrow and highly limited because labour is indeed the end product; the labour component is irreducible (see the collection of papers on the "Baumol's disease" in the Arts in Towse, 1997).

Our challenge to the theory is that many sectors known as "non-progressive" do not fall neatly into the category of live performance arts, although they have been (are) subject to the "Baumol's disease".

Performing arts belong to the *intrinsically* non progressive sector: limits to productivity are inherent; they are inscribed in the very code of the activity; a part of its essence (one cannot play Mozart faster). The intrinsically non-progressive nature of the living arts sector (opera, symphony orchestra), simply links with the existence of a sacred space, of sorts –and one in to which the quest for productivity gains cannot venture.

Education or health or many other services are of a different kind: they are *structurally* non progressive. There is no intrinsic limit to productivity, but rather serious structural problems regarding the modes of production, development and dissemination of new technologies, organizational practices and technical knowledge (Murnane and Nelson, 1984; Foray and Hargreaves, 2003; Foray, 2001 and 2006). Nothing in the "code" of education tells the teacher that she must teach 40 hours of geography to 10 years old pupils. To take another example, nothing in the "code" tells the chef that he needs one hour of cooking time to make a *soufflé*. These are written in recipes which provide instructions assuming a certain level of technical knowledge and practices.

In these sectors, there is no "sanctuary" that technological changes could not, in principle, permeate to drive gains in productivity and quality. Rather, difficulties in advancing technical knowledge in order to perform tasks in a more efficient way are at the core of the structurally non-progressive sectors. A well known innovation economist, R.R. Nelson (2003) precisely pointed out what he refers to as the uneven evolution of human knowledge and know-how. Some sectors are more able to advance practices and practical knowledge than others: "Today it remains astonishing to observe the contrast between fields where improvements in practice are closely reflecting rapid advances in human knowledge – such as ITs, transportation, medical care (surgery and drug therapy) – and other areas where the state of knowledge appears to be far more constraining. The fact is that knowledge is not being developed to the same degree in every sector" (Nelson, 2003).

One obvious explanation concerns resource allocation, and the failure of mechanisms that would otherwise properly gauge the intensity of efforts to improve something (David and Foray, 2002). For example, pharmaceutical companies respond to large markets' demand for new drugs to treat hypertension rather than investing in R&D to improve the availability of drugs for the victims of malaria - a disease which primarily affects poor countries in which drugs markets are much more limited. So the intensity of demand generates price signals that stimulate profit-motivated efforts to satisfy some wants. But differences in effective demand or market incentives account for only a small portion of the uneven evolution of technical knowledge. Our objective is to address some structural factors influencing the production and development of technical knowledge (translated into useful innovation), its dissemination and effective use in sectors which are qualified as *structurally* non-progressive.

B. TOWARD A NEW SECTORAL DYNAMIC TAXONOMY

Novel ways of conceptualising the dynamics and transformations of industries are only useful where they provide new insights. In this case, it becomes clear that the search for potential remedies to "Baumol's disease" requires a different type of response.

The outlook for the intrinsically non-progressive sectors is challenging, and whether to maintain their economic viability will often fall into the domain of political choice. If a society wishes to maintain its performing arts, for example, an ever-growing volume of financial support is likely to be required; a matter of social choice and political decision.

But the answer is different for the structurally non-progressive sector: Yes, "Baumol's disease" can be cured under certain conditions. In such cases, the problem is two-fold: what are the predisposing structural conditions of a progressive sector; and can these conditions be met in the sector under consideration? These are the broad based, general questions addressed by this chapter.

An activity which is stagnant need not remain so forever

The fact that some sectors are *structurally* non-progressive (as opposed to intrinsically non-progressive), means that the dividing line between these two parts of the economy is not fixed once and for all. The process of long-term growth involves non- progressive sectors that change and transform their knowledge processes so as to become progressive. Sometimes this process is obvious because the progress of technologies is obvious. In these cases, there are few alternatives for organizations and individual practitioners other than to join the new "epistemic culture" that provides a more efficient methodology for knowledge advancement (see the case of medicine below)[43].

In other cases, the potential impact of new technologies may be less obvious, and there may be resistance to the adoption of the new epistemic culture (see below for the case of education, where different epistemic cultures and communities co-exist by offering "competitive" alternatives).

The case of medicine is an interesting one, since this sector profoundly transformed its knowledge base to become an "evidence-based" discipline. In his recent book, Tubiana (2007) describes this evolution: "Of course, in 1948, the tools of evidence-based medicine were not so effective, but the concept was there, full of promise. I came back to France with a lot of hope. Medical practices appeared to me as a series of recipes badly interlinked, failing to draw on the extraordinary growth of physiology and biochemistry. French and Wiener medicines were essentially based on discussions at the sick person's bedside... each doctor treated his/her patients according to inspiration and intuition. Of course, some of them achieved remarkable results because of their intuition and experience. But the average level was alarming... However, in 1950, avenues for progress became clear: to transform medicine into an evidence-based discipline. Every patient was to be considered as a source of information and, the conditions were established to build robust diagnosis, and to track every patient so as to collect, accumulate and aggregate data. It was then necessary to group patients into homogeneous series; in order to establish why different patients' reactions to the same treatment were different... We learned to codify examinations and treatments. Such evolution occurred in the space of a few decades, and there were controversies; but without convulsion, since the power of modern methodologies shortens and reduces the length of debates".

---

[43] The methodology a community adopts to determine best practice within its domain will reflect its dominant epistemic culture. An epistemic culture can thus be defined as a means of identifying best practice (Foray and Hargreaves, 2003).

Tubiana's recollection of these events illustrates well how the sector experienced profound changes in the way the practical knowledge and know-how of doctors were developed and used.

Another industry that recently seems to have joined the progressive part of the economy is "business services". These have experienced an acceleration of labour productivity growth since 1995 (Triplett and Bosworth, 2003). The adoption and use of information technologies creates dynamic feedback, such as the development of new practices of human resources management, knowledge management and codification, and service engineering so that information technology capital deepening coupled with organizational capital played a major role in productivity growth in this sector (Brynjofsson and Hirt, 2005).

Summarizing these cases, we believe that the place of any particular activity in the classification is not only a manifestation of the activity's technological structure as a sort of exogenous condition; it also results from a large number of other drivers. These range from the history of firms, organizations and innovation capacities in a particular sector of a particular country, to proactive policy programmes seeking to address specific issues and overcome a knowledge and innovation deficit within the non-progressive sectors.

Exploring transition paths

There are therefore a large number of movements, migrations and transition paths at the boundaries between the non-progressive and the progressive parts of the economy. Baumol himself recognises this in identifying a third category, the so-called "asymptotically stagnant" sectors which combine both a technologically sophisticated component and an irreducible, labour intensive component, such as TV broadcasting (Baumol et al., 1985)[44]. More recently, he even acknowledges the possibility for some services to become technology leaders (Baumol, 2002).

Following, but also critically analysing Triplett and Bosworth's work, Hartwig (2006) estimates productivity growth in various service industries (finance and insurance, wholesale and retail trade, communication services) to highlight some acceleration at the macro level. He finds this, however, limited to what he calls the "productive services", in which the technological dimension of the service is becoming strongly predominant (as in communication services); leaving productivity growth in the other part of the services sectors (those which are not "technology dominated"), at a very low level.

Unsurprisingly, we suspect that the development of ICT applications and the complementary investments in human capital and organizational changes in these sectors have played and still play a great role in boosting productivity. After all, "Baumol's disease" seems to have been diagnosed in the absence of the personal computer and the internet, which have vastly enhanced productivity in many service industries. But while the ICT revolution has played a great role in some activities (see Wolff, 2002; Brynjolfsson and Hirt, 2005), ICT development has had a much more limited impact in terms of productivity in some other sectors (consider education, healthcare and some other cases, for example). So a consideration of ICT alone

---

[44] Baumol shows that the cost and price behaviour of these asymptotically stagnant activities approaches that of the stagnant sector (Baumol et al., 1985).

appears to be insufficient in explaining the productivity miracle in some of the former, non-progressive sectors. There is much more to discover and understand about these transition paths, which involve certain transformations of the processes by which knowledge and innovation about practices are generated, used and disseminated.

C. DIFFERENT MODES OF KNOWLEDGE PRODUCTION AND USE

We now turn to addressing the issue of the existence of different routes to advancing innovation and practical knowledge in different sectors. One route has been deeply studied by innovation economists. This is the model of "science illuminating technologies" (Nelson, 2003), which is characterised by: i) the centrality of R&D as a means of generating knowledge of immediate value for solving problems and developing applications; ii) the ability to identify, understand (analyse), codify and replicate "best practices" in the field; and iii) the dominance of an epistemic culture through which people believe that the problems they are facing in the course of their professional life can be solved by inquiry and science, i.e. by relying on a strong technical core of knowledge that is available in case books and data bases. This is the model at the origin of the greatest advances of technological knowledge, and the model that forms the micro-foundation of the progressive sectors in the economy. The question is whether it can be used and extended as a meaningful benchmark for the other sectors. There are two scenarios that we need to discuss and clarify (Foray et al., 2007):

The first possibility is that the non-progressive sectors have been lagging behind sectors such as IT, transportation, and medical care (surgery and drug therapy), in terms of their research methods and codification activities, and hence their production of reliable know-how. In fact, some of the most advanced sectors were themselves lagging behind just a few decades ago, and the model for advancing knowledge and innovation is, in fact, similar. If so, structural changes are needed. These should involve more efficient and effective applied science, large-scale codification of best practice and the emergence of new incentive structures for practitioners to make use of existing codified knowledge regarding effective practice, as has long been the case for physicians, for example. A virtuous spiral between these various changes may help to develop long-term dynamics towards more intensive and efficient innovation and knowledge development processes.

The alternative view is that companies in these sectors approach knowledge production and use with an entirely different logic because much of their practice cannot be routinized. In such a case, one would be mistaken to think that a small number of structural changes (including massive adhesion of practitioners to a new epistemic culture); will result in the sector joining the "champions" of the knowledge economy. This would suggest a different model for advancing knowledge that remains poorly understood, and requiring analysis. In other words, the success of the established model in the progressive sectors has obscured the fact that there are other ways in which science can interrelate with technology; and that developing these can aid the advancement of knowledge in some sectors.

D. THE CASE OF EDUCATIONAL INNOVATIONS

As an example, we will briefly explore the microeconomic and sectoral evidence on R&D and innovation in the educational sector. The educational sector has been widely known as a non-progressive sector – a sector in which productivity growth is limited, very sporadic and far smaller in magnitude that what is happening in the progressive part of the economy (Roza, 2008). However, our hypothesis is that this is a "structurally" non-progressive sector. In this section, we will turn to some structural factors related to the way new technical knowledge is produced, developed (translated into useful innovation), disseminated and effectively used in the educational sector[45].

We need also to stress that this is a sector where innovation is notoriously very difficult to observe – a difficulty we will seek to mitigate by using patent data (Foray and Raffo, 2009).

A difficult science and poor linkages to practice

The educational sector is often characterised by experts as a sector suffering from an innovation deficit and a structural inability to advance technical knowledge and know-how at the same rate as it occurs in some other sectors[46]. "Consider the efforts to develop more effective educational practices in schools: even if we do know more about educational practices than we did previously, knowledge creation in this domain has been slow and there have been severe difficulties in diffusing "new and superior" knowledge" (Nelson, 2003).

The main difficulty lies in developing a science which can illuminate practices and provide guidance to their systematic improvement. Formal R&D is of secondary importance both for the training of people and for the generation of useful innovation. What Nelson and Murnane wrote more than 20 years ago on education is still by and large true: educational R&D is very weak in producing practical solutions: "R&D should not be viewed as creating *programs that work'*; it only provides tidy new technologies to schools and teachers. It is thus a mistake to think of educational R&D in the same way as industrial R&D" (Murnane and Nelson, 1984). Educational R&D too rarely generates knowledge of immediate value for solving problems and developing applications. There will, of course, continue to be contributions from social science theory to education. However, the goal of this kind of research is not to provide and develop a repertoire of reliable practices and tools to solve immediate problems that teachers meet daily in their professional life: "For novice teachers, practical problems in classrooms are not usually perceived to be solvable by drawing upon the psychology of education or child development, that have been studied in universities" (Foray and Hargreaves, 2003).

This problem of a very weak link between science and the improvement of practices is crucial, since it influences both the supply of and the demand for research. The result is a fundamental inertia in the system, caused by the negative externalities which exist between a weak supply and an insufficient demand.

---

[45] A similar issue is addressed by Curtler (2010) in the case of healthcare.
[46] Technical knowledge involves in this case the broad set of both embodied and disembodied knowledge that enable the development of pedagogical practices and instructional technologies.

There are three factors explaining the relatively weak role of science in shedding light on and influencing practices in education:

On the supply side, educational sciences are simply very hard to do. Berliner (2007) wrote about educational research as the hardest science: "we do our science under conditions that physical scientists would find intolerable". Compared to designing a bridge, the science to help change schools and classrooms is harder to do because the context cannot be controlled, and an inherent lack of generalisability between differing contexts reduces the value of any research method to illuminate a body of practices[47]. There is indeed an educational science, but nothing comparable to an applied science or engineering discipline to develop a body of knowledge and techniques that could illuminate educational practices.

On the demand side, most practitioners who are (or should be), involved in the improvement of practices do not believe that the educational problems they are facing in the course of their professional life can be solved by inquiry, by evidence and by science (Elmore, 2002). They do not believe, for example, that it is necessary to have a developmental theory of how students learn the content and how the pedagogy relates to the development of knowledge and content. Weak incentives for teachers to use research are rooted in a deep cultural norm: namely, the view that teaching is an individual trait, and that the foundation of good performance involves natural quality, inspiration and talent, rather than a set of competences acquired over the course of a career (Elmore, 2002). Because of this cultural norm, it is very difficult to make a case for knowledge management, building databases about evidence on "what works and encouraging teachers to behave as engineers by searching for solutions to problems in cases book. "Teachers are primarily artisans, working alone in a personally designed environment where they develop most of their skills by trial-and-error tinkering…In short, they learn to tinker, searching pragmatically for acceptable solutions to problems their 'clients' present" (Foray and Hargreaves, 2003).

Finally, there is a general deficiency of incentives to codify technical knowledge and know-how, and the resources allocated to codification are weak. Numerous practices remain tacit; unexplained and not articulated, invisible and difficult to transfer. "There is no more in education than a weak equivalent in the field of pedagogical knowledge to the systematic recording and widespread use of cases found in surgery or law and the physical models in engineering and architectural practice. Such records coupled with comments and critiques of experts allow new generations to pick up where earlier ones left off" (Foray and Hargreaves, 2003). Some important mechanisms to support the cumulative nature of knowledge and its progressivity and to materialise the potential for spillovers are simply missing. "The beginner in teaching must start afresh, uninformed about prior solutions and alternative approaches to recurring practical problems. What student teachers learn about teaching is intuitive and imitative rather than explicit and analytical" (*ibid.*). When excessive stocks of knowledge are left in tacit forms, this makes them more costly to locate, to appraise and to transfer. A result may be excessive insularity and a waste of resources resulting in underuse of the existing stock of knowledge. This may therefore lead to private and social inefficiencies.

---

[47] See the special issue of EINT (Foray, Murnane and Nelson, 2007) about the comparison between educational research and research in the biomedical area.

Incentives for change are there, adequate responses are not

To put it in Nelson's words, the key to success in advancing technical knowledge has been the design of practice around what is known scientifically. For various reasons, this is not operating well in education.

As a result, policymakers, industries and society as a whole are asking schools to make improvements in the presence of an extremely weak technical core. "Consider what would happen if you were on an airplane and the pilot came on the intercom as you were starting your descent and said, "I've always wanted to try this without the flaps". Or if your surgeon said to you in your pre-surgical conference, "you know, I'd really like to do this the way I originally learned to do it in 1978". Would you be a willing participant in this? People get sued for doing that in the "real" professions, where the absence of a strong technical core of knowledge and discourse about what effective practice is carries a high price" (Elmore, 2002).

The problem is not so much the lack of incentives for schools and managers to improve educational practices and technologies. These incentives are there - probably less powerful than in other sectors, but pressure for performance of schools, which are channeled through higher standards and accountability, is increasing and thereby creates such incentives. The problem lies rather in the way practitioners, teachers and administrators seek to respond to these incentives and pressures. There is a failure to translate such pressures into innovation, improved practices and the development of instructional know-how and technologies. Practitioners do not try to improve practices by relying on a strong technical core of knowledge that should be available in case books and data bases. Rather, they respond to the increased accountability by changing structures; but changing structure does not change practices. As Elmore (2002) argues forcefully: People and schools put an enormous amount of energy into changing structures and usually leave instructional practice (innovation) untouched.

A small (innovation) explosion?

Even a casual examination of patent data provides us with a slightly different view of innovation in this sector. Looking at the IPC subclass G09B in PATSTAT, it becomes clear that patent applications have increased dramatically from the early nineties in the domain of educational and teaching technologies (figure I.6.1)[48].
In addition, a positive trend is found for these technologies as a share of the total production of technologies, which shows that this traditional sector is growing faster than average in technological terms.

---

[48] In our study (Foray & Raffo, 2009), we consider educational and teaching-related technologies as any patent filed under the G09B IPC subclass. This subclass is defined as Educational or demonstration appliances; appliances for teaching, or communicating with, the blind, deaf or mute; models; planetaria; globes; maps; diagrams. This subclass covers simulators regarded as teaching or training devices, which is the case if they give perceptible sensations having a likeness to the sensations a student would experience in reality in response to actions taken by him; models of buildings, installations, or the like. But it does not include simulators which merely demonstrate or illustrate the function of an apparatus or of a system by means involving computing, and therefore cannot be regarded as teaching or training devices; components of simulators, if identical with real devices or machines.

Figure I.6.1. Evolution of education related technologies

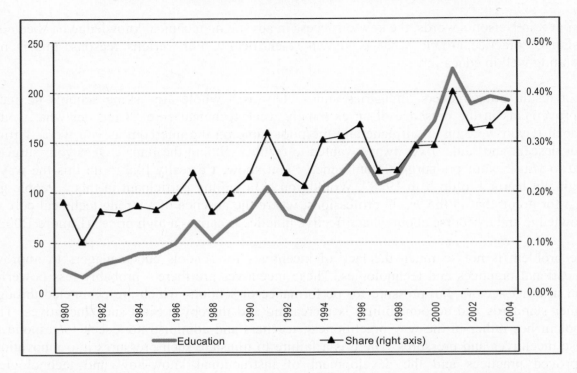

Source: PATSTAT (September 2008). Figures express Triadic patent families declaring a G09B IPC subclass.

But this growth is not only explained by large incumbents' strategic behaviours, as we also observe the formation of a population of small firms which are specialized in the development of technological solutions to educational problems and issues. This is apparent from the entry of new firms (Figure I.6.2), but also in the declining (technological) concentration evidenced by different indicators (Figure I.6.3).

In Figure I.6.3, it can be observed that the concentration – expressed by technological shares held by both the top four and by the top 10 firms – has steeply declined over the past two decades. The inverse Herfindahl-Hirschman Index (HHI) furnishes a similar picture, showing that technological concentration has been reduced from around thirty to sixty "ideal" firms. Furthermore, all three indicators suggest that this evidenced fall in concentration might be slowing down or, if we consider the HHI, even starting to regress. In any case, these preliminary results suggest the emergence and consolidation of an industry specialized in the production of educational and instructional tools and knowledge, strongly rooted in new information technologies.

Figure I.6.2. Firms producing education-related technologies: new entry

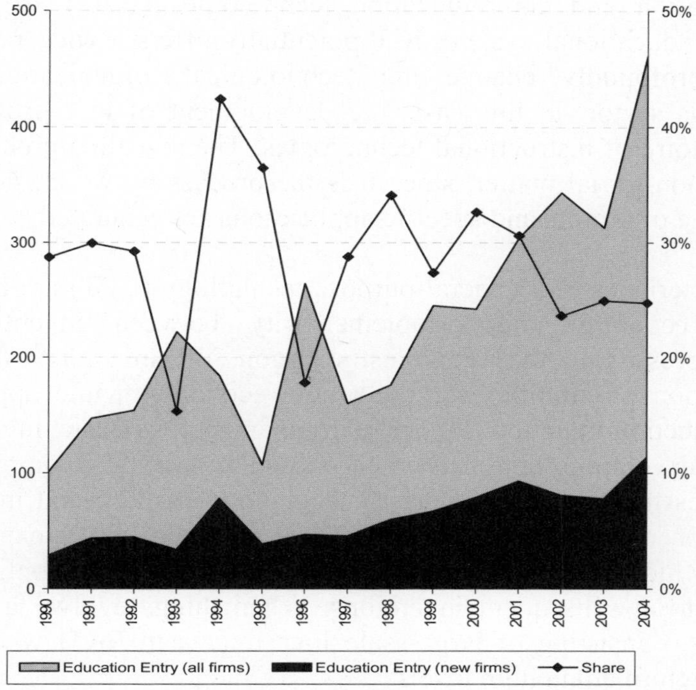

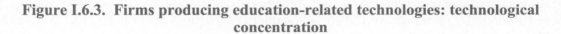

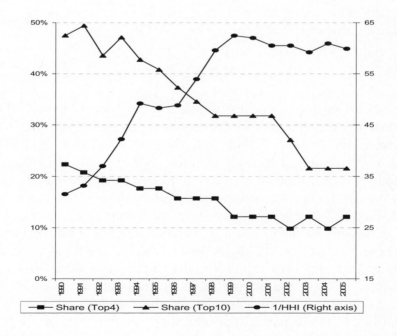

Source: PATSTAT (September 2008). Figures retrieved from firm's Triadic patent families.

Figure I.6.3. Firms producing education-related technologies: technological concentration

Source: PATSTAT (September 2008). Figures built from firms' Triadic patent families portfolios.

Educational innovations driven by a wider technological revolution

The new information and communication technologies (ICTs) are clearly a source of innovation in the educational system. ICT potentially offers a wide range of new tools and instruments to profoundly change the technological, organizational and institutional foundations of this sector. In this case, the development of ICT provides opportunities to broaden the repertoire of instructional technologies. The so-called process of co-invention of applications is a non-trivial matter, since it is the process by which the technology diffuses across a wide range of sectors and specific applications are generated.

In fact, the characteristics of a general-purpose technology (GPT) are horizontal propagation throughout the economy and complementarity between invention and application development. Expressed in the economist's jargon, the invention of a GPT extends the frontier of invention possibilities for the whole economy, while application development changes the production function of one particular sector. Basic inventions generate new opportunities for developing applications in particular sectors. Reciprocally, application co-invention increases the size of the general technology market, and improves the economic return on invention activities related to it. There are therefore dynamic feedback loops in accordance with which inventions give rise to the co-invention of applications, which in turn increase the return on subsequent inventions. When things evolve favourably, a long-term dynamic develops, consisting of large-scale investments in R&D where social and private marginal rates of return attain high levels.

It is clear that the sort of renaissance of innovation in practices and methods of pedagogy and instruction is strongly associated with the dynamics of ICTs. The application of ICT in education is not a single innovation, but an array of technologies that can be applied in a variety of ways. ICTs are viewed, also, as enablers of change: schools engage in a series of activities which could not have been achieved in the absence of ICT. It is, however, premature to claim that the education sector has now reached the position of being a core user sector with the potential to significantly boost the dynamics of ICTs.

E. DISCUSSION

A quite intensive innovation activity is now observable in the development of new methods of pedagogy and instruction technologies. However, the locus of this activity is not really inside the sector, but rather on the supply side. Given our observation and discussion of the innovation deficit in "the core" of the system (the classroom) as explaining in part the non-progressive nature of the education sector, it is good news that a population of entrepreneurs enters and grows on the market for new pedagogical methods. However, there is a need to qualify this trend. Firstly, while an industry structure comprising a population of small and specialized firms has many virtues from a dynamic efficiency point of view, it also brings some concerns. These concerns are mainly related to the increased patenting activity which is needed for small, specialized firms to enter and compete, but which is likely to adversely affect static efficiency through the pricing of ideas and knowledge which were previously freely accessible. Secondly, it is unclear whether the largest market for new methods of pedagogy – which is the public part of the education sector - will match well the business model of myriad entrepreneurs and frenetic innovators seeking high economic returns on intensive R&D.

Problems with the new structure

We observe the development of an industrial structure populated by firms that specialise in one, well-defined set of activities. While innovation in methods of pedagogy continues to be dominated by large integrated firms, a population of small specialized firms is emerging and expanding. Of course, patenting and licensing play a greater role in this new structure - both as a cause and a consequence of the new, vertically disintegrated structure. There are some reasons to believe that the new structure is likely to be more efficient than a structure where only large integrated firms would serve the markets for methods of pedagogy (Cockburn, 2003). Efficiency gains from specialization, market-driven resource allocation and intensified competition are the factors which are discussed in the literature as generating efficiency gains through vertical specialization. But there are also problems.

One of these problems involves the development of a market for instructional tools, which implies that potential users must now pay for access to methods and knowledge of the kind that used to be obtained for free, but is now explicitly priced in the form of licensing agreements. In educational communities, some of these new patents are likely to generate great anxiety as practitioners realise that they are infringing patents and violating the law simply by applying methods and practices that they have been using freely since entering the profession. We know that researchers in biomedical sciences now often tend simply to "ignore" (in the sense of failing to obey), the patents on research tools. And the firms which have been granted these patents either anticipate weak appropriability of their knowledge by granting licenses on a large scale or simply tolerate infractions, especially by academic researchers. This set of norms and practices on both sides results in the reasonably effective reduction of the social inefficiencies potentially generated by the so-called "anti-commons problem" in biomedical research. It is not clear whether school managers and teachers are in a position to exhibit similar behaviours, and what the strategic responses of the small, specialized firms holding the patents would be.

For example, the US patents of Blackboard "for technology used for Internet-based education support system and method", cover 44 different features that make up a learning management system. F.Lowney, Director of the IT management system at the Georgia College and State University Library wrote: "Much of what Blackboard claims to have invented really came from and was freely given by the education community. Now the community is being punished through a gross lessening of competition in this market" (Networkworld, 2008). For an Associate Professor of Medical Education, the real question is: "What are they going to do next, try to patent word processing and charge you royalties if you are using it in a classroom? If obvious uses of technology to facilitate teaching based on standard software applications are allowed to be patented just because they are used to support education we are in real trouble" (Inside Higher Ed, 2006). The problem with Blackboard patents, and we suspect hundreds of patents for educational technologies, clearly involves the now well-rehearsed conflict between open source communities (which are proliferating in the educational world), and for-profit businesses attempting to enforce their claims on some (software) patents. But a new problem arises here, which is about patenting in an area where, traditionally, the norms of public good and free access were strongly dominant.

Another problem with the vertically disintegrated structure concerns the ability of small, specialized companies to capture the benefits of their innovation. Transaction and bargaining costs on these markets for methods of pedagogy are likely to be very high; and patents as a means to capture the value of the innovation might be not so effective (depending partly upon how the first problem is to be resolved). The problems of the firms considered here are rather similar to what has been described by Cockburn (2003) with regard to tools companies in the biotechnology sector.

Is it a good idea to become an "educational entrepreneur"?

This is the big question (analogously raised by Curtler (2010) in the context of health care entrepreneurs). Innovation needs entrepreneurship, or at least needs a complex distribution of firm size and age, including a strong population of entrepreneurs at one extreme of the continuum. Baumol has written extensively and convincingly on the pivotal role played by the entrepreneur or young innovative firm as a mechanism for fueling innovation, and as an organizational form which is needed to complement large companies' modes of operation. However, the educational sector has built severe barriers to entry, which is likely to render entrepreneurial activities in the sector less attractive. The reward structure in this sector is not in favour of competitive entry by new firms and radical innovators willing to take risk and be creative in the search for large private returns on R&D and other innovation activities. Among those barriers, one can mention (Berger and Stevenson, 2007):

- The education sector does not invest in innovation;
- In many countries, there is a so-called "big edu" – an oligopoly of a few very large suppliers of educational resources which solve the problem of a highly atomised demand by building enormous sales forces; entrepreneurs cannot afford to play this game;
- Slow sales cycles, involving too many people "in charge" at different levels (state agencies, districts, schools);
- The constraint of pilot programmes to test an innovative tool means that start-ups cannot always market their product at a scale that is economically viable;
- There is no business culture to manage innovation in the school system: administrators usually choose to solve problems by using in-house staff resources more intensively. This is perceived as costing nothing, since people are already paid but new tools and systems need to be procured. Few school administrators have a formal training in business decision-making or in calculating return on investment;
- Teacher time is a sunk cost; there is no benefit to saving this time;
- It is very often recommended by public authorities that administrators should not meet with entrepreneurs and vendors to avoid any unfair advantages. However, when such a "vendor wall" exists, how do these administrators become informed about anything?
- Because the various barriers described here constrain potential rates of return, and educational companies require too long to generate a meaningful return, venture capitalists (VC) are typically uninterested, and most innovative start-ups in this field

fail to convince professional VCs to fund them. Angel investors can, to a certain extent, act as a substitute; and

- It is commonplace in education that foundations and charities give away for free the very things that entrepreneurs are seeking to turn into business! This unintended consequence of a strategy of building an open access, "commons" type resource is a familiar phenomenon from development economics, and can severely restrict entrepreneurial spirit.

Beyond all the problems identified above, the public sector of education is a particularly special market in the sense that "consumers" do not necessarily wish to buy each year the kind of product that a restless innovative activity needs to offer and commercialise

There are currently national experiments (US, Chile, UK, New Zealand) on the development of quasi-markets in education to foster educational innovations (Lubjenski, 2009). These experiments will be important in order to see whether any greater demand for innovation is associated with such institutional changes. Will the new industry specialized in the development of new methods of pedagogy find more dynamic markets as countries increasingly engage in leveraging quasi-market mechanisms of choice and competition in education?

F. SIGNIFICANCE OF THE ISSUE AND POLICY IMPLICATIONS

The micro-foundation of "Baumol's disease" and of the evolution of some sectors towards the progressive part of the economy remains poorly understood. This is mainly due to the disconnection between two parts of the literature: on the one hand macro-level productivity studies exploring "Baumol's disease"; and on the other the microeconomic conditions, procedures and effects of innovation and knowledge advances. Baumol and others, while illuminating a fundamental property of economic systems, did not proceed far in seeking to understand the very nature of the transformations that are driving some sectors towards the progressive part of the economy. By and large, one could say that innovation economists have failed to connect some of their findings to macro-level productivity studies.

In terms of the economic significance of the issues addressed in our paper, it is clear that the relative economic weight of some of the non-progressive sectors is likely to continue to grow in the near future as a consequence of global challenges such as demographic change, urban crisis, etc. Industries delivering services that involve personal care (healthcare, education, social services), are currently regarded as prime examples of sectors affected by "Baumol's disease". It is therefore crucial to find out more about the conditions that would support further advances in the production of technical knowledge and practices in order to increase productivity in these industries. Our case study on R&D and innovation in the education sector serves perhaps as an example of what needs to be done in many non-progressive sectors.

Policy implications are also important: the history of the transformation or stagnation of sectors shows that differences in national systems of innovation and R&D policy matter a great deal (Aghion et al., 2009). The productivity acceleration in some services has been observed first in the US rather than in Europe; and this has been the consequence of great disparities in innovation capacities involving both producers (of the technologies) and users (services) (see Foray and Van Ark, 2008; Hall and Mairesse, 2009). In the education sector itself, and as a result of the very poor performance of the educational system as a whole, the US has launched a radical R&D policy aiming at accelerating innovation and productivity in this area (Cooke and Foray, 2007). In doing so, the US educational R&D policy has been shaped by the assumption that knowledge and innovation advances in the education sector should follow the same model of "science illuminating practices" that has worked so well in the most advanced sectors of industry (section C, above). This is a brave assumption and such a policy entails high risk. But at least the US federal administration has made a choice between the two scenarios (section C) - "*the problem mainly lies in the weakness of educational applied science and in the (absence of) incentives of practitioners to apply research findings for improving practices*" - and has designed and deployed a R&D policy accordingly.

Although it is too early to know whether this policy is producing some positive effects on innovation and productivity, the fact is that there are plenty of R&D and innovation policy opportunities in sectors that we have qualified as "*structurally non-progressive*".

REFERENCES

Aghion, P., David P. and Foray, D. (2009), "Linking Policy Research and Practice in 'STIG Systems': Many Obstacles, but Some Ways Forward", *Research Policy*, vol.38, Issue 4.

Baumol, W. (1967), "Macroeconomics of unbalanced growth: the anatomy of urban crisis", *The American Economic Review*, vol.57, no.3.

Baumol, W. (1993), "Health care, education and the cost disease: a looming crisis for public choice", *Public Choice*, 77.

Baumol, W. (2002), "Services as leaders and the leaders of the services", in Gadrey and Gallouj (eds.), *Productivity, Innovation and Knowledge in Services*, Edward Elgar.

Baumol, W. and Bowen, W. (1965), "On the performing arts: the anatomy of their economic problems", *American Economic Review*, vol.55, no.1/2.

Baumol, W., Batey Blackman, S.A. and Wolff, E. (1985), "Unbalanced growth revisited: asymptotic stagnancy and new evidence", *American Economic Review*, vol.75, no.4.

Berger, L. and Stevenson D. (2007), "K-12 entrepreneurship: slow entry, distant exit", *American Enterprise Institute Conference on the Future of Educational Entrepreneurship*, Washington D.C., October.

Berliner, D. (2007), "Educational research: the hardest science of all", *Educational Researcher*, vol.31, no.8, pp18-20.

Brynjolfsson, E. and Hirt, L. (2005), "Intangible assets and the economic impact of computers", in Kahin (ed.) *Transforming Enterprises*, MIT Press.

Cockburn, I. (2003), "O brave new industry that has such patents in it! Reflections on the economics of genome patenting", draft, Boston University.

Cooke, T. and Foray, D. (2007), "Building the capacity to experiment in schools: a case study of the Institute of Educational Sciences in the US department of Education", *Economics of Innovation and New Technology*, vol 16, issue 5, pp.385 – 402.

Curtler, D. (2010), "Where are the health care entrepreneurs? The failure of organizational innovation in health care", *NBER Summer Institute 2010*, Cambridge MA.

David, P.A. and Foray, D. (2002), "On the fundamentals of the knowledge society", *International Social Science Journal*, no.171.

Elmore R. (2002), "The limits of change", *Harvard Education Letter*, Vol.18, No.1, January-February.

Foray D. (2001), "Facing the problem of unbalanced development of knowledge across sectors and fields: the case of the knowledge base in primary education", *Research Policy*, Vol.30, Issue 9 (December), pp. 1553-1561.

Foray, D. (2006), *The economics of knowledge* (chapter 9), Cambridge: MIT Press.

Foray, D. and Hargreaves, D. (2003), "The production of knowledge in different sectors: a model and some hypotheses", *London Review of Education*, Vol.1, No.1.

Foray, D. and Raffo, J. (2009), "A small explosion: patents in educational and instructional technologies and methods: What do they tell us?" 4th epip conference, Bologna, Italy.

Foray D. and van Ark B. (2008), "Knowledge for Growth: European issues and Policy challenges". In *Knowledge for Growth: prospects for Science, Technology and Innovation*, European Commission, EUR 24047.

Foray, D., Murnane, R. and Nelson, R. (2007), "Randomized trials of education and medical practices: strengths and limitations", *Economics of Innovation and New Technology*, Vol.16, Issue 5, pp.303 – 306.

Hall, B. and Mairesse, J. (2009), "Corporate R&D returns". In Knowledge for Growth: Prospects for Science, Technology and Innovation, European Commission, EUR 24047.

Hartwig, J. (2006), "Productivity growth in service industries – Has "Baumol's disease"really been cured*?"*, *KOF working paper,* number 06-155.

Hartwig, J. (2008), "What drives health care expenditure? Baumol's model of

Unbalanced growth revisited*",* *Journal of Health Economics,* Vol.27, Issue 3, pp. 603-623.

Hartwig J. (2009), "Can Baumol's model of unbalanced growth contribute to explaining the secular rise in health care expenditure? An alternative test", forthcoming in *Applied Economics.*

Inside   Higher   Ed   (2006),   "Blackboard   Patents   challenged", www.insidehighered.com/news/2006/1201/patent

Lubienski, C. (2009), "Do quasi-markets foster innovation in education? A comparative perspective", CERI, Directorate for Education, OECD.

Murnane, R. and Nelson, R. (1984), "Production and innovation when techniques are tacit: the case of education", *Journal of Economic Behavior and Organization*, vol. 5, issue 3-4, pp.353-373.

Nelson, R. (2003), "On the uneven evolution of human know how", *Research Policy*, vol. 32(6), pp.909-922.

Networkworld (2006), *Software patent ignites firestorm in education*, www.networkworld.com/news/2006/11106-software-patent-ignites-firestorm-in-higher-education.html

Nordhaus, W. D. (2008), "Baumol's Diseases: A Macroeconomic Perspective," *The B.E. Journal of Macroeconomics*, 8(1) (Contributions), Article 9.

Roza, M. (2008), "Must public education suffer from Baumol's disease?" *The Denver Post*, 08/03/2008.

Towse R. (ed.) (1997), *Baumol's Cost Disease: the Arts and other Victims*, Edward Elgar.

Triplett, J. and Bosworth, B. (2003), "Productivity measurement issues in services industries: Baumol's disease has been cured", *FRBNY Economic Policy Review*, September.

Tubiana, M. (2007), *N'oublions pas demain*, Editions de Fallois, Paris.

Wolff, E. (2002), "How stagnant are services?", in Gadrey and Gallouj (eds.), *Productivity, Innovation and Knowledge in Services*, Edward Elgar.

PART II

NATIONAL POLICY EXPERIENCES AND INITIATIVES

1. THE FINNISH EXPERIENCE OF SERVICE INNOVATION POLICY AND MEASURES

Tiina Tanninen-Ahonen and Sami Berghäll,
TEKES, Finnish Funding Agency for Technology and Innovation, Finland

A. INTRODUCTION

Tekes, the Finnish Funding Agency for Technology and Innovation, is the main public funding organization for research and development (R&D) and innovation in Finland. Tekes finances industrial R&D projects as well as projects in universities and research institutes.

Tekes works with the leading innovative companies and research institutes in Finland. Each year, Tekes finances some 1,500 business research and development projects, and almost 600 public research projects at universities, research institutes and polytechnics. Tekes provides grants of around €600 million annually in support of innovative projects aimed at generating know-how and new kinds of products, processes, and service or business concepts. Funding is also available for organizations carrying out development work.

According to its mission statement, Tekes promotes the development of Finnish industry and the service sector by technological means and by supporting innovations. The same idea is reflected in its new name, the Finnish Funding Agency for Technology and Innovation, which emphasises the entire innovation chain from technology development to new services and innovations.

B. TEKES' SERVICES STRATEGY

Services and service concepts are becoming increasingly important, both in relation to expanding product scope and in creating independent businesses. Particular attention will be paid to the development of service business concepts, service quality and service productivity. Services are also important from an employment perspective. For these reasons, services have played an increasingly important role in the strategies of Tekes (2002, 2005 and 2008), and at the same time in the development of programmes (e.g., Serve programme 2006 – 2013), instruments and funding criteria.

Over time, the focus in developing services has changed from technology push services to business opportunity pull service concepts, and more recently to customer- and user-driven solutions.

Table II.1.1. A renewed strategy: services in Tekes' strategy and operations

Past:
• Year 2002 Strategy – emphasis still on technology
• Year 2005 – New strategy – emphasis on service concepts
Key results from 2005 – a process:
• Year 2006 Serve – programme
• Year 2008 – New strategy – emphasis on Customer centric service business
• Year 2009 Serve Re-orientated towards Pioneers of Service Business
Present:
• Year 2009 – National Innovation strategy
• Year 2011 – New Tekes strategy

2006 marked a turning point. In accordance with our 2005 strategy, there was a change of name, mission statement and organization. With these changes, services and non-technological innovations also became more visible. Changes were also made to the relevant legislation to reflect Tekes' new mission.

Tekes promotes a broad-based view of innovation: besides funding technological breakthroughs, Tekes emphasises the significance of service-related, design, business and social innovations.

In 2006, Tekes launched an extensive programme called "Serve - Innovative services". In the first phase, Serve targeted the development of innovative service concepts and cutting edge business service innovations within Finnish companies. As part of the Serve-programme, the evaluation criteria for companies' R&D projects were specified on the basis of the new EU state aid rules. To date, around 156 innovative service concept projects have been financed, mainly in the area of KIBS and industrial services.

After the mid-term evaluation in 2008, Serve has progressed to the 2nd phase where its main objective is to challenge Finnish companies to become global forerunners in the customer-centred, knowledge-based service business. Serve aims at the second wave of service business where out-of-the-box thinking challenges traditional ways of doing things, at both the strategic and operational levels. The volume and timetable of the programme have been extended and the programme continues until the end of 2013 with a total budget of €224 million. In the Serve programme, service innovation has played a key role.

C. SERVICES INNOVATION AS THE KEY

In the development of services and the necessary competences, the key to the Tekes approach has been, and remains, the concept of service innovation. Service innovations are multidimensional in nature. They involve organizational, operational, delivery system, customer interaction and technology-related dimensions. As a result of this multidimensionality, it is necessary to integrate the various disciplines relating to these matters. Only through an interdisciplinary approach can one address issues such as the balancing of short-term profit and long-term market power, the efficiency of supply chain versus the commitment of one's network of partners, developing and maintaining a brand image versus global sourcing of factors of production, etc. This complexity results in a need to build a new theoretical basis of services innovation. Services innovation is seen to arise from new ways of looking at the needs and demands of customers and/or users. Thus, the development of customer-centric (rather than production-based) service business models with a new revenue logic, while balancing network interests and partnerships based on a new division of benefits driven by intangible services, is a significant challenge. In addition, understanding how customers perceive the intangible value generated, and overcoming the various policy obstacles to develop integrated solutions also presents significant hurdles for service innovation and service innovation policy.

The service business and service innovations theme are used to develop service businesses across all industries. The approach chosen is to develop businesses through business skills and competences. In this process, the customer (and customer-need in particular) plays the central role in driving the innovative (or novel) business models. While the result of the development is a business model, the means of arriving at this new model often require a knowledge-intensive approach to businesses and network interaction. The networks (whether company internal or external) therefore demand close interaction and cooperation underpinned by trust. This is because, only in an open atmosphere that favours creativity can one arrive at the novel combinations of concepts and approaches required to meet the needs of one's customers and target market. Therefore, while the values and aspirations of individual consumers create the basis for service business in consumer markets, the same knowledge-creating and communication skills also need to be brought into B2B-planning.

Thus, in developing a business driver based on services innovation, companies acquire a natural, consumer-centred source of innovation. Furthermore, this new centre is, by definition, based on the intangible dimensions of business interaction. In this way, developing and producing services that incorporate clients' roles, tasks and delivery channels as essential parts of the process, companies are also equipped with the tools to build a new foundation for foreseeing client needs. This ability is seen as one of the key tools of modern competition. As in the well-known case of Apple's iPod, it seems that a company can become a market leader by changing the terms of competition in the market itself. This may be achieved through an intuitive understanding of the needs and demands of the market, but then taking a further leap forward. It seems that this is the reason why simple technological skill is increasingly linked to user and customer centricity - being able to communicate effectively results in forward-looking intelligence that, if used innovatively, can build new demand. Thus, an innovative company can shape markets, while competitors are forced to assume the "follower" role.

However, the transformation to a customer-centric service business (and revenue logic) seems to require a novel business philosophy to foster the service innovation activity approach. Increased research and cooperation between researchers and companies is needed, with methodologies (drawing upon ethnographic principles) that are able to provide a solid foundation for developing customer needs, and providing the necessary foresight. That is, a logic that flows from the outside in, rather than from the inside out. To a certain extent, service networks need a new theoretical basis that strikes a balance between building a profitable business, and establishing close relationships. In practice, this means new contract and revenue logics built on partnership, and a fresh perspective on the protection of intelligent property rights.

Therefore, it is Tekes' view that the fostering of innovation in the services business requires a broad based cooperation and an array of new measures by which the various authorities and policymakers can induce and accelerate development. A traditional, product based paradigm may even detract from this objective.

D. TWO APPROACHES TO SERVICE INNOVATION

At present, we can identify two distinct philosophies in relation to the origin of service innovation. On the one hand, we have what could be described as a producer-centric approach, where the focus of services innovation is to develop new models to enhance the product-service balance, supply chain or service delivery in general, the optimization of service systems, tailoring pricing in relation to company offerings, etc. The other perspective could be described as a user-, customer-demand centric approach. However, there is an important distinction to be made – namely that, while both the producer- and user-centric approaches talk of customer centricity, the approach taken to optimization differs. The producer-centric approach regards customers as responding passively to a company's offerings in a way that is relatively stable and predictable through time. In such cases, the relevant horizon for consideration in the optimization exercise often ends with the next member of the supply chain or, at the extreme, with the final industrial customer in the network. Thus, end-user focus is new to this approach. The customer-centric approach seeks to build the same chain, but starting from a completely different point in the chain. The driving principle is that it is the wants and needs of the consumer that will ultimately determine who survives in the competitive environment. A better understanding of one's customers provides the means to innovate and experiment with new forms of delivering value to the market.

While the two approaches outlined above are by no means mutually exclusive in practice, they characterize some radical differences that exist. Both approaches have a strong tradition in the academic and business communities. In a pure service relationship, the transaction is wholly intangible and results in a co-created exchange setting. The service provider (i.e., the producer) sells something that the customer may (or may not) perceive to be of a similar value. For the producer, it is critical to understand the value of the service in order to accurately price it. However, as services are perishable at the time of provision, the broadening of the relationship is dependent on an accurate assessment of one's competitive advantage in relation to the competition. Therefore, the context is determined along multiple dimensions, including customer values, needs, perceived alternative providers, time of provision, accuracy of communication and a wide range of organizational and cultural-related issues. Figure II.1.1 outlines the key concepts underpinning the two approaches.

Figure II.1.1. Producer- and consumer-centric approaches

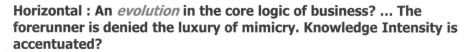

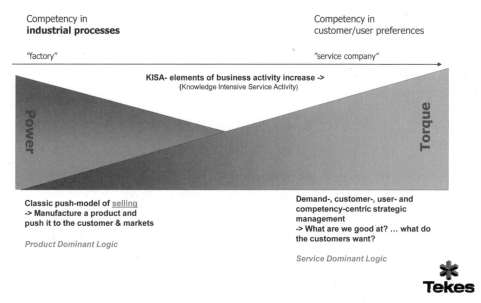

While these two contexts appear quite distinct, even a producer-orientated view encounters similar, intangible questions once placed in a forerunner or 'pioneer' position in a market. In such a situation, it is necessary to 'shape' the market, given a lack of forerunners to follow. Customer needs must be anticipated more rapidly than followers are capable of mimicking one's products and eating away the margins of the 'pioneer' technology. The discussion that follows explores the Service Innovation phenomenon via its three core scientific dimensions.

E. COMPANIES ARE INTERESTED IN SERVICE INNOVATION AND INNOVATION IN THE SERVICES SECTOR

2008 seems to have marked a turning point in terms of R&D funding disbursed by Tekes for company projects. For the first time in our 26 year history, the service sectors have overtaken manufacturing (including construction) in terms of the share of our R&D expenditure, which totaled €300 million in 2008. This trend continued in 2009, with approximately 85% of Tekes funding for R&D in the services sector being directed to Knowledge-intensive Business Services (KIBS), which includes software, technical engineering, architecture, management and R&D services consultancy, with the remaining 15% going to wholesale, retail trade and healthcare services.

Projects involving non-technological innovation received €234 million, or 41% of total funding. Examples of these include business and service concepts, branding, service practices, management and organization of work related to new services, design, inquiries into consumer behavior, etc.

Figure II.1.2. Tekes' R&D funding by sector

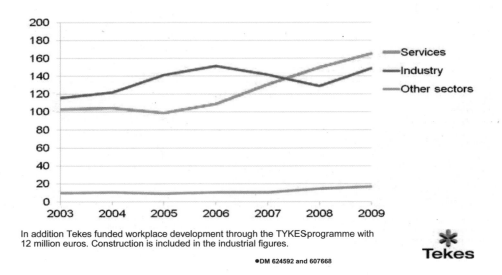

In addition Tekes funded workplace development through the TYKESprogramme with 12 million euros. Construction is included in the industrial figures.

●DM 624592 and 607668

F. FUTURE TRENDS IN THE SERVICES BUSINESS

The future of the services business seems to point towards a more holistic view of the business entity. We may anticipate a shift from developing individual products and services towards providing solutions and experiences. This is equally reflected by a shift in emphasis from a product-dominated approach to a more service-driven logic. Thus, the service as "experienced" by the consumer will determine the design, manufacturing process and financial outcome - essentially, the entire business logic - with hardware and software viewed as platforms and tools for competitive and innovative services business.

Another consequence of such an approach is that customers are viewed as partners, rather than passive consumers to be manipulated. Customer-centric thinking requires knowledge of the customer and his or her preferences. 'Pioneers' search for this information proactively, defining and shaping the market by delivering services that satisfy latent needs - all others follow. While services are activities as such, they may also be used as a tool for effective communication – if this is made a priority. Thus, if, and only if, customer feedback is actively sought, customers increasingly play a role as co-creators of the company's service portfolio. In such a way, companies can tap in to a vast array of resources outside of the company's own resources – and it is an array of resources that competitors cannot control or manage. Therefore, to argue in favor of co-development or co-creation is not to pursue an idealistic agenda, but to point to the sheer magnitude of untapped business development potential that present day business practices have overlooked. While the developed countries might be losing their competitive edge in manufacturing, they certainly are not losing advantage at the forefront of customer knowledge.

G. CONCLUSIONS

At present, we regard services innovation as one of the most crucial concepts in developing a competitive foundation for Finnish companies. The concepts of user-centricity, customer-centricity and demand-centricity provide the guidelines for developing new businesses. However, for the policymaker, this necessitates constant revision and renewal of the strategic approach to policy. We also need to communicate the rationale and the practical actions related to this strategic renewal – which is often not an easy task. Further, the necessary agility requires a critical approach to our mission and the current structures – it is no time to hark back to past achievements.

The core challenge of the services phenomenon is its degree of embeddedness within the present economy – it exists as an important horizontal phenomenon, but is not always sufficiently accounted for in official statistics, nor can it be effectively managed from the centre. Thus, the horizontal approach requires tools and activities applied to different sectors and clusters. At the same time, we need a vertical approach between the policymaking, implementation and the operational tiers. Services are a growing phenomenon everywhere – and, while we see this trend, there is a lot further to go to fully understand it.

2. FOSTERING SERVICE INNOVATION IN RENEWABLE ENERGY AND SUSTAINABLE CONSTRUCTION: OSEO PILOTING OF EU SUPPORTED[49] INNOVATION VOUCHER SCHEMES

Vincent Morfouace and Serge Galant (TECHNOFI) and Jacques Gautray (OSEO), France

A. INTRODUCTION

OSEO, the French Public Agency for Innovation, Financing and Guarantee support, is piloting an innovation voucher scheme in France. This is being done with the support of the technology clusters (the so called "Pôles de Compétitivité"), in order to boost the development of innovative services by SMEs active in the renewable energy and sustainable construction sectors. This pilot is being carried out simultaneously in several European Union Member States with the support of the European Commission's Directorate-General for Enterprise and Industry. Innovation in services involves both technical expertise and business expertise to help the selected SME managers to value the innovative contents, both within France and abroad. This support is provided through external expertise, supported by a grant of up to €15,000, which should initiate a higher second stage funding to realize market applications, through either public or private investments. A qualification scheme to prepare the external experts has been designed and tested to share common tools which will, in turn, aid the delivery of high quality support services to candidate SMEs in France. Replication in other Member States based on the experiences gained in France and other participating countries can then be considered, with the lessons learned being used to maximize impacts in these high growth sectors.

B. THE EUROPEAN CONTEXT

The European Directive 2009/28/EC was settled on 23 of April 2009, acknowledging that each Member State commits to increase its share of energy consumption from renewable energies, initiating efforts to boost the EU-27's share from 8.5% today to 20% by 2020.

For France, the objective is to jump from 10.3% of consumed renewable energies in 2005 to a 23% share in 2020. Achieving this objective will require not only investment in energy generation units, but also in a wide range of associated services to enable the implementation and operation of the distributed power plants. Estimates[50], as shown in Table II.2.1, amount to €50 billion turnover of services for €85 billion worth of equipment from 2006 to 2020 to achieve the above 23% target.

---

[49] Directorate-General for Enterprise and Innovation, European Commission.
[50] KIS-PIMS project (co-funded by the EC, DG ENTR) Deliverable D1.1 "Mapping of the PIMS sectors in Austria, Finland and France". Public access at www.europe-innova.eu/kis-pims/publications-tools/

Table II.2.1. The role of services in meeting France's renewable energy objectives for 2020

French Renewable Energy Market	Turn-key investments	Services included in-investments	Operation & maintenance services	Fuel-supply services (biomass)	Total Services
Value 2006 - 2020 (€ billion)	113.0	28.1	10.0	12.0	50.1

The above figures show that the cost of services will impact significantly upon the final unit cost of energy derived from renewable sources, beyond the impacts of capital investments. The role of innovation vouchers, as promoted by OSEO in France, is to support innovative SMEs involved in providing these services through external business expertise to address:

- The potential European competition they may face in the provision of such services, based on innovative solutions aiming to reduce costs;
- The potential market perspectives if they prove to possess robust and competitive know-how; and
- The rationale for developing such innovative services for at least the European market, since all Member States will be involved in the development of renewable energy sources in one way or another.

C. AN INNOVATION VOUCHER SCHEME TO HELP SME SERVICE BUSINESSES TAKE OFF

Innovation vouchers were pioneered in the Netherlands through the pioneering work of Senternovem[51]. They may be viewed as flexible financial instruments customized to meet the needs of innovative SMEs, and comprise grants to finance speedy access to external expertise for feasibility assessments and the elaboration of business models. They may therefore lead to complementary actions (needing internal and/or external funding), where relevant.

In France, pilots have been carried out with the financial support of OSEO, in accordance with OSEO's working rules. Namely, grants cover 50% of the total expenses incurred in the framework of acquiring external expertise up to a maximum of €15,000 per project. It is allocated to an SME upon acceptance of a project proposal in response to the Calls for innovative services in the areas of renewable energies (KIS-PIMS), but also sustainable construction (GreenConServe). The KIS-PIMS Call was opened in December 2008 and will close in early 2011 when the KIS-PIMS pilots are completed, whereas the GreenConServe Call started in April 2010 for an initial period of one year.

This voucher scheme is a specific instrument in the sense that technology is just one way to enable the delivery of a service to customers. Thus, innovative features can come from the business model itself (e.g. financial service innovation), or from new tools (such as information and communication solutions), opening up new ways of delivering customer support. Consequently, the proposed innovation voucher gives access to business expertise

---

[51] Senternovem has recently merged with EVD to become the NL Agency.

(risk analysis, business model definition, sensitivity analysis, international competition, etc.), in addition to purely technical skills. The voucher scheme can involve more than one expert working within a single, voucher-funded project.

After running the SME support scheme for a year, an expert qualification scheme has been implemented. The procedure operates through a two-day training session to transfer knowledge and know-how about the tools chosen or specifically developed to perform voucher-based assistance. This training includes an evaluation of the ability of trainees to use the tools autonomously. The candidate experts are pre-selected on the basis of their CV, which ensures that a minimum level of experience in the renewable energies/construction sectors and SME support in an international context has been acquired during their professional careers.

D. LESSONS LEARNED FROM THE PILOTS COMPLETED SO FAR

Firstly, services innovation and innovation based on services often appear to SMEs as somewhat "fuzzy" concepts. Examples of sector services are insufficient to explain the added value of innovative services. A pedagogical approach has been developed to explain the meaning of value-added services.

Secondly, shifts in mindset towards selling value-adding services together with technology supplies remain in their infancy.

Thirdly, cash flow generation is the key issue for young SMEs seeking to make use of external expertise. The original voucher scheme from Senternovem has been successful because it enabled access to external expertise without cash flow concerns.

Fourthly, the pilot has shown that more than 50% of vouchers supported SMEs in accessing significant development funding beyond the voucher scheme.

Last, but not least, benchmarking with other EU27 Member States (involving EC support in organizing partnering events), is highly valuable for the cross-fertilization of ideas and knowledge.

E. CONCLUSIONS

The voucher scheme under pilot in France in the renewable energy and sustainable construction sectors is shown to be a suitably relevant tool, when implemented using simple administrative procedures. Taking full account of in-house expenses incurred in terms of personnel time support for the expert and in order to provide the required data, it is a good option, which allows funding of up to 100% of the external expertise (i.e., no cash out).

Due to the modest amounts of grants involved, it is essential to minimize the administrative costs of innovative service proposal selection. Web-based management of this instrument will surely be a promising option.

The experts likely to support SMEs should be subject to a qualification process to assure the quality of the support process. Furthermore, the voucher scheme proves to be another scheme supporting business internationalization, helping entrepreneurs to better grasp the dynamics of the business environment within which they must operate.

REFERENCES

ADVANSIS, Heidenreich, M. and TECHNOFI (2009), KIS-PIMS project (co-funded by the European Commission, DG Enterprise), Deliverable D1.1 "Mapping of the PIMS sectors in Austria, Finland and France", www.europe-innova.eu/kis-pims/publications-tools/

3. FOSTERING SERVICES INNOVATION THROUGH RESEARCH IN GERMANY: THE "INNOVATION IN SERVICES" PROGRAMME

Zrinka K. Fidermuc Maler and Klaus Zuehlke-Robinet,
German Aerospace Centre, Bonn, Germany

A. INTRODUCTION

This article aims to provide an insight into the research programme "Innovation in Services". Since the mid 1990s, there has been a strong services research initiative, largely supported by a funding concept developed by the Federal Ministry for Education and Research (Bundesministerium für Bildung und Forschung). An enhanced and updated programme of services research was initiated in 2006, with the objective of improving the interaction between services research and services innovation. The same programme also represents an integral component of the Federal Government's innovation policy. Currently, the programme supports almost 300 ongoing research projects, all of which are focused upon the theme "Productivity of Services".

This paper is structured as follows. Section B provides an overview of the work of the Project Management Agency at the German Aerospace Centre. This is followed in section C by a brief account of the development of publicly funded services research in Germany, while section D will outline the current research programme "Innovation in Services", with priorities covered in section E, and implementation and funding in sections F and G. We then consider how services research is interconnected with the Federal Government's innovation policy – for example through integration in both the Federal Government's "High-Tech Strategy" and in the "Action Plan 2020". Finally, the article concludes with a brief summary and some conclusions.

B. THE PROJECT MANAGEMENT AGENCY

"Der Projektträger im Deutschen Zentrum für Luft- und Raumfahrt (PT-DLR)"[52] is a research funding organization supporting the Federal Ministry of Education and Research (BMBF) and the Federal Ministry of Economics and Technology (BMWi), along with other federal ministries, in the implementation of programme related project funding. Bearing in mind the necessity and importance of research and development for both science and for Germany as a business location, the PT-DLR is committed to the general interest. It carries out the specifications of its principals competently and swiftly, thus supporting the acquisition and utilization of scientific knowledge and technological progress.

The scope of services provided by the PT-DLR is fourfold:

---

[52] The Project Management Agency forms part of the German Aerospace Centre.

- *Conceptual work:* The creation of position papers on the state of the art in science, the conception of funding foci, the preparation and determination of promotional measures;
- *Controlling:* Professional and administrative project management, interim and final outcome evaluation and financial control;
- *Evaluation:* External assessments of applications, evaluation of funding concepts, staging of seminars; and
- *EU-wide and international cooperation*: Support of the BMBF in the conceptual and organizational design of cross-border research projects and funding.

The PT-DLR team comprises over 750 employees who, over the past year, have managed around €800 million. More than 50% of the employees are scientists, drawn from all fields of research. They have an in-depth knowledge of the latest developments in science, research and development, including extensive experience of the design, financing, support and evaluation of research projects.

The "Work Design and Services" department is situated within the PT-DLR, and its primary responsibility is to implement the "Innovation in Services" research funding programme.

C. A SHORT HISTORY OF SERVICES RESEARCH IN GERMANY

Today, we can look back upon almost fifteen years of services research funded by the Federal Ministry of Education and Research. Without rapid gains in the importance of services for employment, economic growth, prosperity and innovation, this would probably not have been possible. The promotion of services research and the crucial role played by the BMBF will be described in more detail.

In 1995, the German Federal Ministry of Education and Research responded to the perceived lack of a service mentality among the country's business and research organizations by launching its 'Initiative on Services for the 21st century', thus laying a vital foundation for the comprehensive development of services in Germany. The Initiative's main approach involves promoting ideas, concepts, strategies and models intended to contribute to the successful, stable realization of Germany's potential as a location both for living and for doing business, while also securing employment. The Initiative's overall objectives were:

- To support the development of the services sector;
- To encourage a more positive attitude towards research and development;
- To incentivise private initiative;
- To draw attention to the benefits of training and recognized qualifications, and support appropriate implementation strategies; and
- To promote networking with other economic sectors of the economy.

A total of six announcements were published prior to the launch of the new programme in 2006, as follows:

- Benchmarking to boost innovation, growth and employment in the service sector;
- Knowledge-intensive Services (KIS);

- Service Engineering und Service Design;
- Standardization and quality in the service sector;
- Work organization, management and tertiarization; and
- Innovative services in small to medium-sized enterprises (Craft Trades).

Some significant achievements were achieved during this first phase. One good example is in Services Engineering. Until the establishment of a project in this area, set up by a call, there had been no systematic, practical tools for the planning of service operations. Based on a broad knowledge of the engineering sciences, it was possible to initiate and sustain significant developments in services[53]. Now, Services Engineering is widespread in companies, and related degree programmes form part of university curricula. Another example is provided by the standardisation of services and service processes. Standardization improves the marketability of services, and defines minimum standards for services. A distinguishing feature of this first stage was the cross-sectional nature of the work. In addition, a more comprehensive approach to funding was adopted after 2006.

D. THE CURRENT PROGRAMME "INNOVATIONS IN SERVICES"

The BMBF programme "Innovations in Services" (BMBF, 2006a), which began in 2006, is still ongoing. The programme was officially announced in 2006 at the 6th Service Conference of the Federal Ministry, which takes place according to a two-year cycle. For the first time, a fully-defined approach for research funding was introduced.

The intention of the programme may be viewed as forward looking – i.e., to enhance and support the dissemination of a new understanding of innovation policy. Innovation is here understood in a very broad sense:

- As the cooperation with and involvement of entrepreneurial innovation in societal developments;
- Innovation in order to overcome the technological determinism; and
- As a means of competitive differentiation through services. This public funding addresses an area of innovation policy previously neglected by policymakers in the innovation field.

In the book "Services Made in Germany – A Travel Guide"[54], service innovation was defined as follows: "Service innovation directly facilitates customers, meeting their needs and desires. It can be understood both as a process of development within an organization and as the resulting configuration of new activities (both by the company and by customers, suppliers, and other actors), within a specific context."[55]

The programme includes a brief survey and describes both economic and social trends in the service industry, and service development. It also lists relevant action areas for research policy, and areas for future research. Furthermore, there are specified tools for the

---

[53] Bullinger and Scheer, 2006.
[54] For more details see here Chapter 7: Other activities.
[55] Reichwald et al 2008, p. 11.

implementation and control of the programme, with a six year time frame and public budget of €70 million. The programme also lists new societal trends such as: Developments in the consumption and sales markets, convergence of material goods and services, the progress of information and communication technologies, and not least the (underestimated) importance of innovation in services. The action areas of the programme include innovation management, new areas of growth and services work.

E. CENTRAL THEME OF THE PROGRAMME "INNOVATION IN SERVICES"

The strong interaction between services research and practice must be viewed as providing a foundation for innovation in the services sector. The programme "Innovation in Services" therefore prioritizes the promotion of such research-practice interactions. This is a means of targeting knowledge and insights of real world applicability, ensuring their direct transfer and, consequently, simultaneous learning effects for science and industry, which the support of this programme.

The prerequisite for success is excellence in service research and the services sector. The programme's central theme is therefore: "Using research and development to help Germany achieve the same excellence in the service field as it exhibits in the field of industrial production. This applies to both service research and the service sector"[56].

The excellence of the manufacturing sector is particularly well captured in the term "Made in Germany". However, the trademark "Made in Germany" - as described above – cannot be assigned to the area of services. In order to reach that goal, to close the existing gap and to accelerate the dynamics of economic and social innovation, it is necessary to make best use of services research to discover potential applications in business, research, education and society. In practice, this has meant a systematic development of services for business and society through publicly funded service research.

The programme "Innovation in Services" is neither sector nor industry specific in its orientation. The central research questions in both services and service development, together with related aspects of the processes and products, are comprehensively addressed and translated into business and science related research questions. Such an approach certainly makes it possible to address issues of a commercial nature. The success of this programme will depend on two variables:

- On the capacity to establish relevant thematic priorities; and
- On the programme's capacity to respond to change. In a dynamic market environment, it is indispensable that the planning, implementation and control processes at the programme implementation stage are sufficiently responsive to change.

Therefore, the programme itself must be "capable of learning" – in fact, the programme "Innovation in Services" was devised as a learning programme. Working closely with the research sector, industry and the social partners, and with regard to the recommendations issued by participants in the campaign "Partners for Innovation", funding policy objectives

---

[56] BMBF 2006a, p. 8.

were translated into the following thematic fields of action. These fields of action provide the starting point for the funding provided by this learning programme:

- Innovation management
- Innovation in growth sectors
- People in service companies.

In order to ensure quality of funding in the thematic fields of action, it will be essential that the programme ensures sustained cooperation between theory and practice, as well as public debate. These cross-cutting tasks arise in all fields of action, and constitute the interface between well structured funding at the research stage, and the continual responsiveness to change that is embedded in the framework of a learning programme[57].

The funding available through the research programme gives the universities, colleges and research institutes an opportunity to increase the depth and breadth of knowledge in the field of service science. Furthermore, by means of research projects, the programme supports the so called "Community Building" that aims to enhance cooperation between companies, universities, research institutions and intermediary organizations, and sustain contact with the international research community. Service research, in the form of both conceptually and application-oriented joint research projects between the scientific and business spheres, is intended to fill remaining gaps in the systematic development of services, and to strengthen its role in the innovation process. Services science has been enjoying an increase in research activity for some time now, which is one means of ensuring that services science research receives adequate institutional support[58].

Innovation policy is understood to be a cross-cutting instrument. Services represent a mediating, leading and shaping force in this policy field. Innovation is driven not only by technology - rather, it is a more comprehensive process.

Typical forms of innovation in services such as process changes and improvements, the bundling of complementary services to address complex problems in production, or in relation to sustainability or demographic change require multidisciplinary approaches rather than sector specific ones.

The programme is intended to induce learning processes in and between science and industry, theory and practice. In order to realise these ambitious objectives, the programme takes into account specific support instruments. These instruments guarantee that the conditions for the programme – so that it is possible for it to be considered a learning one - are met.

A broad public debate is intended to provide the foundation for the progressive development of the "Innovation in Services" programme. This debate is being supported by the work and experience of focus groups, annual status reports and meetings of experts. A short explanation of their tasks follows:

---

[57] BMBF 2006a.
[58] The central portal for the presentation of results is the homepage www.DL2100.de.

- Focus groups consisting of funding recipients and parties interested in a particular funding priority will be used, *inter alia*, to ensure internal networking, increase visibility and develop recommendations for research activities and future action.
- A conference will be held over several days every two years or so, with the aim of presenting and discussing current findings from funded projects in various forums[59].

Open programme structures are indispensable to a learning programme. The programme structures also require feedback loops that embed learning to ensure, for example, the progressive development of suitable funding instruments or content priorities. As a consequence, a number of activities will be carried out, including:

- Meta studies on individual funding priorities. The findings from these studies will be incorporated into the respective ongoing research funding activities.
- Regular international monitoring activities that are used to give domestic funding activities an international perspective, and which provide a platform for critical discussions (with the advisory board, for example), on the progressive development of the Ministry's "Innovation in Services" funding programme[60].
- Impact analyses and strategic audits will target the "Innovation in Services" funding programme as a whole after approximately five years, and contribute to the overall assessment of funding measures with regard to their direct and indirect impacts, and the programme's progressive strategic development.

F. IMPLEMENTATION OF THE FUNDING PROGRAMME

The programme "Innovation in Services" is implemented through thematically oriented, public announcements. These announcements contain information about relevant references, research and action areas, as well as the application procedure. The typical structure for research funding is the so called "Joint Research Project". This represents a work-sharing cooperation between several independent partners such as universities, research institutes, companies or organizations. Under the umbrella of a common theme, these partners work independently and contribute individually to address common research questions. This ensures close collaboration between stakeholders from the beginning. For instance, the companies' requirements can be sent directly to the relevant research institution for consideration. In a reciprocal sense, institutions' research questions can also be "road-tested" directly by companies in terms of practical relevance. The duration of projects is generally three years.

Once an announcement is published in the Federal Gazette, project outlines may be submitted to the relevant project management agency for consideration. Proposals must be based on the latest accomplishments in research and development (R&D), with work to be completed in the respective thematic field. Proposals should also take into account relevant international R&D, along with findings and insights from earlier programmes and ongoing projects. The participation is open to research institutions, as well as to businesses and organizations that operate in the relevant fields.

---

[59] www.dienstleistungstagung.de
[60] Spath/Ganz 2008; http://www.service-monitoring.eu/

Conditions for funding

The approved projects will receive funding subject to the prevailing budgetary situation. Funding for commercial enterprises is subject to the regulations regarding cost-based grant applications. Therefore, a funding rate of up to 50% is the rule for commercial businesses. Small and medium-sized enterprises may be granted an additional 10%[61].

Ongoing funding projects deal with cross-sectoral issues in order to obtain new knowledge and applicable "pilot" results for research institutes, universities and companies. Moreover, results must be generalized so as to be of use to other stakeholders.

G. CURRENT AREAS OF RESEARCH FUNDING

In the previous programming period there were five strategic priorities, whereas in the current programme there are only four. The following table shows briefly the duration of the funding streams, the number of funded projects and the available public funds. Since the funded companies must make their own financial contribution, it is likely that the overall budget will be around one third larger.

Table II.3.1. Current areas of research funding

Funding area	Duration	Number of projects	Public budget in € millions
Exportability and Internationalization of Services	2004 - 2009	66	24
Integration of Product and Services	2006 - 2010	83	19
Service Quality and Skilled Service Work	2008 - 2011	57	16
Technology and Services in the Wake of Demographic Change	2008 - 2011	80	25
Service Productivity Management	2010 - 2014	120	31

A brief explanation of each of the funding priorities follows.

(a)   "Exportability and Internationalization of Services"

Funding is provided for service research in order to address gaps in the evidence base, increase the competitiveness of the service sector and to improve employment opportunities by creating new and attractive employment opportunities in the services sector. Their particular, intangible nature has previously been a considerable obstacle to the export of services. But now the development of information, communication and automation technologies and greater mobility of people, knowledge and capital provide a basis for the introduction of new forms of trading in services. Germany will need to innovate further in the services sector if it wants to expand its trade in services on a European and international scale.

---

[61] BMBF 2006a, p. 23.

Activities are focused on three thematic areas:

- Basic aspects of service exports, including studies on enabling and obstruction factors, and general conditions for the successful export of services;
- New visions for corporate organization, including "Management Processes", "Organizational Concepts" and "Organization/Technology Interaction"; and
- Creation of international networks of stakeholders from the fields of teaching, research and practical application.

(b)   "Integration of Products and Services"

This call covers those research subjects dealing with "hybrid value creation" and "customized solutions through the bundling of material assets and services".

In order to develop new growth areas and to secure their competitive position, especially in the light of growing competition from low wage countries, manufacturing industries are developing increasingly as providers of customized solutions that combine material assets and services. As a result, hybrid value creation as a form of business-related service has become increasingly important, and viewed as a way to increase and to sustain the international competitiveness of the German manufacturing sector. This call takes into account the fact that the boundaries between the provision of material goods and the provision of services are becoming increasingly blurred. The projects deal with issues such as the pricing of hybrid products, organization design and change management[62].

(c)   "Service Quality and Skilled Service Work"

Innovation and success in the services area and the scope for growth and increased employment will be influenced significantly by the qualifications, skills and motivation of the work force. In comparison to other sectors of the economy, it is notable that many areas of the services sector lack attractive and professionalized, modern working practices.

This fact applies primarily to the non-academic area of "specialized services". Qualification and design efforts should therefore focus not only on the academic professions related to the service, but include also other sections of the workforce.

The constituent elements of expert work, such as skills and qualifications, taking pride in work, appreciation, respect, professionalism and commitment, which are key success factors of the German innovation system, have to be developed systematically in the area of service innovation as well. The planned funding measures are intended to target precisely the remaining and unexploited potentials to professionalize, in order to create attractive employment opportunities[63].

---

[62] More information can be found under http://www.zukuenftigetechnologien.de/
[63] For more information visit http://www.servprof.de/home

(d)   "Technology and Services in the Wake of Demographic Change"

In Germany, social and economic structures have changed in recent decades. The funding activity "Technology and Services in the wake of Demographic Change," focuses on three of these structural changes: 1) The structural transformation from an industrial to a service economy resulting from an increase of automation and productivity; 2) Micromechanical Engineering Systems (MMES) playing a more significant role for growth and employment; 3) Demographic change resulting in a higher proportion of elderly and very elderly people in the population.

On the one hand, the German economy can maintain and expand its position of international leadership in MMES, and hence need to integrate technological developments into services and markets. On the other hand, innovative service companies will open up new market opportunities by using MMES. Thus, it is important to tighten the relationship between technology and new services. Therefore, the results of the funding activity should help identify new opportunities from demographic change and enable German companies to design services supported by innovative technologies – especially for elderly people or patients suffering from chronic disease[64].

(e)   "Service Productivity Management"

The "Service Productivity Management" call was issued in 2009. The idea was to look into the question of services productivity with focused energy - how to measure it, evaluate, increase and improve it. The main research question for science and business therefore becomes how to improve the productivity of services.

The wider economy benefits from the results of this research, because the optimization of productivity has a direct impact on all business entities due to the incorporation of services in all economic processes. A specific feature of this call is the establishment of a strategic partnership instrument entitled "Productivity of Services". This instrument - based on the model of a Public-Private Partnership - facilitates a close cooperation between industry, science and policymakers.

In general, the tasks of a strategic partnership are to accompany the call and to provide a stimulus for the enhancement of the programme "Innovation in Services". Such a partnership contributes to the networking of national, European and international activities in services research and innovation policies, thereby anchoring and strengthening the topic in the public consciousness. Furthermore, such a partnership facilitates a broad knowledge transfer between science and industry R&D and formulates recommendations to the relevant stakeholders (businesses, education institutions, intermediary organizations, politics, and science) in terms of productivity guidelines[65].

---

[64] For more information visit www.dienstleistungundtechnik.de
[65] http://www.service-productivity.de/

H. "ACTION PLAN SERVICES 2020" AND THE "HIGH-TECH STRATEGY"

The vital role of services in the development of innovation is also emphasized by the fact that the services research programme has become a part of the Federal Government's "High-Tech Strategy"[66]. This strategy reflects the idea that innovation is not associated solely with technological innovations. Rather, services are seen as a mediator between technology and the market on one side, and businesses and customers on the other.

In 17 future fields identified as "high potential" economic areas, which includes services, special effort should be made in relation to innovation in order to bundle, generalize and make available existing results from services research for other areas of research. In the current legislative period, the High-Tech Strategy has been continued and enhanced. The original 17 fields are now merged into five demand areas and the services represent - as a cross-cutting theme - an integral part in all demand areas: Health, Climate/Energy, Security, Mobility and Communication. Two research projects funded under the umbrella of the programme "Innovation in Services" explore specific issues in services research, and seek to establish better ways of embedding these within the "High-Tech Strategy".

The High-Tech-Strategy continues the adopted approach of incorporating early results in services research with other research areas defined in the "Action Plan Services 2020" of the Federal Ministry of Education and Research[67]. The Ministry paved the way for new innovation policies with the "Action Plan Services 2020", which advocates close cooperation with technical and technological research from the outset. This is primarily about linking new technologies with the key concepts for service infrastructure in order to make them marketable. Finally, services are drivers of new technological developments, and pave the way to the market and to customers. It is essential that technological developments be connected to services from the outset in order to release their maximum potential.

Several measures have already been tested in pilot projects such as "Health Regions of the Future", "Energy-Efficient City" and "Mobility and Assistance in an Aging Society." The focus for further activities will be not only on such areas as environment, climate, sustainability, and security studies and research. Of equal importance will be those activities in which there is an explicit interdependence between technology and services, and where services could act as a driver for technological developments.

I. OTHER ACTIVITIES

This section will give a brief overview of some specific activities under the funding programme, together with some detail around the international aspects of national funding and research activities: EPISIS (European Policies and Instruments to Support Innovation in Services), "Service Made in Germany – A Travel Guide", and "Service-Engineering - the Drivers of Innovation in SMEs".

---

[66] BMBF 2006b.
[67] BMBF 2009.

EPISIS

The main objective of the EPISIS project is to facilitate transnational cooperation between policymakers and innovation agencies in the field of services innovation through parallel policy, strategic and operational level activities. The project offers an open platform for the discussion of policy recommendations, tests new policy approaches in support of services innovation and organizes three policy oriented, international conferences.

Project Overview

Services innovation is a phenomenon that cuts across all sectors of the economy. Services innovation is developed in all industries, from the service sector to traditional manufacturing sectors. Services innovation can create new business opportunities for companies from very different backgrounds, and can therefore facilitate the transformation and renewal of industries, networks and clusters as a whole. What distinguishes services innovation from the traditional understanding of R&D and innovation is its less technological nature. In the strict sense services innovation is, first and foremost, non-technological. Technology is understood rather to be an enabling platform for new service concepts and for services-based business models. The integration of services and technology is important for the development of services innovation, but the driver for innovation is not the technological solution in itself, but the value it can create for both the service provider and customer. Public services are not specifically addressed by the project.

Specific objectives

The heterogeneous character and the multidimensional, multilayered nature of services innovation call for an approach that involves parallel policy, strategic and operational level activities. The main policy level objective of the project is to advance a broad-based innovation approach to innovation policy by identifying emerging policy challenges for services innovation, and designing appropriate policy responses. The project's main objective at the strategic level is to enhance the understanding of services innovation, and to promote further the change in mindset required for the recognition of services and services innovation as powerful economic forces in the EU. The project's main operational level objective is to encourage the development of the necessary policy tools and measures in the field of services innovation.

Activities

The project has established a "European Services Innovation Think Tank" to be engaged in policy and strategic level discussion and agenda development. The "Think Tank" covers representatives from the EPISIS partners (Finland, Sweden, UK, Germany and Denmark), as well as non-partner countries and organizations (Austria, Estonia, Finland, France, Germany, Ireland, the Netherlands, Norway, Slovenia) and will meet twice a year for the project duration. The aim of the "Think Tank" is to act as an open platform for discussion between the public authorities responsible for supporting services innovation, as well as to develop concrete policy recommendations and validate the findings of project activities. The project also includes three policy-focused "International Conferences on Service Innovation," to disseminate results to the wider innovation policy community. The ultimate goal of the project is to develop new policy tools in the field of services innovation, and to pilot and validate new service innovation support schemes on selected areas.

Germany is a partner in the EPISIS project, leading Work Package 3 on improving knowledge transfer and service innovation, as well as heading Task Force 3 on the integration of services and technologies. The Ministry of Education and Research appointed PT-DLR to execute its tasks within the EPISIS project.

A central objective of any research funding is to disseminate key findings beyond the network of directly funded stakeholders. Particular attention is paid to this aspect of effectiveness. Two examples are outlined below.

Service Made in Germany – A Travel Guide

The first example is a project entitled "Service Made in Germany - A Travel Guide". The aim of this travel guide is to illustrate the impressive transformation of Germany into a services champion. The content is based on innovation fora that were held between September 2007 and February 2008 in services champion locations nationwide. The guide presents services excellence on the part of businesses and research institutions to a wider public of experts, who we hope will visit the locations described and personally observe the quality of "Services Made in Germany[68]".

The Travel Guide is working through the key issues in relation to services research in a very concrete and clear manner. The guide includes areas such as Service Innovation, Service Engineering, Service Standardization, Service Exports[69] and invites readers to visit the companies and research institutions involved.

Service-Engineering - the Drivers of Innovation in SMEs

The second example is the project "Service-Engineering - the Drivers of Innovation in SMEs". The project focused on the exemplary testing of innovative methods, models and tools in selected pilot farms. It included the organization of a set of events and workshops aimed at an immediate knowledge transfer. More than ten pilot enterprises were grouped together to develop and test exemplary and transferable service management processes. As part of this, the Ministry of Education and Research jointly organized, with the federal states' chambers of commerce, knowledge transfer events for companies[70]. The results of the project demonstrated to small and medium-sized enterprises the benefits of a deliberate and systematic design of services, and raised their awareness of the key issues.

---

[68] Reichwald et al. 2008, p. 4.
[69] http://innofor.clicresearch.de
[70] http://www.service-engineering-kmu.de

J. CONCLUSIONS

With the programme "Innovation in Services", German research policymakes a significant and visible contribution to strengthening the innovative capacity and readiness to innovate in the area of services. The research projects deal with the main questions in the context of services innovation. The federal programme creates a bridge between research and the innovation system in the services sector.

The success of this approach and of the related course of action can be measured by the fact that other public research programmes build on the results of this programme.

The programme is particularly effective because of the cross-cutting, multisectoral approach to the research. In addition, services and their potential contribution to the innovation system as a whole are taken into account in the wider innovation funding system.

Raising public awareness of the results of the programme has also helped to increase significantly the relevance and impact of the role of services innovation throughout the innovation process. The role and significance of services research is set to increase in the future. Without innovations in services, it will not be possible to address societal challenges in the sense of sustainability at the social, economic and ecological levels. As part of this process, services research will remain a durable, key factor in helping find the answers to the challenges that lie ahead.

REFERENCES

BMBF (2009), "Zukunft gestalten mit Dienstleistungen. Aktionsplan DL 2020", Federal Ministry of Education and Research, Bonn/Berlin

BMBF (2006a), "Innovation in Services", *BMBF-Funding Program*, Federal Ministry of Education and Research, Bonn/Berlin

BMBF (2006b), "The High-Tech Strategy for Germany", Federal Ministry of Education and Research, Bonn/Berlin

Bullinger, H.-J. and Scheer, A.-W. (Hrsg.) (2006), "Service Engineering: Entwicklung und Gestaltung innovativer Dienstleistungen", 2., vollst. überarb. u. erw: Aufl., Springer Verlag, Heidelberg, Germany.

Reichwald, R., Möslein, K. M., Huff, A. S., Kölling, M. and Neyer, A.-K. (2008), "Service Made in Germany. A Travel Guide", Center of Leading Innovation & Cooperation, HHL – Leipzig Graduate School of Management.

Spath, D. and Ganz, W. (Eds.) (2008), "The Future of Services. Trends and Perspectives", Carl Hanser Verlag, München, Germany.

4. SERVICES INNOVATION IN THE NETHERLANDS

Hans Simons, NL Innovation, the Netherlands

A. INTRODUCTION

The services sector is extremely important for the Dutch economy, accounting for approximately 70% of the country's Gross National Product and 80% of its employment. The services sector presents major opportunities for growth, given the increasing trend towards the liberalisation of services on a global level. New, ICT-enabled innovative service concepts can be duplicated in relatively straightforward fashion and then exported. The focus here is on those service sectors that are prominent internationally, both technologically and in terms of market potential.

In 2007, two new initiatives aiming to initiate an innovation programme were launched: Service innovation & ICT and Logistics & Supply Chains. Companies and research institutes have jointly taken the first steps to formulate a document outlining the vision and ambitions in these areas. In January 2009, their proposals for innovation programmes were discussed in the Strategic Advisory Committee for Innovation Programmes. This Committee advised the Dutch Ministry of Economic Affairs to implement both programmes.

B. SERVICES INNOVATION & ICT

Financial sector and creative industries

This programme is targeted at the financial sector and creative industries. Companies and organizations operating in the important creative and financial industries (including Philips, IBM, ING and ABN/AMRO), have joined forces in this innovation programme to integrate their ambitions with respect to services innovation and ICT.

Creative industry

As part of this process, the creative industry is focusing on the growth area of creative and ICT solutions. The industry's overall objectives are to transform the Netherlands into a European Hub for Smart Content, Experiences and Connectedness; achieve revenue growth of €7.9 billion; double the number of start-ups and medium-sized businesses involved in cross-media content; increase the number of new lifestyle products and services at an annual rate of 6%; and generate 10% annual growth in creative value-added services offered by ICT service providers.

Information, communication and media

The industry is looking to implement invisible and intuitive technology in products and services, centred around information, communication and the media. As today's consumers are fickle, interactive and demanding, personalised services are vital to meeting their needs and requirements. Finally, another key industry challenge is to connect three 'spheres' that currently remain insufficiently integrated: small and medium-sized businesses operating in the creative industry; the creative production industry; and first-rate educational and research institutions. Bringing these spheres together will create opportunities for economic growth and innovation.

Three growth areas: content, experience and connectedness

To achieve this objective, three interrelated growth areas have been designated: content, experience and connectedness.

- With respect to content, the industry aims to achieve a position of international leadership in terms of the amount of content to be stored, enhanced, published and distributed;
- In terms of experience, the objective is to transform the Netherlands into an international centre of excellence for lifestyle and work-style products and services;
- Finally, in terms of connectedness, the industry intends to play a leading role in the international transition from infrastructure-related services to creative value-added services.

Financial sector

The financial industry has equally put the creation of a hub at the top of the Holland Financial Centre's innovation agenda. The objective is to turn the Netherlands into an international centre of excellence in financial logistics, to establish the most efficient processing system for value data of any country, and to achieve an internationally leading position in value-added services related to financial logistics. This should generate an annual growth of more than €950 million in revenue and reduce the administrative burden for Dutch businesses by €600 million per year.

Financial logistics is a rapidly growing market that calls for pre-competitive collaboration between stakeholders. Following the introduction of the Single Euro Payments Area (SEPA) in 2008, national payment markets are integrated in a single European market for payment processing: 315 million consumers and 17 million companies will be using electronic payment methods, as well as new systems such as iDEAL and e-invoicing. SEPA has a major relational impact on the European payment market. The market for Personal Identification Number (PIN) payments (i.e. making purchases by debit card using an in-store payment terminal) is volume-driven, and the national European payment brands lack the economies of scale needed to compete with major credit card companies such as VISA and MasterCard. One challenge here is that, while there is currently no viable, pan-European alternative to these US-based companies, this area is in fact relatively important to the Dutch financial sector.

However, the opportunities and challenges are not limited to the market for payment processing: financial logistics services are set to become tradable goods, thereby creating significant opportunities for innovative, high value-added services throughout the financial sector. This requires effective cooperation, a common European approach, standardisation and exploitation of the innovative power of challengers and new entrants in the sector.

Positioning of the Netherlands

The objectives in each area are aligned with the positioning of the Netherlands as a Portal to Europe (as chosen by the Innovation Platform), as well as with the Platform's aim of developing the Netherlands into the most creative economy in Europe, and one of the three most creative economies worldwide.

Three parallel initiatives

Following the recommendation of the Strategic Advisory Committee for Innovative Programmes of the Dutch Ministry of Economic Affairs regarding the Service Innovation and ICT initiative[71], substantial efforts have been made to create focus and mass within these specialized areas. As part of these efforts, the programme will comprise three parallel initiatives:

- A plan to establish an innovation programme for the service industry: 'Service Innovation — people driven, ICT empowered';
- Developing the innovation agenda as set out by the Holland Financial Centre (one of the initiators), for the purpose of strengthening the Netherlands' position as a financial centre; and
- The strategic research agenda of IIP Create (also one of the initiators), as a platform for innovation in those segments of the creative industry where innovation is technology-related.

Achieving the objectives of the innovation programme could have potentially significant impacts on other areas. It is also anticipated that several new technological and service concepts will swiftly find their way to other industries, both in manufacturing and in services.

Dedicated approach

At this stage, around one hundred companies in total have joined the initiative. Although investing independently, participants also acknowledge the importance of joint action, as this provides added value both to them and the wider industry. This added value is to be generated through joint research projects and promotional activities, standardisation, infrastructure development, education and labour market development.

In these industries in particular, given there is rarely an established tradition of R&D and innovative action, it is essential that an innovation programme be dedicated from the outset to creating an impact across the chain, from knowledge development through to implementation. The companies are investing in industrial research and value realization (i.e. commercialization) in roughly equal measure. Additionally – although to a lesser extent – their investment focuses on developing scientific research and education. The parties involved

---

[71] Arising from discussions in June 2008.

are applying for a government grant in support of all three components of the programme. The main portion of this grant will be used for knowledge development, while implementation will require the smallest commitment.

Governmental instruments

A combination of new and existing instruments will be used to support implementation, comprising:

- A dedicated programme (see below for further information);
- A system of tax credits;
- A voucher scheme in support of innovative activity; and
- Regional projects (local initiatives receiving governmental support);

The main emphasis for Government support is through the dedicated programme, which has the following thematic components:

- R&D support: 25 – 50% of eligible costs
- Leading scientific research on services innovation and engineering
- E-identity and e-profiling
- A productivity enhancing work environment
- A platform facility to strengthen the infrastructure of other parts of SII programme:
    o A Virtual Creative Collaboration Platform (an interactive platform and integrated market place);
    o National innovation accelerator (a matchmaker between incubators, firms and financiers); and
    o An e-invoicing platform (a platform for e-billing Business to Consumer (B2C), unlocking internet banking for Business Service Providers (BSP).
- Human Capital: an academic exchange programme and international guest lecturers
- Dissemination and application of findings:
    o Public relations: an annual event and website to raise awareness, etc.;
    o Seminars, master classes;
    o Innovation voucher projects; and
    o International embedding of best practice (e.g. via Enterprise Europe Network).

Time frame and financial dimension

The programme will run for eight years, divided in to two four-year phases. The total investment will be €61 million per year during the first four years (private and public). For the first two years, the Dutch Government has set aside €125 million.

Governance

The SII programme is coordinated by the Programme Office for Service innovation and ICT, in which the private sector takes the lead.

C. LOGISTICS & SUPPLY CHAINS

Like all innovation programmes in the Netherlands, the Logistics & Supply Chain Programme is realized through public-private collaboration.

A special Committee called "The Van Laarhoven Committee" has formulated a vision that includes the goal of transforming the Netherlands into the European market leader by 2020 in managing transnational flows affecting one or more European countries, and that are managed through the centralized management functions of market parties.

This ambition is based on the vision that there will be strong global growth in traded goods, and hence an increase in the complexity and the dynamic of supply chains. That complexity is increasing so rapidly that individual management centres (of particular companies) will no longer be sufficient. There is a major opportunity for the development of practices for effective management of multiple supply chains. New technological and ICT developments make it possible to more effectively control and manage complexity in the supply chain. The Netherlands can be a 'first mover' by developing a cluster of international expertise to manage the flow of goods and logistical nodes, as well as facilitating the structuring and harmonisation of logistical chains. These chain management and configuration activities have the potential to be combined in a Supply Chain Campus, where individual and joint management centres could be established and cooperate with knowledge institutes.

Concrete themes:

- *Cross Chain Control Centre (4-C)* involves the contemporaneous management and configuration of several supply chains using the latest technological and professional developments, resulting in efficiency benefits and new services.

- *Service logistics* must capitalise on opportunities to optimise international logistic service chains through the application of innovative concepts in chain management and configuration, and enable the Netherlands to become a market leader over a period of around four to six years.

- *Defining role of nodes* deals with the development of chain management and configuration concepts with greater coordination from the nodes/main ports so that the reliability of distribution can be improved in the future. This could generate major benefits for the Netherlands, such as a reduction in the number of shipments, the stimulation of multi-modal transport and improved accessibility.

- *The Supply Chain Campus* aims to provide the space for the above-mentioned activities and research, as well as hosting leading training courses. The campus also seeks to attract logistical management centres from the business sector. This should enable the Netherlands to maintain its leading reputation in the area of chain management and configuration.

Activities

The following activities will be performed:

- R&D - comprising cutting edge applied research in the 4C domain (cross chain control centres); major ports control function and service logistics;
- Demonstration projects;
- Stimulation of SME buy-in by linking into existing SME networks (i.e., Dinalog Friends and Line organizations);
- Fostering human capital via further education and continuous professional development (CPD); and
- Embedding results and knowledge into the training curricula in the three major domains: academic, professional and vocational.

The latter will also seek to stimulate open innovation.

Running period and financial dimension

The programme will run in 2009-2013. The total investment will be €68 million, of which the Dutch Government will supply €25 million.

Governance

The private Dutch Institute of Advanced Logistics (Dinalog) will take the lead on this programme. It will initiate and control all activities, alongside its other functions in the area of research and development (R&D).

5. PROMOTING SERVICES INNOVATION BASED ON BETTER PRACTICES: DECONSTRUCTING BUSINESS AS USUAL

Irene Martinsson, Vinnova, Sweden

A. INTRODUCTION

This chapter is a contribution to the discussion of how economic activity in business life is becoming more service-oriented. A growing focus on services within the study of marketing has evolved into a theory of a transformation from a goods-dominant logic (G-D logic) to a service-dominant logic (S-D logic). A central concern of marketing scholars focusing on S-D logic is this evolution of a new logic. It is assumed that there is a transformation in progress. The present chapter seeks to contribute to this line of literature by deconstructing business as usual and defining nine commonalities among the heterogeneous service companies, and proceeding to further the understanding and potential of knowledge transfers across sectors. In an attempt to inject service research into the policy literature, we also develop a new model for case-based policy recommendations in the field of services.

It is suggested that services are different from goods (Bolton, 2004; Lovelock & Gummesson, 2004; Aitken, Callantyne, Osborne & Williams, 2006; Vargo & Lusch, 2008; Vargo, Maglio and Akaka, 2008). Vargo and Lusch (2008) acknowledge a difference and suggest that the provision of goods as the basis of economic exchange should be replaced by an emphasis on the provision of services. One approach is to relate an emerging Service-Dominant Logic (S-D Logic) to management studies (Johnston & Clark, 2005; Metters, King-Metters, Pullman & Walton 2005; Chase, Aquilano & Jacobs, 2006; Fitzsimmons, 2006; Ford & Bowen, 2008; Jacob & Ulaga, 2008). Jacob and Ulaga (2008) suggest that in recent years, manufacturers around the world have made increasing efforts to orient their businesses towards service, as an addition to their traditional business, in order to remain competitive. Several researchers claim that figures in developed economies indicate that services dominate the economy (Spohrer & Riecken, 2006). The current study asks the following: Can we promote service innovation based on better practices from empirical examples?

Services account for the lion's share of economic activity in most countries, and the service sector within manufacturing is growing steadily (World Investment Report, 2004). Services account for 30 percent of total Swedish exports (Ekonomifakta, 2008).

Researchers are investigating manufacturing companies that have increased their efforts to provide service as an addition to their traditional business (Ford & Bowen, 2008; Jacob & Ulaga, 2008). Existing work also uses S-D Logic as a new language to convey concepts that emphasize skill and knowledge as objects of exchange. Furthermore, researchers suggest that the focus of market exchange should shift from products to an understanding of the process of value creation within the exchange itself (Bolton, 2004; Lovelock & Gummesson, 2004; Aitken, Callantyne, Osborne & Williams, 2006; Vargo & Lusch, 2008; Vargo, Maglio and Akaka, 2008). Previous research has neglected to explore the differences and commonalities of new service development across sectors i.e. in service companies[72] as well as manufacturing companies that "servify" their business. One reason why academic scholars have not focused on how new service development is performed across sectors may be that it draws from and integrates a number of academic disciplines such as engineering, management and computer science in addition to a number of sectors such as manufacturing, transport, construction as well as the service sector. Could manufacturing companies learn from the way that service companies develop new services? It is noteworthy to highlight that service companies may also learn from the way manufacturing companies make R&D investments visible. If business is transforming and becoming service-oriented, service companies may give us some hint as to what transformation to "servification" may entail. Most service companies have not undergone a transformation; rather they have always developed services. Without an understanding of business as usual in service companies as a reference point, it may be difficult to transfer knowledge across sectors and different types of organizations.

B. METHOD

This study is based on data from a quantitative survey (Frankfort-Nachmias & Nachmias, 1996). The sample consists of 4000 Almega member companies; Almega represents service companies whose employees total 400,000. The focus on Almega-member companies offers an opportunity to locate an S-D Logic in Swedish service companies since this would be where S-D Logic may appear in business as usual. The target population was also selected because Almega has gathered data focusing on innovation and research activity in their member companies. The selection of service companies was based on the fact that they were Almega members. The companies in the target population were each contacted and asked to fill in a questionnaire focusing on innovation and research. A total of 778 service companies responded (20% of those polled).

The research design of this chapter incorporates a quantitative survey and qualitative case examples. The quantitative survey described above gives a more generalisable description of service companies. The quantitative survey is also complemented with examples of qualitative case studies from the VINNOVA project portfolio in order to render a more detailed examination of the issues at hand. Three project managers were asked to describe their most important project results and if they see any possible future challenges.

C. BUSINESS AS USUAL IN SERVICE COMPANIES

Solutions, sometimes combined with knowledge, are now sold as product packages that are customized for every consumer. Although this is an empirical statement, we still must regard and measure each company according to their hard assets. With increasing competition and internationalization, manufacturing companies will be forced to wrap knowledge and services around their core goods in the near future. Manufacturers will have to provide fuller and more complete economic offers and solutions based upon the customer's demands and desires. Pine and Gilmore (1999) suggest that eventually, many manufacturers will shift away from a goods mentality to become predominantly service providers.

---

[72] Service companies are defined as companies whose core business is to deliver services.

In order to explore commonalities among the heterogeneous service companies and define key aspects of "business as usual" the present study uses survey data gathered by the Employer and Trade Organization for the Swedish Service Sector (Almega). It is a quantitative survey of 778 service companies that responded to a questionnaire. The results below indicate key aspects of service business. Service companies are defined as companies that have not undergone a transformation from production to service, but rather that their core business has always been that of delivering services.

The key aspects of "business as usual" in service companies are summarized below:

- Business-to-business markets dominate;
- New technology is not the main driver to start the business;
- Businesses operate across industries;
- Laws, rules and structures do not address the service market;
- Companies do not use buzzwords such as "research," "innovation" and "service development";
- The development process is continuous;
- New ideas stem from employees and end users/customers;
- New ideas are generated from within the organization;
- Companies perceive that they are at the forefront of service innovation.

D. SERVICE INNOVATION IN THREE SWEDISH CASES

Service production is a complex operation requiring the performance of several interrelated activities on the company level. To understand growth the company cannot be perceived as a black box, rather we need to further our understanding of the economic activity (Weber, 1968) performed in services production.

To further our understanding of service innovation at the company level three cases from the VINNOVA service innovation portofolio are exemplified below. The cases focus on different aspects of service innovation. A central aspect is value creation for the customer based on the interaction between customer and supplier. Service delivery is built up of processes in which communication is central and where the offering is often made possible and enhanced by technology.

The first case is part of a three-year project on the theme "Dynamic Business Models and User Driven Service Innovations"[73] which was started in 2007 as part of VINNOVAS call on Service Innovations. The core of the project consists of three service innovation cases: one in the building construction industry and two cases in the media industry. Common to all three cases is the focus on information and communication supported services in the two industries. In the building construction industry case, a new mobile service was developed and implemented using wireless communication technology (ICT) to support a set of central activities on building construction sites (so-called self control activities). In the two media

---

[73] Contacts: 1) Per Andersson, Center for Information and Communication Research (CIC), Stockholm School of Economics (Per.Andersson@hhs.se) 2) Hans Malmqvist, Consulting H. Malmqvist AB (hans@malmqvistab.se). Special thanks to Per Andersson and Hans Malmqvist who contributed with the first case description.

industry pilots, one focused on a new wireless supported ICT service to support the physical distribution of newspapers, and the other on a new software to support the planning procedures for certain media production operations. The three service development processes all build on the idea of user involvement. For these processes a set of project targets were developed: 1) develop a new user oriented process for service development, 2) focus on information- and communication supported services, 3) focus on professional services, and 4) involvement of large application areas like construction and media. The process model used build on the idea of high degree of user involvement and was further developed in the service design process.

The second case is part of a three-year project on the theme "Meta Business Models for mobile services (MeMo)"[74] which was started in 2008 as part of VINNOVAS call on Sustainable Business Models for eServices. The mobile services industry needs sustainable business models in order to manage rapidly changing business structures while capturing new business opportunities. The objective of a current project (MeMo) is to explore business models for mobile services and present a meta-business model to create future efficient businesses for mobile service providers. As the project is in progress and the analyses are not finalized the results are preliminary. However, certain patterns can be identified and these indicate that:

- The revenue component, which is only one part of a full business model, still receives disproportionate attention among most actors in the value chain. For many actors, the revenue component solely forms their business model, despite the increased business model complexity in the sector.
- The awareness, among different actors, of the variety of available and suitable business models is limited. Increased knowledge about the components that constitute a business model could enhance the actors' possibilities to achieve sustainable competitive advantage in the value network.
- Standardization, on various levels (e.g. infrastructure, service development and mobile devices) is a crucial driving force for further development within the mobile industry and its related business models. In some respects, standardization is the driving force for innovation.;
- Cooperation within the value chain in the mobile industry is crucial. However, actors within this industry differ enormously in, for example, size, power and maturity. This implies that the actors have to deal with particular challenges related to the partnership component of their respective business model.
- Although some actors integrate the innovation process and the business model development process, there is still a lack of theoretical models that describe and explain such integration.

---

[74] Contacts: 1) Michael Nilsson, Centre for Distance-Spanning Technology (CDT), Luleå University of Technology (Michael.nilsson@cdt.ltu.se). Special thanks to the research team and Michael Nilsson who contributed with the second case description. Further information available at http://www.cdt.ltu.se/~memo

The final case is part of a three-year project on the theme "Methods to create innovative services (MASIT)"[75] which was started in 2007 as part of VINNOVAS call on Service Innovations. The case implied collaborative project work involving a manufacturing firm in the automotive industry, one of their business-to-business customers (a transportation firm), as well as a university, all in Sweden. The general aim of the project was to develop and apply methodology for service co-creation involving both suppliers and customers, while having the focus on the early phases of service development. Problem orientation is a central starting point underlying the developed methodology, meaning that the search for solutions is based on problems, needs, and potentials that have been identified in the customer's operations. The project was carried out adopting an action-based research approach. Thus, the research team selected and developed methods and work practices for problem analysis, idea generation, refinement, and evaluation of services. The proposed approaches were then applied in a service development experiment mainly based on workshops. The experiment was followed up by an analysis of the resulting output, an interview series, and an evaluation by peers in focus groups. Central findings of the experiment are:

- The participants were highly engaged – the approach worked well both practically and socially; and
- The resulting service concepts were holistic in nature and each one addressed many of the identified customer needs;

In the more general sense, project results included:

- Methodology for development of service concepts, having the focus on the early stages of the process. This methodology now constitutes the basis for early service development at the automotive firm, and has been integrated in their ordinary development process.
- Process output consisting of a problem analysis of the operations at the transportation firm, more than 50 ideas on a detail level, and four synthesized concept proposals.

Two academic papers, one of them (Almefelt et al., 2009), describes the methodology in detail and its practical application. The other one is in the pipeline and will report on experiences from the experiment along with process improvements and application guidelines.

E. USING CASES TO GENERATE POLICY RECOMMENDATIONS

The cases presented above exemplify areas where companies have initiated service innovation. From a policy point of view the aim of cases is to highlight areas where countries need to develop adequate policies to support companies in the management of service innovation activities.

---

[75] Contacts: 1) Lars Almefelt, Product development, Chalmers University of Technology, (lars.almefelt@chalmers.se). Special thanks to the research team and Lars Almefelt who contributed with the final case description.

Building on Yin and Heald (1975) the present chapter argues for a bottom-up approach, where a collection of heterogeneous cases is used to aggregate categories. This is in contrast to a top-down approach where classification and statistics incrementally divide the area into smaller segments. The rationale behind a bottom-up approach is that it allows for different sectors to be involved. The intention is to go from a number of cases towards wider concepts and categories by means of qualitative analysis.

The current chapter suggests that case descriptions can be used to illustrate how existing policy affects and influences companies on a practical level. The cases demonstrate potential policy-level challenges that have not yet been addressed. Do we need new polices? Could the derived concepts and categories be used to proceed towards policy recommendations that support better practices? The ambition of this chapter is to show that a possible way for governments to support economic growth is to develop policies based on knowledge from companies with excellent operations and track record. It is not argued that a limited number of cases alone could generate statistically justifiable conclusions rather that case descriptions can serve as a basis for generating effective policy recommendation.

Extending Martin and Scott (2000) policy discussion to the service innovation field the current study argues that it is important to take full advantage of insights offered by empirical studies. Policy recommendations can benefit from taking explicit accounts of features from the real world that are often neglected in a more theoretically informed policy discussion.

The guiding principle when developing a new model for case-based policy recommendations grew from an understanding that if policies are designed to promote economic growth companies cannot be perceived as black boxes. Figure II.5.1 shows the new model of how to build policy-level recommendations based on cases in a bottom-up process. The use of case survey method to analyze policy has been neglected in the evidence-based policy literature (Martin & Scott, 2000; Hull, Kumar, Qutub, Unmehopa & Varney, 2004; Hart & Vromen, 2008; Neylan, 2008). There could be serious consequences if this neglect continues; efforts to develop adequate policy recommendations in the field of services will suffer if the nature service production remains unexplored. Currently little efforts have been made to provide a basis in the form of a case-based policy recommendation model that allows for an injection of the in-depth study of service production.

The first motive for extending current theories is to highlight that adequate policy recommendations in the field of services will suffer if the nature of service production on company level remains unexplored. The second proposed motive for extending existing theories is to acknowledge the difficulty of supporting renewal embedded within the company in opposition to separate R&D projects. The third motive for extending current theories is to recognize how companies manage non-linear and market-driven innovation, such as open and user-driven innovation[76] A final motive for extending current literature is to highlight that if policy recommendations are to promote economic growth, companies cannot be perceived as black boxes, rather we need to further the understanding of economic activity in service production.

---

[76] For an extended discussion on bringing new ideas and research to meet the needs of the market place the reader is kindly referred to Wessner (2005) article on "Driving innovation across the valley of death".

Figure II.5.1. A new model for case-based policy recommendations

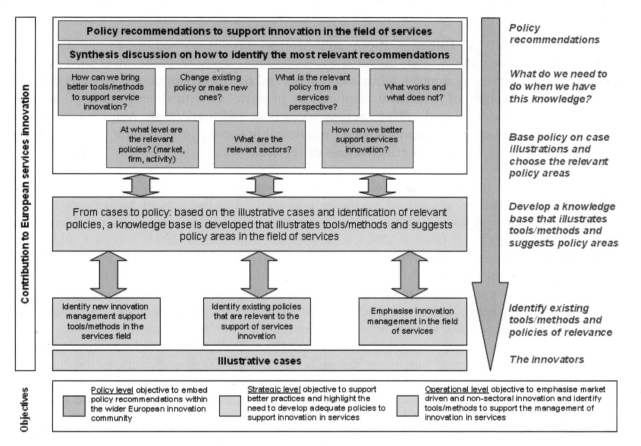

The new model illustrated above extends Yin and Heald's (1975) bottom-up approach to a service innovation context. Initially a collection of heterogeneous cases is drawn from a non sectoral service innovation portfolio. The bottom-up process proceeds as three aggregate themes specific to the service innovation field are defined. The first theme is identifying new innovation management support tools. Second, to illustrate if and how existing policies may be relevant. Finally, to focus on how to manage innovation in the field of services. Given the large number of policy instruments available, the illustrative cases are complemented with an exploration of existing policies that may be relevant. Based on this knowledge policy advice informed by the case illustrations focus on what is relevant to promote innovation in the field of services; a) How can we bring better tools/methods to support service innovation?[77] b) Should we change existing policies or make new ones? c) What works and what does not work? d) At what level are the relevant policies located (market, firm, activity)? e) What are the relevant sectors? f) How can we better support service innovation? The answers to these questions are synthesized to identify the most relevant policy recommendations.

---

[77] The present chapter emphasizes one point which may have implication for future research. Is there an actual difference between what is defined as policies or tools? Could it be that the organizational affiliation of the individual who introduces a policy or a tool has bearing on where it is defined as a policy or a tool regardless of the content?

F. ANALYSIS AND DISCUSSION - PROMOTING SERVICE INNOVATION BASED ON BETTER PRACTICES

While the research of Bitner, Ostrom and Morgan (2008) alerted us to the fact that corporations, governments and universities worldwide have recently awakened to the realization that service dominates global economies and drives economic growth, this chapter indicates the absence of a critical exploration of how activities performed in service companies can create desired utilities across sectors. In addition Vargo, Maglio and Akaka (2008) claim that there is tremendous need for renewal in service production to fuel economic growth and raise the quality and effectiveness of services.

It was established in the introduction that researchers advocating a S-D Logic emphasize skills and knowledge as objects of exchange and argue that the unit of analysis of market exchange should shift from products to an understanding of the process of value creation within the exchange itself (Bolton, 2004; Lovelock & Gummesson, 2004; Aitken, Callantyne, Osborne & Williams, 2006; Vargo & Lusch, 2008; Vargo, Maglio and Akaka, 2008). Previous research has neglected to explore the differences and commonalities of new service development across sectors i.e. in service companies as well as manufacturing companies that "servify" their business. The present chapter explored service production and challenges the assumption that all types of service production are unique to a specific sector.

The current results suggest that there are at least nine observable aspects to the business activities performed in service companies. First, the business-to-business market dominates, as other firms are the main customers. Second, it was somewhat surprising to find that new technology was not the main driver in starting a new service business. Third, service firms operate across a wide range of industries. Fourth, the current empirical evidence indicates that present laws, rules and structures are not designed to address the business performed in service companies. The fifth aspect to business in service companies is a deep unfamiliarity with what the respondents perceive as "buzzwords" such as research, innovation and development. The sixth aspect of service business is a continuous development process. Yet another aspect of service business is that new ideas are mainly produced by employees, as well as end users/customers, rather than as a result of traditional R&D projects. In contrast to, for example, open innovation, empirical evidence from the present survey supports the claim that new ideas mainly stem from within the organizational context and customers whereby little attention is given to inter-organizational collaboration. A final aspect of "business as usual" is that service companies perceive themselves as being at the forefront of service innovation. This was surprising, as the respondents had previously answered that they were unfamiliar with such concepts as research, innovation and development.

The present evidence, as illustrated in figure II.5.2, supports the idea that the renewal of innovation in service businesses can be thought of as a circle encompassing both service production and embedded service renewal (ESR). These activities are intertwined, constantly ongoing processes that create incremental renewal of the services produced. This result is surprising and stands in opposition to traditional R&D activities, which are separate from production.

Figure II.5.2. R&D in traditional production versus embedded service renewal in service production

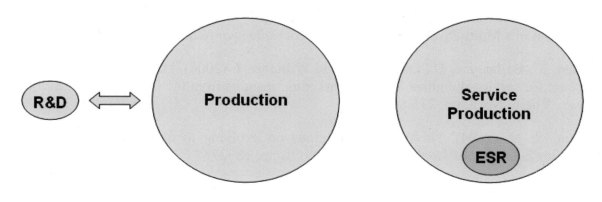

ESR = Embedded Service Renewal

The results of this study underscore that when knowledge and solutions constitute a service business, new service development i.e. renewal, is embedded as employees must understand their customers' needs and be participants in the development of new service concepts. Using Derrida's (1976) concept of deconstruction the present study suggest that in service firms a deconstructive force is "always already" at work. The deconstructive force, currently defined as the embedded service renewal, juxtaposes the daily service production making the concept of "business as usual" complicated and elusive, ESR is always already at work.

It was previously established that the current results indicate that that present laws, rules and structures are not designed to address the business performed in service companies. There is a gap in existing policies. Despite the revival of evidence-based policy formulation through statistics (Neylan, 2008) and think tanks (Hart & Vromen, 2008) there has been relatively little attention given to in-depth case descriptions (Yin & Heald, 1975) of service production in actual companies. The present chapter continues along the avenue of evidence-based research but complement existing knowledge by developing a new model for case-based policy recommendation that explicitly seek to describe what policies are relevant in service production. S-D researchers have suffered in the past from a failure to state in-depth the assumption of value creation in service production across sectors. S-D researchers in building up a theory of value creation often omitted to examine the foundation upon which value creation form across sectors. How is value created? The current chapter argues that this examination is essential not only to prevent misunderstanding, which arise from a lack of the assumptions of value creation, but also because researchers, policymakers and companies must choose between a rival set of assumptions when furthering their understanding of value creation in service production. Is renewal formed in R&D or ESR? Is there a close relation between various forms of innovation in manufacturing and services? Does traditional production also perform ESR in addition to the formal R&D?

REFERENCES

Almefelt L, Rexfelt O, Zackrisson D and Hallman T (2009), "Methodology for service innovation in a Multi-Disciplinary context", *Proceedings of ICED '09*, Vol. 5, pp.405-416.

Aitken, R., Ballantyne, D., Osborne, P. and Williams, J. (2006), "Introduction to the special issue on the service-dominant logic of marketing: insights from the Otago forum", *Marketing theory*, Vol. 6, No. 3, pp. 275-80.

Bolton, R. N. (2004), "Invited commentaries on evolving to a new dominant logic for marketing", *Journal of Marketing*, Vol. 68, No. 1, pp. 18–27.

Bitner, M., Ostrom, A. and Morgan, F. (2008), "Service blueprinting: A practical technique for service innovation, California Management Review", Vol. 50, No. 3, pp. 66-94.

Chase, R. B., Aquilano, N. J. and Jacobs, F. R. (2006), "Operations management for competitive advantage", Tata McGraw-Hill.

Derrida, J. (1976), "Of grammatology", Baltimore, Johns Hopkins University Press.

Ekonomifakta, Nationalräkenskaperna (www.ekonomifakta.se 2008-11-14)

Fitzsimmons, J. A. and Fitzsimmons, M. J. (2006), "Service management: Operations, strategy, information technology", McGraw Hill.

Ford, R. and Bowen, D. (2008), "A service dominant logic for management education: It's time", *Academy of management learning & education*, Vol. 7, No. 2, pp. 224-243.

Frankfort-Nachmias, C. and Nachmias, D. (1996), "Research methods in the social science", St Martin's press Inc.

Hansson, J. (2005), "Kompetens som konkurrensfördel", Nordstedts akademiska förlag, Sweden.

Hart, P. and Vromen, A. (2008), "A new era for think tanks in public policy? International trends, Australian realities", *The Australian journal of public administration*, Vol. 67, No. 1, pp. 12-19.

Hull, R., Kumar, B., Qutub, S., Unmehopa, M. and Varney, D. (2004), "Policy enabling the service layer", *Bell Labs Technical Journal*, Vol. 9, No. 1, pp. 5-18.

Jacob, F. and Ulaga, W. (2008), "The transition from product to service in business markets: An agenda for academic inquiry", *Industrial marketing management*, Vol. 37, pp. 247-53.

Johnston, R. and Clark, G. (2005), "Service Operations Management" (2 Ed.), Essex: Pearson.

Lovelock, C. and Gummesson, E. (2004), "Whither service marketing? In search of a new paradigm and fresh perspectives", *Journal of service research*, Vol. 7, No. 20, pp 20-41.

Martin, S., Schott, J. (2000), "The nature of innovation market failure and the design of public support for private innovation", *Research Policy*, Vol. 29, pp. 437-447.

Metters, R., King-Metters, K. H., Pullman, M. and Walton, S. (2005), "Successful service operations management", Thomson South Western Publishing.

Neylan, J. (2008), "Social policy and the authority of evidence", *The Australian journal of public administration*, Vol. 67, No. 1, pp. 12-19.

Pine, J. and Gilmore, H. (1999), "The experience economy", Boston Massachusetts, Harvard Business School.

Spohrer, J. and Riecken, D. (2006), "Services Science: Introduction", Special Issue Editors, *Communications of the ACM*, Vol. 49, No. 7, pp. 30–32.

Vargo, S." and Lusch, R. (2008), "From goods to service(s): Divergence and convergence of logic", *Industrial marketing management*, Vol. 37, pp. 254-259.

Vargo, S., Maglio, P. and Akaka, M.-A. (2008), "On value and value co-creation: A service system and service logic perspective", *European Management Journal*, Vol. 26, pp. 145-152.

Weber, M. (1968), "Economy and Society", Vol.1, New York, Bedminister.

Wessner, C. (2005), "Driving innovation across the valley of death", *Research technology management*, Vol. 48, No. 1, pp. 9-12.

World Investment Report. (2004), "The Shift Towards Services", United Nations, New York and Geneva.

Yin, R. and Heald, K. (1975), "Using the case survey method to analyze policy studies", *Administrative science quarterly*, Vol. 20, pp. 371-381.

PART III

SECTOR APPROACHES AND BUSINESS PERSPECTIVES

1. TOWARDS POLICIES THAT UNLOCK THE POTENTIAL FOR SERVICE INNOVATION TO CREATE NEW MARKETS AND FOSTER INNOVATION IN OTHER SECTORS

Mette Koefoed Quinn[78], European Commission,
Directorate-General for Enterprise and Industry

A. INTRODUCTION

Service innovation is a real phenomenon, but it is difficult to measure and even more difficult to promote, taking into account its cross-sectoral nature and its many different facets. Many service sectors innovate as much as manufacturing, in particular the knowledge-intensive services. But it is also evident that innovation in services is quite different from innovation in manufacturing. For example, the role of R&D is less important in most service sectors than it is in manufacturing. However, user-centred and employee-driven innovation plays a much stronger role, and the "time to market" for innovative solutions is comparably short in services.

B. THE CHALLENGE OF CAPTURING SERVICE INNOVATION

A key statistical problem is that service activities are performed in all industries, from service sectors to traditional manufacturing sectors, and service innovation therefore happens both in services and in manufacturing. The Community Innovation Survey 2010 (CIS 2010), for instance, takes this aspect into account by asking questions with regards to product innovation for both products and services – thus recognising that service innovation cuts across sectoral boundaries. Capturing service innovation statistically remains nevertheless a thorny task. More research work is needed here. The EPISIS INNO-Net[79] is making a start by working on improving the service typology and indicators on service innovation.

Although some major improvements were achieved in recent years to measure services and service innovation, the fundamental measurement problems will be difficult to overcome. Many service innovations are not recognised as such, as they are part of new or improved "package" solutions. It is therefore unlikely that service innovation can ever be fully captured, considering the conflict between academic interests to know more about this phenomenon and the public policy objective not to impose undue administrative burdens on enterprises for the collection of data.

---

[78] The opinions expressed in this article are those of the author alone and not necessarily those of the European Commission.

[79] The European Policies and Instruments to Support Service Innovation INNO-Net is a project under the PRO INNO Europe® initiative funded by the Competitiveness and Innovation Programmes (CIP) of the European Commission, for further information: www.proinno-europe.eu/episis

C. THE POLICY VIEW: THE EUROPE 2020 STRATEGY

From a policy point of view the question is less "What is service innovation and where does it happen?", but more "What is the economic impact of service innovation and how to influence it in a positive manner?" Policymakers are not very interested in measuring and promoting service innovation as such, but rather in its impact on competitiveness, growth and jobs or in its potential to better address societal challenges. This requires a fundamentally different approach towards the economic analysis of service innovation that goes beyond the question of statistical measurement.

The European Commission's Europe 2020 Strategy provides the framework for assessing why and how service innovation should be supported through policy measures in the future. This requires, first of all, a clear understanding of how service innovation is supporting smart, sustainable and inclusive growth. To this end, an Expert Panel on Service Innovation in the EU has been set up by the Commission's Directorate-General for Enterprise and Industry that will issue policy recommendations by early 2011 on how to further promote service innovation as a catalyst for economic and societal change at the EU level.

D. BEYOND MARKET AND SYSTEMIC FAILURES

In order to raise the political interest in service innovation, it is not sufficient to better understand where service innovation happens and what drives it. Service innovation has many different expressions, and not all of them require or deserve political attention or support. In the first instance, more information and economic analysis is needed on existing market and systemic failures that hamper service innovation in Europe. But this kind of information is even more difficult to obtain than capturing service innovation statistically. And yet another kind of information is needed to demonstrate how service innovation can contribute to better addressing societal challenges, like decoupling growth from the consumption of natural resources. What do we really know about the ecological footprints that new internet services leave? And if we knew how to improve eco-efficiency through service innovation, what policy conclusions does this suggest in order to promote environmentally sustainable services?

Potentially, many market or systemic failures exist that may hamper service innovation. The Commission Staff Working Document "Challenges for EU support to innovation in services – fostering growth and jobs through service innovation," presented the available evidence on market and systemic failures in the field of service innovation. Its analysis showed that the empirical knowledge on barriers to service innovation is still rather poor. Theoretically, many barriers may exist for service innovation, but most of these are difficult to prove empirically. It is therefore nearly impossible to base any meaningful policy conclusions on the available information on market or systemic failures, which remains too general and significantly incomplete.

E. TOWARDS A MORE PROACTIVE AND STRATEGIC APPROACH

The rise of the service economy is well documented and it is clear that the relative weight of service activities, specifically market services, in the overall economic activity in the EU greatly outstrips that of manufacturing. There is broad agreement that services and service innovation are important drivers of innovation and competitiveness. However, this in itself is not sufficient to call for specific actions in support of service innovation. The Commission Staff Working Document "Challenges for EU support to innovation in services," follows an alternative route of argumentation that goes beyond the concept of market and systemic failures: the cross-sectoral approach. Rather than addressing only existing or perceived market and systemic failures, it could be considered opportune to proactively promote the emergence of new industrial sectors driven by service innovation, and to facilitate structural change towards a service economy.

Service innovation takes place in all sectors – manufacturing and services – but it can be assumed that, sooner or later, it finds its expression in new businesses that are specialized in services. Most of the service innovation that is currently taking place in manufacturing will eventually be outsourced and further professionalized – thereby creating new businesses, new markets and sometimes entirely new sectors. Service innovation is therefore to be seen as a catalyst for industrial change and entrepreneurship, which quite often results in new enterprises, sectors and markets. Building industrial policy strategies on this transformation process would make a real contribution to the further implementation of the Europe 2020 Strategy.

F. HOW BEST TO SUPPORT SERVICE INNOVATION?

Service innovation may be supported at four different levels: (1) at the activity level, for example, through research projects and financial support for the development of new business models; (2) at the firm level by enhancing the capacity of service companies to innovate faster and better, for example, by supporting start-ups, improving the innovation management of firms or facilitating access to finance; (3) at the sectoral level by creating a favourable business environment for service innovation, such as through clusters; and (4) at the market level through the liberalization of service markets, effective consumer protection or standards that support the trust in, and interoperability of innovative services.

In other words, the difference between supporting service innovation at the activity level and at the firm level is that, in the first case, the development of specific new business models is supported whereas, in the second case, the innovation capacity of a service firm is targeted in general, irrespective of the type of service innovation. Supporting service innovation through cluster initiatives at sectoral or cross-sectoral level goes yet a step further by improving, more generally, the business environment in which service firms operate and innovate. Finally, the liberalisation and deregulation of markets as well as the privatization of public services is a strong driver for the emergence of new services that may fundamentally reshape our economies.

These different approaches to support service innovation may co-exist and mutually reinforce one another. At the European level, it seems most promising to concentrate on a combination of sector-level policies with the promotion of open and competitive markets. Supporting service innovation to have a real impact at the activity level results in projects that would need to be combined with accompanying measures, such as business incubation and access to finance. This is best done at the regional or even local level, as it is much more difficult to use synergies between different support mechanisms for innovative service firms at the European level.

G. HOW DO SERVICES CLUSTER?

It is often overlooked that many service industries geographically concentrate or "cluster" their activities as they also benefit from the spatial proximity of partners, technology and service providers like traditional clusters.[80] The European Cluster Observatory[81] provides strong statistical evidence of this. Some service sectors, like transportation and logistics, financial services and publishing, lean very much towards clustering whereas other services, like retail, public services or healthcare, can be found practically everywhere. It seems that knowledge-intensive services in particular tend to cluster, with the exception of those that are publicly provided with a wide geographical coverage, like healthcare.[82] A particularly interesting case is that of creative industries, which in many regions contribute to economic prosperity and job creation. The creative industries not only comprise an important sector in themselves in terms of their contribution to growth and job creation - there are also many positive spill-over effects from the creativity and dynamic interaction of this sector with others, for example, through supply-chain relationships and labour mobility, that stimulate innovation. This makes it a sector of strategic importance.

A recent sector report on the creative and cultural industries conducted by the European Cluster Observatory in April 2010 looked further into where and how creative industries cluster. The analysis showed that creative industries firms operate within complex social environments and that they cluster together like other industries, but that the clustering is based on different types of collaborations. Creative industries are heavily clustered in large urban areas and capital city regions such as London, Paris, Amsterdam, Bucharest or Prague. However, there are also examples of medium-sized cities where clusters and cluster initiatives in creative industries are significant.

H. SERVICE INNOVATION AND INDUSTRIAL POLICY

To be globally competitive, regions and countries will have to develop their own visions of where in the global market they would like to position themselves in the years to come. Most often, they still bet on technological leadership in specific sectors, such as ICT, biotechnology or nanotechnology. In the meantime, some regions have understood that services may offer new opportunities for them. In theory, service innovations can happen everywhere but certainly not with the same probability. They require a specific "eco-system" that supports creativity and openness towards new solutions. Following a cross-sectoral approach implies that creating generally favourable framework conditions for service innovation is not enough. Different services flourish under different conditions, and many of these are determined by the sectoral boundaries within which companies operate and innovate.

---

[80] See section 1.5 on "Services and the concept of innovation clusters" in the Commission Staff Working Document SEC (2009) 1195 "Challenges for EU support to innovation in services – Fostering new markets and jobs through innovation".

[81] For more information of the European Cluster Observatory, see http://www.clusterobservatory.eu/

[82] See also the European Cluster Observatory priority sector report on knowledge-intensive business services of March 2009 that is available at http://www.clusterobservatory.eu/upload/kibs.pdf

Although the term "industry" refers to both manufacturing and services, European industrial policy has traditionally been concerned mainly with manufacturing, and thereby no longer fully reflects the economic reality. The rise of the service economy is now considered as one of the most profound underlying structural changes affecting growth, jobs and wealth in the EU. In this respect, services are important not only as an 'outcome' of structural change but also in terms of their potential role in facilitating the adaptation of industry in response to broader pressures for change, such as globalization or better protection of the environment and more effective use of limited natural resources.

In future, it should not only be understood that services are a driver of innovation and competitiveness in general, but it should also become evident that services help all industrial sectors to become or remain competitive. New service industries will emerge that require different policies and support. Thus, it will be necessary to follow a more integrated approach to services and manufacturing. An industrial policy that is concerned with "speeding up the adjustment of industry to structural changes," should therefore accommodate a significant services dimension.

As a first step towards a more service-minded industrial policy, the European Commission has announced the launch in 2011 of a new cross-sectoral initiative to support the creative industries and their interaction with other industries, as well as a cross-sectoral initiative on innovative mobile services. These new initiatives will examine in greater depth entrepreneurship, access to finance, clusters and framework conditions for the development of these emerging industries. The aim of both initiatives is ultimately to generate greater regional and national innovation support for these industries so as to fully unlock their economic potential.

REFERENCES

European Commission (2010), "Europe 2020: A strategy for smart, sustainable and inclusive growth", Commission communication, March 2010. http://ec.europa.eu/eu2020/index_en.htm

European Commission (2009), "Challenges for EU support to innovation in services – Fostering new markets and jobs through innovation", European Commission staff working document SEC (2009) 1195, September 2009. http://ec.europa.eu/enterprise/policies/innovation/files/swd_services.pdf

Power, D. and Nielsén, T (2010), "Priority Sector Report: Creative and Cultural Industries", Europe INNOVA European Cluster Observatory, March 2010.
http://www.europe-innova.eu/web/guest/news/-/journal_content/56/10136/199295

2. THE CREATIVE ECONOMY: LEADING TRADE AND INNOVATION

Edna dos Santos-Duisenberg and Sudip Ranjan Basu[83],
United Nations Conference on Trade and Development[84], Geneva

A. INTRODUCTION[85]

The ongoing global economic and financial crisis has ushered in a new era of re-thinking of international economic policymaking. The current crisis has forced countries to step onto a path that would encourage an in-depth look at their national dynamics to promote skills and technological development as an integral part of sustainable development strategies.

With a steady decline of global demand in the most advanced countries since the last quarter of 2008, the majority of the developing and transition countries have seen a sharp fall in their exports which led to a deterioration in disposable income and increased unemployment numbers. The crisis has uncovered that while the traditional manufacturing industries were seriously hit, the more knowledge-based creative sectors were more resilient to external shocks.

The global economic recovery process remains fragile, despite mitigating policy measures initiated by G-20 countries since early 2009, and it is now clear that the recovery cannot depend solely on raising consumer demand in developed countries. Developing and economies in transition countries should continue enhancing the development of their creative capacities, progressively looking for new market opportunities and promoting technology and innovation.

Since the publication of the first United Nations *Creative Economy Report – 2008: the challenge of assessing the creative economy towards informed policy-making*, the creative economy has become a much talked about issue of the international economic and development agenda, calling for informed policy responses in both developed, economies in transition and developing countries. Adequately nurtured, creativity fuels culture, infuses a human-centred development and constitutes the key ingredient for job creation, trade expansion and innovation while contributing to social inclusion, cultural diversity and environmental sustainability.

[83] The authors would like to thank Cheng Shang Li for excellent research support. Thanks are also due to the participants' comments at the Applied Policy Seminar, Promoting Innovation in Services Sector, 25 March 2010, Geneva, Palais des Nations, organized by the United Nations Economic Commission for Europe (UNECE).
[84] The views expressed in this paper are those of the authors and do not necessarily reflect the views of the United Nations Secretariat or its members. Any mistakes and errors in this paper are those of the authors' own.
[85] This chapter is largely based on the analysis and information of the *Creative Economy Report - 2010: creative economy a feasible development option, United Nations, New York and Geneva. Visit* http://www.unctad.org/creative-programme for further information. Email: *creative.industries@unctad.org*

At the outset, it may be worth noting that analysis of the creative economy provides new insights into the impact of recent developments in the global market. The quantitative evidence indicates that an important lesson from the global economic and financial crisis is that the market, contrary to conventional wisdom, does not have a near-miraculous capacity to address socio-economic imbalances. Hence, policies and actions to foster development should be rooted on a balanced role for policy interventions and market interactions. In this context, the debate around the development dimension of the creative economy gained momentum in a search for a new development model better adapted to the realities of the contemporary society and increasing market participation of transition and developing countries. Therefore, any attempt to identify trends, strengths and weakness, as well as challenges and opportunities in the creative economy should be addressed in national strategies with respect to the changing global environment.

Clearly, there is a need for a better understanding of the dynamics of the creative economy in our globalized world. A more holistic approach to development is needed. It is time to take some distance from the global and look more deeply to the local, identifying specificities and identities of countries and recognizing their cultural and economical differences in order to capture their real needs and surrounding environment. It seems crucial to explore the linkages between creative capacities, trade, investment and technology, and innovation and see how this can be translated into a vibrant creative economy that can contribute to economic prosperity and poverty reduction.

The key contextual feature is that the world economy has faced the most severe recession since the Great Depression of the 1930s, and this has seriously undermined global growth, employment generation and quality of life. Many believe that the crisis pointed to the limitations of mainstream economic policies, giving clear signs of the need for profound economic and financial reforms, new approaches to development strategies and better balance between the roles of the market and the government. New development routes are needed to reorient policies towards more equitable, sustainable and inclusive growth strategies that are able to accelerate socio-economic growth, create jobs and raise living standards. Against this background, the creative economy is a feasible development option.

We now outline a course for the remainder of the paper. Section B presents a brief sketch of UNCTAD's work on the Creative Economy. Section C discusses concepts, definitions, classification and measurement issues related to the creative economy, with sections D and E specifically outlining UNCTAD definitions of the creative industries and creative economy. UNCTAD global database on the creative economy is reported in sections F, with section G providing some preliminary analysis of the UNCTAD trade statistics on the creative economy. Section H concludes the paper.

B. UNCTAD'S WORK ON THE CREATIVE ECONOMY

The United Nations activities have placed development at the heart of global policy concerns and actions. In particular, UNCTAD's work in this area seeks to demonstrate that the creative economy is not the only solution, but rather a feasible option that can contribute to fostering development during this time of global crisis. By dealing with economic, cultural, social and technological issues, it offers some possible ways to support developing and economies in transition countries' efforts to advance development in line with the MDGs. This section highlights the UNCTAD's mandate in areas related to the creative economy.

The creative economy concept emerged within an international policy framework highly influenced by the Millennium Declaration that was unanimously adopted at the United Nations General Assembly in 2000 by the international community, comprising 189 Member States. For achievement of the eight Millennium Development Goals (MDGs) by 2015, a series of policy instruments have been articulated by the United Nation's bodies to assist developing countries in the process of responding to these challenges. Since 2000, UNCTAD has been proactive in promoting international policy action to assist developing countries to enhance their creative industries and hence their creative economy for trade and development gains.

At the tenth session of UNCTAD (UNCTAD X) held in Bangkok, Thailand, and attended by representatives of 168 Member States, the UNCTAD secretariat was mandated to carry out research and analysis with a view to formulating policy recommendations in the area of trade in services, including audiovisuals[86]. An intergovernmental Expert Meeting on Audiovisual Services was convened by UNCTAD in 2002 in close collaboration with UNESCO. This intergovernmental forum provided insights to assist developing countries to examine the issues relating to trade in audiovisual services and formulate positions in the context of WTO negotiations, particularly as regards the General Agreement on Trade in Services (GATS) and the Agreement on Trade-Related Aspects of Intellectual Property Rights (TRIPS Agreement).

At the Third United Nations Conference on the Least Developed Countries, organized by UNCTAD in its capacity as the United Nation's focal point for issues relating to the LDCs and held in Brussels in May 2001, the music industry became the subject of intergovernmental debates[87]. The rationale was to sensitize governments of LDCs to the fact that the wealth of the poorest countries lies in the abundance of their talents translated into cultural expressions such as music and dance, which in turn have significant economic value. Recalling that recorded music products worldwide were part of a $50 billion market, far exceeding the markets for traditional commodities, the Secretary-General of UNCTAD emphasized that "the music industry feeds into a wider policy discussion about how to diversify economic activity in LDCs"[88]. In follow-up, a series of studies was carried out to examine the economic potential of the music industry to improve earnings from trade and intellectual property rights (IPRs) in a number of developing countries, particularly in the LDCs and SIDS[89]. These studies paved the way for policy initiatives and technical assistance projects to strengthen the music industry in some countries, particularly in Africa and the Caribbean. The fourth United Nations Conference on Least Developed Countries will be held in Turkey in 2011.

---

[86] See "Audiovisual services: Improving participation of developing countries", note by the UNCTAD secretariat (UNCTAD document TD/B/COM.1/EM.20/2), September 2002.
[87] See Third United Nations Conference on Least Developed Countries, " Music Industry Workshop: Proceedings of the Youth Forum (Document UNCTAD/LCD/MISC.82, New York and Geneva, 2003.
[88] Opening statement by R. Ricupero, Secretary- General of UNCTAD, at the Youth Forum, 19 May 2001, cited in "Music Industry Workshop: Proceedings of the Youth Forum"(document UNCTAD/LCD/MISC.82).
[89] Reference to case studies by the UNCTAD/WIPO research project on the Caribbean music industry.

In 2004, at the UNCTAD XI Ministerial Conference held in São Paulo, Brazil, the topic of creative industries was introduced into the international economic and development agenda[90] for the first time on the basis of recommendations made by the High-level Panel on Creative Industries and Development. The São Paulo Consensus, negotiated among 153 countries[91], stated that:

> "...Creative industries can help foster positive externalities while preserving and promoting cultural heritages and diversity. Enhancing developing countries' participation in and benefit from new and dynamic growth opportunities in world trade is important in realizing development gains from international trade and trade negotiations, and represents a positive sum game for developed and developing countries" (para. 65).
>
> "...The international community should support national efforts of developing countries to increase their participation in and benefit from dynamic sectors and to foster, protect and promote their creative industries" (para. 91).

Member States "recognized that creative industries represent one of the most dynamic sectors in the global trading system" and that "their dual economic and cultural functionality calls for innovative policy responses"[92]. The High-level Panel, with the presence of the United Nations Secretary-General, stated that "special measures were needed for the development of creative industries at the international level, particularly in the trade and financing arena and in ensuring cultural diversity in developing countries," and that "The need for increased and better coordinated international efforts was needed for the promotion of more collaboration among different international agencies and the investment community."[93]

In discharging its mandates, UNCTAD shaped a number of international and national policy initiatives in the area of creative industries and the creative economy. In this regard, it built synergies among the United Nations organizations, aiming at exploring complementarities, undertaking joint technical cooperation projects and promoting more effective concerted international actions. In this spirit, the United Nations Multi-Agency Informal Group on Creative Industries was set up by UNCTAD in 2004. The Group, which brings together ILO, ITC, UNCTAD, UNDP, UNESCO and WIPO, maintains a regular dialogue and meets annually in Geneva. This has paved the way for partnerships and prompted a new impetus for collaborative initiatives, taking into account the competencies, mandates and differentiated approaches of the bodies involved. A concrete example of such initiatives was the first Creative Economy Report - 2008, which was a pioneer example of cooperation involving the contributions of five agencies from the UN family in a joint endeavour to improve policy coherence and the impact of international action on issues relating to the creative economy.

---

[90] Deliberations based on "Creative Industries and Development" (UNCTAD document TD (XI) BP/13), 4 June 2004.

[91] See São Paulo Consensus, contained in the report of United Nations Conference on Trade and Development on its eleventh session (UNCTAD document TD/412), 20 August 2004.

[92] See High-level Panel on Creative Industries, 13 June 2004, Summary prepared by UNCTAD secretariat (UNCTAD document TD/L.379), 16 June 2004, para.4. See: http://www.unctad.org/en/docs/tdl379_en.pdf

[93] Ibid., para.7.

A High-level Panel on Creative Economy and Industries for Development met on 14-15 January 2008 in Geneva as an UNCTAD XII pre-conference event. The session was attended by eminent government officials, policymakers, experts and practitioners from the cultural and creative community and academia from 49 countries, 19 international organizations and nine non-governmental organizations. The Panel was convened by the Secretary-General of UNCTAD with the aim of assisting Member States in their deliberations on this topic at UNCTAD XII[94]. It was recognized that, in line with its mandate (São Paulo Consensus, paras.65 and 91), UNCTAD has been playing a key role in sensitizing Governments to the potential of the creative economy to foster trade and development gains, promoting policy-oriented initiatives and enhancing cooperation with countries, institutions and the international community at large[95].

Furthermore, two other important events were held during the twelfth session of the quadrennial Ministerial Conference of UNCTAD held in Accra, Ghana, from 20 to 25 April 2008: (a) The launching of this first *Creative Economy Report 2008*[96] by the Partnership UNCTAD-UNDP Special Unit for South-South Cooperation as the first multi-agency study to present the United Nations perspective on this emerging topic; and (b) the launching of the UNCTAD Creative Africa Initiative[97].

The Creative Economy Report 2008 became a world reference on this new topic that in a few years has become well-integrated in the international economic and development agenda. There is evidence that the report has been instrumental in facilitating policy formulation in international, regional, national and municipal governmental spheres. The report concluded that the creative industries was one of the most dynamic sectors of the world economy due to the increasing demand for knowledge-based goods and services that associate creativity, culture, arts, media, design and creative services with new lifestyles. The forthcoming Creative Economy Report – 2010 aims to show that the creative economy is not a panacea but is a feasible option to foster a human-centred, inclusive and more sustainable development path in this post-crisis period.

C. CONCEPTS, DEFINITIONS, CLASSIFICATION AND MEASUREMENT

This section provides an overview of the development of the concepts of "creativity", "creative products", "cultural industries", "creative industries" and "creative economy" in an effort to reach not a final consensus but at least a shared vision as a basis for comparative analysis and informed policy-making. It also considers the emergence of the associated concepts of "creative class", "creative cities", "creative clusters" and "creative districts". So fundamental to an understanding of the creative economy - what it comprises and how it

---

[94] See Secretary-General's high-level panel on creative economy and industries for development, Background paper prepared by the UNCTAD secretariat (document TD (XII)/BP/4), 17 January 2008, available at: http://www.unctad.org/en/docs/tdxiibpd4_en.pdf. For further details about the meeting, consult: http://www.unctad.org/Templates/Meeting.asp?intItemID=1942&lang=1&m=14639&year=2008&month=1

[95] See Outcome of the Secretary-General's high-level panel on creative economy and industries for development, Note prepared by the UNCTAD secretariat (document TD(XII)/423), February 2008

[96] http://www.unctadxii.org/en/Programme/Other-Events/Creative-Africa/Launch-of-the-Creative-Economy-Report/

[97] http://www.unctadxii.org/en/Programme/Creative-Africa/

functions in the economies of both developed and developing countries - are the evolving concepts of "cultural industries" and "creative industries". Much debate surrounds these terms.

Concepts and definitions

There is no simple definition of "creativity" that encompasses all the various dimensions of this phenomenon, and likewise no straightforward definition of the term "creative economy"[98]. Indeed, in the field of psychology, where individual creativity has been most widely studied, there is no agreement as to whether creativity is an attribute of people or a process by which original ideas are generated. Nevertheless, the characteristics of creativity in different areas of human endeavour can at least be articulated. For example, it can be suggested that:

- Artistic creativity involves imagination and a capacity to generate original ideas and novel ways of interpreting the world, expressed in text, sound and image;
- Scientific creativity involves curiosity and a willingness to experiment and make new connections in problem-solving; and
- Economic creativity is a dynamic process leading towards innovation in technology, business practices, marketing, etc., and is closely linked to gaining competitive advantages in the economy.

All of the above involve technological creativity to a greater or lesser extent and are interrelated, as shown in figure III.2.1. Regardless of the way in which creativity is interpreted, there is no doubt that, by definition, it is a key element in defining the scope of the creative industries and the creative economy.

Another approach is to consider creativity as a measurable social process. From the economic point of view, however, a relationship between creativity and socio-economic development is not apparent, particularly the extent to which creativity contributes to economic growth. In this case, it is important to measure not only economic outcomes of creativity but also the cycle of creative activity through the interplay of four forms of capital - social cultural, human, and structural or institutional - as the determinants of the growth of creativity - the creative capital. The accumulated effects of these determinants are the "outcomes of creativity". This is the framework of the creativity index, also known as the 5Cs model. There are debates about a possible establishment of a European Creativity Index to be applied to the countries of the European Union; the proposal builds upon existing indices and suggests a model with 32 cultural-related indicators grouped in five pillars of creativity, namely: human capital, technology, the institutional environment, the social environment, openness and diversity[99]. The goal of such an index would be to highlight the potential of including culture-based indicators in existing frameworks related to creativity, innovation and socio-economic

---

[98] See *Boston's Creative Economy*, BRA/Research, United States of America for a discussion of definitional issues http://unitus.org/FULL/BostonCreativeEconomy.pdf

[99] This model was developed by a research team of the Centre for Cultural Policy Research of the University of Hong Kong that was led by Prof. Desmond Hui. See *A Study on Creativity Index*, 2005. http://www.hab.gov.hk/en/publications_and_press_releases/reports.htm

development with a view to assessing the creative performance of EU Member States and facilitate policymaking.

Figure III.2.1. Creativity in the modern economy

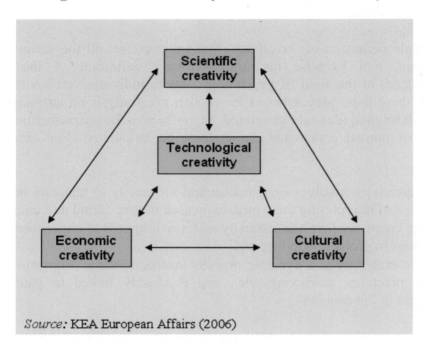

Source: KEA European Affairs (2006)

Figure III.2.2. Interplay of the 5Cs: outcomes of creativity + 4 capitals

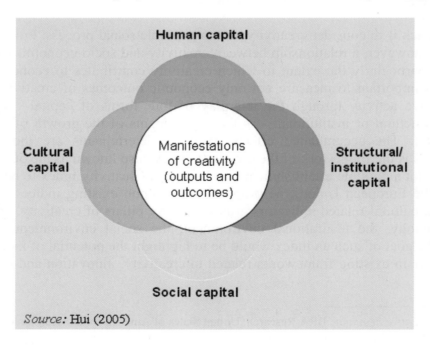

Source: Hui (2005)

Creativity can also be defined as the process by which ideas are generated, connected and transformed into things that are valued. In other words, creativity is the use of existing knowledge to produce new ideas. However, creativity is not the same as innovation. Originality means creating something from nothing or reworking something that already exists. In this conceptual debate it should be pointed out that creativity is not the same as innovation. Nowadays the concept of innovation has been enlarged, it is not only of a functional, scientific or technological nature but it also reflects aesthetic or artistic changes. Latest studies point to the distinction between "soft" and technological innovation, but recognize that they are interrelated[100] There are high rates of soft innovation in the creative industries, particularly in music, books, arts, fashion, film and video-games. The focus is mainly on new products or services rather than processes.

The scope of the creative economy is determined by the extent of the creative industries. Defining "creative industries", however, is a matter of considerable inconsistency and disagreement in the academic literature and in policy-making circles, especially in relation to the parallel concept of "cultural industries". Sometimes a distinction is made between the creative and the cultural industries; sometimes the two terms are used interchangeably. A sensible way to proceed is to begin by defining the goods and services that these industries produce.

The concept of "cultural products" can be articulated if the notion of "culture" is accepted whether in its anthropological or its functional sense. It might be argued, for example, that cultural goods and services such as artwork, musical performances, literature, film and television programmes, and video games share the following characteristics:

- Their production requires some input of human creativity;
- They are vehicles for symbolic messages to those who consume them, i.e., they are more than simply utilitarian insofar as they additionally serve some larger, communicative purpose; and
- They contain, at least potentially, some intellectual property that is attributable to the individual or group producing the good or service.

An alternative or additional definition of "cultural goods and services" derives from a consideration of the type of value that they embody or generate. That is, it can be suggested that these goods and services have cultural value in addition to whatever commercial value they may possess and that this cultural value may not be fully measurable in monetary terms. In other words, cultural activities of various sorts and the goods and services that they produce are valued - both by those who make them and by those who consume them - for social and cultural reasons that are likely to complement or transcend a purely economic valuation. These reasons might include aesthetic considerations or the contribution of the activities to community understanding of cultural identity. If such cultural value can be identified, it may serve as an observable characteristic by which to distinguish cultural goods and services as compared with different types of commodities.

---

[100] Stoneman P., Soft innovation: economics, product aesthetics and the creative industries, Oxford University, UK, 2010.

Defined in either or both of these ways, "cultural goods and services" can be seen as a subset of a wider category of goods that can be called "creative goods and services". These are man-made products whose manufacture requires some reasonably significant level of creativity. Thus the category "creative goods" extends beyond cultural goods as defined above to include products such as fashion and software. These latter goods and services can be seen as essentially commercial products, but their production does involve some level of creativity. This distinction between cultural and creative goods provides a basis for differentiating between cultural and creative industries, as discussed in the following sections.

In the present day, there remain different interpretations of culture as an industry. For some, the notion of "cultural industries" evokes dichotomies such as elite versus mass culture, high versus popular culture, and fine arts versus commercial entertainment. More generally, however, the proposition that the cultural industries are simply those industries that produce cultural goods and services, typically defined along the lines outlined above, has gained greater acceptance.

In UNESCO, for example, the cultural industries are regarded as those industries that "combine the creation, production and commercialization of contents which are intangible and cultural in nature. These contents are typically protected by copyright and they can take the form of goods or services". An important aspect of the cultural industries, according to UNESCO, is that they are "central in promoting and maintaining cultural diversity and in ensuring democratic access to culture"[101]. This two fold nature - combining the cultural and the economic - gives the cultural industries a distinctive profile.

Many politicians and academics, particularly in Europe and Latin America, use the concept of "cultural economics" or the term "economy of culture" when dealing with the economic aspects of cultural policy. Moreover, many artists and intellectuals feel uncomfortable with the emphasis given to market aspects in the debate on the creative industries and hence the creative economy. "Cultural economics" is the application of economic analysis to all of the creative and performing arts, the heritage and cultural industries, whether publicly or privately owned. It is concerned with the economic organization of the cultural sector and with the behaviour of producers, consumers and governments in this sector. The subject includes a range of approaches, mainstream and radical, neoclassical, welfare economics, public policy and institutional economics[102]. While the theoretical and economic analysis in this report takes into account the principles of cultural economics as a discipline, the purpose is to better understand the dynamics of creativity and its overall interactions with the world economy, including its multidisciplinary dimension in which cultural policies interact with technological and trade policies.

Usage of the term "creative industries" varies among countries. It is of relatively recent origin, emerging in Australia in 1994 with the launching of the report, *Creative Nation*. It was given wider exposure by policymakers in the United Kingdom in 1997, when the Government, through the Department of Culture, Media and Sport, set up the Creative Industries Task

---

[101] http://portal.unesco.org/culture/en/ev.php-URL_ID=34603&URL_DO=DO_
TOPIC&URL_SECTION=201.html
[102] According to the definition by the *Journal of Cultural Economics*, an academic quarterly periodical published in cooperation with the Association of Cultural Economics International.

Force. It is noteworthy that the designation "creative industries" that has developed since then has broadened the scope of cultural industries beyond the arts and has marked a shift in approach to potential commercial activities that until recently were regarded purely or predominantly in non-economic terms[103].

A number of different models have been put forward over recent years as a means of providing a systematic understanding of the structural characteristics of the creative industries. The following paragraphs review four of these models, highlighting the different classification systems that they imply for the creative economy. Each model has a particular rationale, depending on underlying assumptions about the purpose and mode of operation of the industries. Each one leads to a somewhat different basis for classification into "core" and "peripheral" industries within the creative economy, emphasizing once again the difficulties in defining the "creative sector", as already discussed.

Classification and measurements

A significant landmark in embracing the concept of the "creative industries" was the UNCTAD XI Ministerial Conference in 2004. At this Conference, the topic of creative industries was introduced onto the international economic and development agenda, drawing upon recommendations made by a High-level Panel on Creative Industries and Development.

The UNCTAD approach to the creative industries relies on enlarging the concept of "creativity" from activities having a strong artistic component to "any economic activity producing symbolic products with a heavy reliance on intellectual property and for as wide a market as possible"[104] (UNCTAD, 2004). UNCTAD makes a distinction between "upstream activities" (traditional cultural activities such as performing and visual arts) and "downstream activities" (much closer to the market, such as advertising, publishing or media-related activities), and argues that the second group derives its commercial value from low reproduction costs and easy transfer to other economic domains. From this perspective, cultural industries make up a subset of the creative industries.

Creative industries are vast in scope, dealing with the interplay of various subsectors. These subsectors range from activities rooted in traditional knowledge and cultural heritage such as arts and crafts, and cultural festivities, to more technology and services-oriented subgroups such as audiovisuals and the new media. The UNCTAD classification of creative industries is divided into four broad groups: heritage, arts, media and functional creations. These groups are in turn divided into nine subgroups, as presented in Figure III.2.3.

The rationale behind this classification is the fact that most countries and institutions include various industries under the heading "creative industries", but very few try to classify these industries into domains, groups and subsectors. Yet doing so would facilitate an understanding of the cross-sectoral interactions as well as of the broad picture. This classification could also be used to provide consistency in quantitative and qualitative analysis. It should be noted that all trade statistics presented in this Report are based on this classification. According to this classification, the creative industries comprise four groups,

---

[103] See *Creative Industries and Development*, UNCTAD (document TD (XI)/BP/13, June 2004).
[104] See *Creative Industries and Development* (document TD (XI)/BP/13, 4 June 2004).

taking into account their distinct characteristics. These groups, which are heritage, arts, media and functional creations, are outlined in Figure III.2.3.

Figure III.2.3. The UNCTAD classification of creative industries

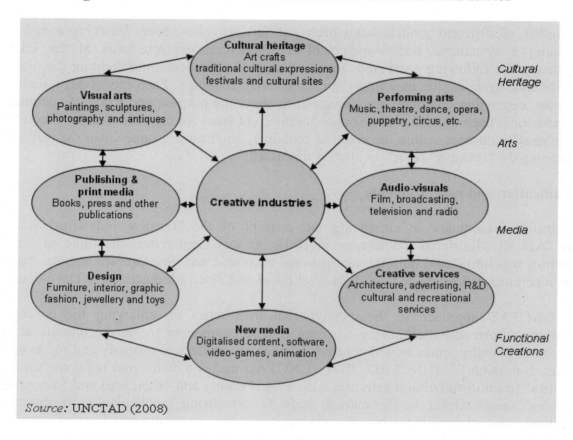

Source: UNCTAD (2008)

D. UNCTAD DEFINITION OF THE CREATIVE INDUSTRIES

The creative industries:

- Are the cycles of creation, production and distribution of goods and services that use creativity and intellectual capital as primary inputs;
- Constitute a set of knowledge-based activities, focused on but not limited to the arts, potentially generating revenues from trade and intellectual property rights;
- Comprise tangible products and intangible intellectual or artistic services with creative content, economic value and market objectives;
- Are at the cross-roads of the artisan, services and industrial sectors; and
- Constitute a new dynamic sector in world trade.

The UNCTAD classification indicates the following subgroups to help understand the creative industries information and analysis.

Heritage. Cultural heritage is identified as the origin of all forms of arts and the soul of cultural and creative industries. It is the starting point of this classification. It is heritage that brings together cultural aspects from the historical, anthropological, ethnic, aesthetic and societal viewpoints, influences creativity and is the origin of a number of heritage goods and services as well as cultural activities. Associated with heritage is the concept of "traditional knowledge and cultural expressions," embedded in the creation of arts and crafts as well as in folklore and traditional cultural festivities. This group is therefore divided into two subgroups:

- Traditional cultural expressions: arts and crafts, festivals and celebrations; and
- Cultural sites: archaeological sites, museums, libraries, exhibitions, etc.

Arts. This group includes creative industries based purely on art and culture. Artwork is inspired by heritage, identity values and symbolic meaning. This group is divided into two large subgroups:

- Visual arts: painting, sculpture, photography and antiques; and
- Performing arts: live music, theatre, dance, opera, circus, puppetry, etc.

Media. This group covers two subgroups of media that produce creative content with the purpose of communicating with large audiences ("new media" is classified separately):

- Publishing and printed media: books, press and other publications; and
- Audiovisuals: film, television, radio and other broadcasting.

Functional creations. This group comprises more demand-driven and services-oriented industries creating goods and services with functional purposes. It is divided into the following subgroups:

- Design: interior, graphic, fashion, jewellery, toys;
- New media: software, video games, and digitalized creative content; and
- Creative services: architectural, advertising, cultural and recreational, creative research and development (R&D), digital and other related creative services.

There is an ongoing debate about whether science and R&D are components of the creative economy, and whether creative experimentation activities can be considered R&D. Recently more empirical research has been analyzing the interactions between research, science and the dynamics of the creative economy. In UNCTAD's approach, creativity and knowledge are embedded in scientific creations in the same way as in artistic expressions. In order to nurture the creative economy, governments should regularly assess the conditions for technology acquisition and upgrading and should implement and review their science, technology and innovation policies, including ICTs and their implications for development. Lately, the term Science 2.0 and Expansion of Science (S2ES) has been used with different meanings. It is usually related to Web 2.0 enabled scientific activities, but it has also been related to the expansion of science by means of new concepts and theories, or new modes of producing knowledge[105].

---

[105] A World Multi-Conference on Systemic, Cybernetics and Informatics held in July 2010 in Florida, USA addressed issues related to the Second Order Cybernetics (2), and the Systems Approach.

UNESCO approached this matter in the context of increased cooperation between science and industry as well as between the public and private sectors in the promotion of scientific research for long-term goals, prior to the discourse about the creative economy, in the context of the World Conference on Science in 1999. As pointed out in the Declaration, the two sectors should work in close collaboration and in a complementary manner. However, from reviewing follow-up activities, it seems that scientists from the public and private sectors have not yet articulated this cooperation even if the private sector is a direct beneficiary of scientific innovation and science education and an increasing proportion of funds for creative-industry-related scientific research are financed by the private sector.

Sport and its role in the creative economy are also debatable. Some classifications of creative industries include sport. In most cases, this is because ministries of culture are also in charge of sport matters. This is also justified by the fact that sport is an important source of revenue and generates positive externalities in various other sectors of the economy. Another practical and methodological reason is that in national accounts, sport is aggregated with recreational services. From the conceptual viewpoint adopted by the present report, sport is associated more with training, rules and competition rather than with creativity. Therefore, sport is not included in the UNCTAD classification of "creative industries".

As noted earlier, there is no unique definition of the "creative economy". It is a subjective concept that is still being shaped. There is, however, growing convergence on a core group of creative industries and their overall interactions both in individual countries and at the international level. This Report adopts the UNCTAD definition of the "creative economy", which is summarized in the following box[106].

For countries in the developing world, recognition of the development dimension of the creative industries and hence of the creative economy has been more recent. The São Paulo Consensus arising from UNCTAD XI was a decisive step in this respect. Subsequently, UNCTAD has enlarged the focus of its policy-oriented analysis, emphasizing four key objectives in its approach to the creative economy:

- To reconcile national cultural objectives with technological and international trade policies;
- To deal with the asymmetries inhibiting the growth of creative industries in developing countries;
- To reinforce the so-called "creative nexus" between investment, technology, entrepreneurship and trade; and
- To identify innovative policy responses for enhancing the creative economy for development gains.

E. UNCTAD DEFINITION OF THE CREATIVE ECONOMY

The "creative economy" is an evolving concept based on creative assets potentially generating economic growth and development.

---

[106] Reference made to the definition by the UNCTAD Creative Economy and Industries Programme, 2006, and in particular "Creative Economy Report 2008", UNCTAD/ UNDP.

- It can foster income-generation, job creation and export earnings while promoting social inclusion, cultural diversity and human development;
- It embraces economic, cultural and social aspects interacting with technology, intellectual property and tourism objectives;
- It is a set of knowledge-based economic activities with a development dimension and cross-cutting linkages at macro and micro levels to the overall economy; and
- It is a feasible development option calling for innovative, multidisciplinary policy responses and inter-ministerial action.

At the heart of the creative economy are the creative industries.

Against this background, the UNCTAD secretariat is developing an economic model to assist developing countries in optimizing trade and development gains from the creative economy. The basic premise is the recognition that trade plays an increasing role in promoting socio-economic growth, employment and development. Trade alone, however, is a necessary but insufficient condition for strengthening creative capacities. On the one hand, the contribution of domestic and foreign direct investment (FDI) to capital formation is essential to induce technology-led innovation, artistic creativity and technical inventiveness. On the other hand, creative entrepreneurship can provide the basis for well-adapted and results-oriented market strategies.

Moreover, in order to positively influence export performance while enhancing creative capacities, effective cross-cutting mechanisms should aim at strengthening institutional and regulatory instruments, particularly to reinforce intellectual property regimes, competition law and fiscal policies. Such a framework can facilitate the following: better access to financing, including micro-credit for independent creative workers and micro enterprises; the formation of creative clusters for sharing know-how and infrastructure facilities; investment promotion and public-private partnerships; greater efficiency in the functioning of networks of local creative firms; and increased competitiveness of creative products and services in global markets. In this schema, tailor-made capacity-building activities to improve entrepreneurial skills and trade- and investment-related policies are highly recommended.

The conceptual approach of this scheme is inspired by ongoing, policy-oriented research in UNCTAD's areas of competence (see Figure III.2.4). This model is in its embryonic stage, still requiring empirical analysis with a view to understanding how the economic and technological spillovers interact or, in other words, how the so-called "positive externalities" may occur in practice. It should also be recalled that creative industries comprise a vast and heterogeneous group of firms with distinct and usually flexible organizational structures specific to each creative subsector. Certainly, the model is still a set of testable propositions requiring practical application to provide evidence for and validate these assumptions. Indeed, to date, little is known and there is insufficient evidence about the impact of the creative industries on the wider economy, particularly their spillovers into other segments of the economy.

Figure III.2.4. The Creative Nexus: the C-ITET model[107]

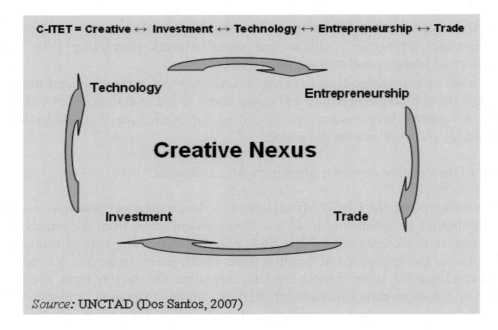

Source: UNCTAD (Dos Santos, 2007)

F. UNCTAD GLOBAL CREATIVE ECONOMY DATABASE

UNCTAD proposed a possible model applicable worldwide that was immediately tested and used through the UNCTAD Global database of trade statistics for creative goods and services, without incremental cost for any country. The purpose of the first Creative Economy Report in 2008 was to start a process of advancing the debate on the importance of mapping, and how to measure the impact of the creative industries at the national and global levels. Now for the Creative Economy Report - 2010, this work moved a step further and considerable improvements have been made in the quality and coverage of the creative industries trade data presented.

In order to achieve this goal, UNCTAD makes a comparative analysis of current methodologies used for statistics for the creative industries, taking into account the new 2009 UNESCO framework for cultural statistics, as well as ongoing work being carried out by other international institutions and individual countries in this regard. As a result of this work, complementary measures for the improvement of the world trade statistics for the creative industries are proposed and presented in this report. The creative economy is booming and governments from developing countries need some analytical tools and comparative analysis to support their efforts to put in place the necessary national and international policies to embark on this new and promising terrain.

The exercise of revising the UNCTAD model for creative industries trade statistics in 2010 takes into account, and complements the work carried out and adopted by relevant international organizations. For example: EUROSTAT published a pocketbook for cultural

---

[107] See "Creative Economy Report 2008", UNCTAD/ UNDP.

statistics in 2007[108]; Convenio Andrés Bello proposed a classification of cultural goods for MERCOSUR countries in 2008[109]; and UNESCO launched the new framework for cultural statistics in 2009[110]. Besides these important references, UNCTAD has also contacted some countries' statistical authorities and gathered feedback and comments. In this way, it was possible to have a clearer idea about the coverage of creative products selected in the international scene.

The intention was, therefore, to conduct an evidence-based comparative analysis of classifications for trade of creative/cultural goods in a global context, with the purpose of not only refining the UNCTAD taxonomy of creative goods, but also to present a pragmatic methodological tool for developing countries with varying capacities to organize their cultural statistics framework. There are different types of cultural statistics such as activities, occupation, trade goods and service, expenditure, time-spending/ participation, etc. The UNCTAD model focuses exclusively on statistical methodologies for 'trade' goods and services, but hopefully in the near future it will also cover trade in digitalized creative products.

There are four potential means of measuring creative industry activity: employment, time use, trade and value added, and copyright and IPR. However, these means are unevenly and inadequately applied to benchmark the creative industries in both the developed or developing world. The identification of a comprehensive data set would be extremely costly and require organizational resources that are unrealistic. Hence, our approach is twofold: first, to try to identify at least one pragmatic measure that can be used for the sector; and second, to help to stimulate further data collection and monitoring by public agencies worldwide. In part, this latter task will require the use of new survey instruments.

In this regard, the role of the relevant United Nations organizations is essential, in particular UNCTAD, UNESCO, WIPO and ILO which are already working with a view to ensuring that official data are collected and analyzed for all countries in the areas of their competence. It is important to ensure equivalence and coherence between various international and national efforts in this endeavour. In part, some of this new data can be collected by marginal extension of existing official census and survey instruments, and it is important that a clear, overarching aspiration be shared between different organizations locally.

The Creative Economy Report argues that it is possible to use existing taxonomies of trade to partially describe the dynamics of the creative economy. This by definition resulted in an underestimate of world trade of creative industries. Yet, UNCTAD made a start in 2008 by creating the basis for a systematic collection and trade analysis of data on the creative economy, highlighting critical areas. Now in 2010, a step further is being taken in revisiting and sharpening the list of creative goods, providing expanded data for creative services, and deepening the trade analysis with greater focus on its South-South dimension.

---

[108] EUROSTAT's *Pocketbook for Cultural Statistics* can be accessed at:
http://epp.eurostat.ec.europa.eu/cache/ITY_OFFPUB/KS-77-07-296/EN/KS-77-07-296-EN.PDF
[109] See: *Nosotros Y Los Otros: El Comercio Exterior de Bienes Culturales En América del Sur*, accessible at:
http://sinca.cultura.gov.ar/sic/comercio/comercio_exterior_sm.pdf
[110] *UNESCO 2009 Framework for Cultural Statistics*: http://www.uis.unesco.org/ev.php?ID=7226_
201&ID2=DO_TOPIC

The UNCTAD classification emphasizes the undiscovered creativity of the Global South by providing elements to identify potentialities. Therefore, the majority of products in the UNCTAD classification are Design and Art crafts. Indeed it was the Creative Economy Report 2008 that first presented world trade statistics for these two categories on a universal basis, since these categories are those for which developing countries have higher market shares and opportunities in international trade. The UNCTAD classification is pragmatic in the sense that it not only analyzes the evolution of statistical methodology, but at the same time shows the balance of trade data currently available.

The UNCTAD global database of trade statistics has migrated to the new classification and the reason for migrating from the HS 1996 to HS 2002 version are two fold. Firstly, the version of HS 1996 has been established for more than 10 years and therefore the composition of codes in HS 1996 cannot be expected to reflect recent developments in creative industries, and a more recent version of HS codes provides for a better disaggregation. In this case, HS 2007 is the latest version and indeed provides the best disaggregation of codes, but the trade data for HS 2007 is only available after the year 2007 making it impossible to conduct a comparative analysis for the evolution of world trade in creative industries.

Secondly, the data availability is another reason to suggest this migration. UNCTAD needs to adopt a classification which is capable not only of capturing the largest number of data but also to maintain the number at the same level. The data availability of HS 2007 is the poorest in the entire time series; only 102 countries' data was available in 2008. On the contrary, although HS 1996 has the largest number of data comparing with other versions, the number of reporting countries decreased nearly 12%, from 166 to 147 between 2005 and 2008. In this context, the 2002 version of HS codes seems to best meet our requirements, and has therefore been selected as the methodology for this report.

UNCTAD is fully aware that there is no single definition and classification of creative industries, neither a "one size fits all" approach that applies to all countries. Rather, there is a multiplicity of approaches, and certainly no consensus model. In this context, international comparison remains highly problematic because of the limitation of methodologies and the gaps in the statistical tools for quantitative and qualitative analysis.

G. TRENDS IN INTERNATIONAL TRADE IN CREATIVE GOODS AND SERVICES

UNCTAD's database attempts to provide a picture of international trade flows of creative goods and services in global markets for the period 2002-2008. The database also contributes to improve market transparency but much more needs to be done at the national and international levels, in order to provide better tools to assist governments in policy formulation, and provide a clear understanding of the dynamics of the creative products in world markets for the creative community.

In 2008, the global economic downturn and recession undermined opportunities in many countries for jobs, growth and economic and social well-being. With falling global import demand, world trade sharply declined by 12%. Export sectors continue to play an important role in the development process through productivity growth, income and employment creation and technology diffusion. The contribution of exports to GDP in developing countries, increased from 26% in 1990 to 44% in 2008, revealing the increasing openness of their economies[111]. Although in global economic upturns trade openness allows countries to secure gains from trade, in global economic downturns negative external shocks are readily transmitted. Falling global import demand has severely affected those countries most successful in export-led growth, calling for a reassessment of export-led growth strategies. Unlike previous crises largely confined to particular countries/regions, this time global demand contraction has limited the ability of countries to use trade to boost recovery. Therefore, international trade may take longer than previously expected to reach its pre-crisis level. In 2010, while the signs of recovery are visible across many countries, concerns remains regarding how robust and sustained the recovery will be.

By contrast, in the case of the creative industries international trade continued to grow, despite the effects of the economic crisis on international trade in 2008. During this decade, creative industries emerged among the world's most dynamic sectors, offering vast opportunities for cultural, social and economic development. Since 2000, exports of creative industry products have been growing at an unprecedented rate, as compared with the traditional sectors of the world economy. More recently, this upward trend in the international trade of creative products became more pronounced, recording an annual growth rate of 14.4% during the period 2002-2008. World trade in creative goods and services surged to US$592 billion in 2008 as compared with US$267 billion in 2002 according to UNCTAD. Over the period 2002-2008, the creative industries gained shares in global markets, growing at an annual rate of 14%.

Noteworthy that creative services are rising extremely fast, in the period 2002-2008 annual growth reached 17.1%, as compared with world services exports which grew at an annual rate of 13.5%. Developed economies accounted for 83% of total exports of creative services in 2008,while developing economies had an 11% market share, and economies in transition had 6% of the world total. This is evidence of the dynamism of the creative economy in contemporary society.

Exports of creative goods accounted for the vast majority of world trade of creative industries. In 2008, they reached US$407 billion, a level twice higher than the US$205 billion in 2002 (see Table III.2.1) and representing an annual growth rate 11.5% over the period. Exports of creative services increased by 17% annually, rising from US$62 billion in 2002 to US$185 billion in 2008 although this increase is also indicative of the growing number of reporting countries, as explained earlier. In any case, trade in creative services grew faster than trade in creative goods.

While developed countries continue to lead both export and import flows, developing countries year after year have increased their share in world markets for creative products and their exports have increased faster than those from developed countries (see Tables III.2.2 and III.2.3). Exports of creative goods from developing economies accounted for 37% of world exports of creative goods in 2002 and reached 43% in 2008. This significant growth

---

[111] UNCTAD, Evolution of the international trading system and of international trade from a development perspective: impact of the crises, UNCTAD TD/B/56/7, Geneva, September 2009.

reflects the remarkable increase in production and trade of creative goods in China, which remained as the world's leading exporting country of creative goods in 2008 with an impressive market share of 20% of total world exports of creative goods. Exports of creative services from developing countries account for 11%, while developed countries exports reached 83% of world exports of creative services in 2008.

Exports of creative goods from the developed economies showed positive trends during the period 2002-2008. Export earnings increased from US$128 billion in 2002 to $227 billion in 2008. Design products provided the highest contribution to the trade balances of these economies, followed by publishing. Exports of arts crafts increased in value but the developed economies lost market share as a result of the increase in exports by developing economies. The United States ranked first in 2008 thanks to its competitive position in design, which includes, among other items, interior objects.

Exports of creative-industry products during the period 2002-2008 were led by Europe. The 27-member European Union (EU-27) is the leading regional economic grouping in exports of creative goods, dominating the market with about 40% of world exports of these goods. It should be recalled, however, that this increase also reflects the growing number of countries in the European Union. Conversely, there are fewer countries grouped as economies in transition, one of the reasons for their very low level of exports. European Union exports of creative products increased markedly during the period 2002-2008 for both goods and services. Its exports of creative goods totaled US$89 billion in 2002, rising to US$163 billion in 2008. However, economies in transition countries export and import flows are much lower as compared to country groups. The group of economies in transition experienced a sharp increase in exports from US$1.2 billion in 2002 to US$3.7 billion in 2008, but this represents only 0.9% of world total exports of creative goods in 2008. Over the past few years there has been growing interest among policymakers in these countries to explore the potential of the creative industries to harness trade expansion and economic development.

In recent years, UNCTAD trade analysis has been providing evidence of new opportunities in the steadily growing markets of the South. Emerging trading and economic dynamism in the South has created a new set of relationships among North and South economies. In 2008, South exports of all goods to the world have reached US$6.1 trillion dollars, up from US$1.4 trillion dollars in 2002. While, in the case of South exports to South, the total figure increased from US$828 billion dollars in 2002 to US$3 trillion dollars in 2008, and is little less in the case of South exports to North economies. Exports from South to South has increased faster than exports from South to North in the same period, which provides further opportunities for developing countries to engage in trading relationships with other developing countries.

In the case of creative industries, South-South trade of creative goods reached nearly US$60 billion in 2008 and has tripled in only six years. The South-South trade in creative goods grew at an astonishing rate of 20% annually over the period of 2002-2008, while South exports to the North has been growing at an annual rate of 10.5%.

The list of the world's 20 leading exporters of creative goods in 2002 and 2008 is presented in Table III.2.4. China headed the list while the positions of the United States, Germany, Italy, the United Kingdom, France and the Netherlands were at the top in 2008 as they had been in

2002. India, Turkey, Mexico, Thailand and Singapore are the other developing economies that ranked among the top 20 exporters of creative goods in 2008. India showed the greatest growth in exports of creative goods during the period 2002-2008.

Another point to underscore is that of trade balance in creative goods. The export and import statistics of the individual countries could clearly indicate if a country has a trade surplus or deficit. For creative goods, China has posted the highest trade surplus that increased from US$29 billion in 2002 to US$79 billion in 2008, which is evident given their dramatic surge in exports. Contrary to the China story, the United States registered a very large trade deficit of US$55 billion in 2008. This result corresponds to the global discussion that China's share of trade deficit in the US is the largest among all other group of economies.

The world trade figures for creative industries clearly provide evidence that creative industries constitute a new dynamic sector in world trade. The magnitude and potential of the global market for creative-industry products are vast and have only recently been recognized. The creative economy in general and the creative industries in particular are indeed opening up new opportunities for developing countries to leapfrog into high-growth sectors of the world economy and increase their participation in global trade. The creative industries are already driving trade and development gains in a growing number of countries, in both developed and developing countries and particularly in Asia.

H. CONCLUDING REMARKS

Creative products and cultural activities have real potential to generate economic and social gains. The production and distribution of creative products can yield income, employment and trade opportunities, while fostering social cohesion and community interaction. Thus, knowledge and creativity are becoming powerful drivers of economic growth in the contemporary globalizing world. They have profound implications for trade and development.

Globalization and the rapid uptake of new ICTs have opened up huge possibilities for the commercial development of creative products. Indeed, it is the adoption of new technologies and a focus on market expansion that are distinguishing characteristics of the creative industries as dynamic sectors in the world economy. Undoubtedly, a major driver of the growth of the creative economy worldwide has been the rapid advances of new information and communication technologies (ICTs). Of course, ICTs benefit the whole economy but their role in the creative industries is of particular significance. ICT tools offer new distribution channels for creative products; allow the adoption of innovative entrepreneurial business models; and strengthen the links between creativity, arts, technology and business.

Research being carried out by UNCTAD affirms that ICTs contribute positively to economic growth in both developing and developed economies[112]. They boost productivity by improving the efficiency of individuals, firms, sectors and the economy as a whole. ICTs can also generate positive side effects in the economy through learning-by-doing, faster transfers of know-how and increased transparency. ICT adoption creates unprecedented opportunities for industries and businesses in developing countries to overcome the constraints posed by

[112] UNCTAD (2006). Using ICT's to achieve growth and development, background paper (document TD/B/COM.3/EM.29/2), September 2006. Available at: http://www.unctad.org/en/docs/c3em29d2_en.pdf

limited access to resources and markets. They also provide an opportunity for enterprises in developing countries to obtain better access to finance through improved online credit information structures. Most importantly, ICTs lower transaction costs and facilitate trade, thereby opening new international business opportunities. Developing countries with better and more efficient ICT infrastructure attract more foreign investment and outsourcing contracts and, generally, more trade. It is also important to observe that the economies in transition countries have recently been able to speed up their trade integration through ICT-related policies in order to reap the benefits of their positive spillover effects.

Together with technology and innovation, they open up a huge potential for countries to develop new areas of wealth and employment creation consistent with new trends in the global economy. For such countries to realize this potential, it is necessary to carefully formulate specific policies for enhancing creative capacities through strategic actions to be taken by governments at local, national and regional levels, while possibilities for international cooperation and strategic alliances should also be explored.

In conclusion, the UNCTAD secretariat will continue to fulfill its mandates and assist governments on issues related to the development dimension of the creative economy and industries, in line with the three pillars of UNCTAD's work: (i) consensus-building, by providing a platform for intergovernmental deliberations; (ii) policy-oriented analysis, by identifying key issues underlying the creative economy and the dynamics of creative industries in world markets, and (iii) technical cooperation, by assisting developing and economies in transition countries to enhance their creative economies for trade and development gains.

Table III.2.1. World exports of all creative industries (goods and services), by subgroup, 2002 and 2008

Subgroup	Value (million of US $)	As % of all creative industries	As % of total world export (2)	Value (million of US$)	As % of all creative industries	As % of total world export (2)	Growth rate (%)
	2002 (1)			2008 (1)			2003-2008
All creative industries (3)	267,175	100.00	-	592,079	100.00	-	14.4
All creative goods (4)	204,948	76.71	3.52	406,992	68.74	2.73	11.5
All creative services (5)	62,227	23.29	3.79	185,087	31.26	4.80	17.1
Heritage	25,007	9.36	-	43,629	7.37	-	-
Art crafts goods	17,503	6.55	0.30	32,323	5.46	0.22	8.7
Other personal, cultural and recreational services	7,504	2.81	0.46	11,306	1.91	0.29	7.3
Arts	25,109	9.40	-	55,867	9.44	-	-
Visual arts goods	15,421	5.77	0.27	29,730	5.02	0.20	12.8
Performing arts goods	9,689	3.63	0.17	26,136	4.41	0.18	17.8
Media	43,960	16.45	-	75,503	12.75	-	-
Publishing goods	29,817	11.16	0.51	48,266	8.15	0.32	7.3
Audiovisual goods	462	0.17	0.01	811	0.14	0.01	7.2
Audiovisual and related services	13,681	5.12	0.83	26,426	4.46	0.69	11.0
Functional creations	194,283	72.72	-	454,813	76.82	-	-
Design goods	114,692	42.93	1.97	241,972	40.87	1.62	12.5
New media goods	17,365	6.50	0.30	27,754	4.69	0.19	8.9
Advertising and related services	8,914	3.34	0.54	27,999	4.73	0.73	18.4
Architecture and related services	18,746	7.02	1.14	85,157	14.38	2.21	20.9
Research and development services	12,639	4.73	0.77	31,111	5.25	0.81	14.8
Personal, cultural and recreational services	21,927	8.21	1.34	40,821	6.89	1.06	10.4

Notes: (1) Reported official figures for creative goods based on 92 reporting countries in 2002 and 138 countries in 2008; creative services based on 102 reporting countries in 2002 and 125 countries in 2008. (2) This column shows the percentage of creative goods in total world merchandise trade, and percentage of creative services in total world trade in services, respectively. (3) All Creative Industries are composed of All Creative Goods and All Creative Services. (4) All Creative Goods are composed of art crafts goods, visual arts goods, performing arts goods, publishing goods, audiovisual goods, new media goods, and design goods. (5) All Creative Services are composed of advertising, market research and public opinion polling services; architectural, engineering and other technical services; research and development services; and personal, cultural and recreational services. Audiovisual and related services and other cultural and recreational services are sub-items of personal, cultural and recreational services. For definitions, please refer to sections C, D and E.

Source: UNCTAD secretariat calculation based on official data in UN COMTRADE database.

Table III.2.2. Creative goods: exports, by economic group, 2002 and 2008
(in US$ millions)

	World		Developed economies		Developing economies		Transition economies	
	2002	2008	2002	2008	2002	2008	2002	2008
All Creative Industries	**204,948**	**406,992**	**127,903**	**227,103**	**75,835**	**176,211**	**1,210**	**3,678**
Art Crafts	17,503	32,323	8,256	11,443	9,202	20,715	45	164
Audio Visuals	462	811	425	726	35	75	3	10
Design	114,692	24,1972	60,967	117,816	53,362	122,439	362	1,716
New Media	17,365	27,754	11,422	13,248	5,908	14,423	36	82
Performing Arts	9,689	26,136	8,947	22,539	698	3,323	43	274
Publishing	29,817	48,266	25,970	38,753	3,157	8,138	690	1,376
Visual Arts	15,421	29,730	11,916	22,578	3,474	7,097	31	56

Source: UNCTAD, based on official data in UN COMTRADE database.

Table III.2.3. Creative goods: imports, by economic group, 2002 and 2008
(in US$ millions)

	World		Developed economies		Developing economies		Transition economies	
	2002	2008	2002	2008	2002	2008	2002	2008
All Creative Industries	**225,590**	**420,783**	**187,170**	**317,058**	**36,692**	**93,721**	**1,728**	**10,003**
Art Crafts	20,341	29,272	15,336	20,836	4,858	7,641	147	795
Audio Visuals	411	699	326	483	83	181	2	34
Design	129,232	248,358	106,388	185,810	21,905	56,376	939	6,172
New Media	17,681	36,361	14,519	26,878	3,031	9,064	132	420
Performing Arts	11,134	28,022	9,651	22,241	1,421	5,322	61	458
Publishing	29,633	49,107	25,166	36,351	4,068	10,915	399	1,841
Visual Arts	17,158	28,964	15,784	24,460	1,327	4,222	48	282

Source: UNCTAD, based on official data in UN COMTRADE database.

Table III.2.4. Creative goods: top 20 exporters worldwide, 2002 and 2008

Rank		Value (US$ millions)		Rank	Market share%	Growth rate%
2008	Exporter	2008	2002	2002	2008	2003 - 2008
1	China	84,807	32,348	1	20.8	16.9
2	United States	35,000	18,557	3	8.6	13.3
3	Germany	34,408	15,213	6	8.5	14.7
4	China, Hong Kong SAR	33,254	23,667	2	8.2	6.3
5	Italy	27,792	16,517	4	6.8	9.7
6	United Kingdom	19,898	13,657	7	4.9	6.5
7	France	17,271	8,999	9	4.2	10.2
8	The Netherlands	10,527	3,686	15	2.6	11.6
9	Switzerland	9,916	5,141	11	2.4	13.5
10	India	9,450	..	-	2.3	15.7
11	Belgium	9,220	5,387	10	2.3	6.7
12	Canada	9,215	9,327	8	2.3	-0.9
13	Japan	6,988	3,976	13	1.7	14.7
14	Austria	6,313	3,603	16	1.6	8.5
15	Spain	6,287	4,507	12	1.5	4.9
16	Turkey	5,369	2,154	23	1.3	15.0
17	Poland	5,250	1,983	24	1.3	14.9
18	Mexico	5,167	3,797	14	1.3	9.1
19	Thailand	5,077	2,899	18	1.2	10.3
20	Singapore	5,047	2,619	21	1.2	6.0

Source: UNCTAD, based on official data in UN COMTRADE database.

REFERENCES

BRA/ Research (2003), "Boston's Creative Economy, Boston, USA

EUROSTAT (2007), "Pocketbook on Cultural Statistics", Luxembourg, see http://epp.eurostat.ec.europa.eu/cache/ITY_OFFPUB/KS-77-07-296/EN/KS-77-07-296-EN.PDF

Hui, D. (2005), "A Study on Creativity Index", Home Affairs Bureau, Hong Kong Special Administrative Region Government.

KEA, European Affairs (2006), "The Economy of Culture in Europe, study prepared for the European Commission (Directorate-General for Education and Culture), Brussels, Belgium, p. 42.

MERCOSUR Cultural (2008): "Nosotros Y Los Otros: El Comercio Exterior de Bienes Culturales En América del Sur (Argentina/ Brasil/ Chile/ Colombia/ Perú/ Uruguay/ Venezuela)", Venezuela
See http://sinca.cultura.gov.ar/sic/comercio/comercio_exterior_sm.pdf

Stoneman P. (2010), "Soft innovation: economics, product aesthetics and the creative industries", Oxford University, UK

UNCTAD (2002), "Audiovisual Services: Improving Participation of Developing Countries", UNCTAD secretariat, Document TD/B/COM.1/EM.20/2, Geneva.

UNCTAD (2003) 3rd United Nation's Conference on Least Developed Countries, "Music Industry Workshop: Proceedings of the Youth Forum", Document UNCTAD/LCD/MISC.82, New York and Geneva.

UNCTAD (2004), "Creative Industries and Development", Document TD(XI)BP/13, 11th session (São Paulo).

UNCTAD (2004), "Report of the United Nations Conference on Trade and Development on its Eleventh Session", São Paulo, Brazil, 13-18 June 2004, UNCTAD document TD/412.

UNCTAD (2006), "Using ICT's to achieve growth and development, background paper", UNCTAD TD/B/COM.3/EM.29/2, Geneva

Available at: http://www.unctad.org/en/docs/c3em29d2_en.pdf

UNCTAD (2008), Secretary-General's high-level panel on the creative economy and industries for development, pre-conference event, Geneva, 14–15 January 2008, UNCTAD document TD (XII)/BP/4.

UNCTAD (2008), "Outcome of the Secretary-General's high-level panel on creative economy and industries for development", Note prepared by the UNCTAD secretariat, document TD(XII)/423, Geneva.

UNCTAD and UNDP (2008), "Creative Economy Report 2008: The challenges of assessing the creative economy: towards informed policy making", New York and Geneva.

UNCTAD (2009), "Evolution of the international trading system and of international trade from a development perspective: impact of the crises", UNCTAD document TD/B/56/7, Geneva.

UNESCO (2009), "2009 Framework for Cultural Statistics", Montreal, Canada. See http://www.uis.unesco.org/ev.php?ID=7226_201&ID2=DO_TOPIC

3. POLICY RECOMMENDATIONS ON INNOVATION IN SERVICES[113]

Corinna Schulze[114], IBM Europe

A. THE IMPORTANCE OF THE SERVICE ECONOMY

According to available statistics, the services' share of the global economy has grown, rising from 56% of GDP in developed countries in 1971 to 72% in 2006. Services are essential for the efficient operation of all economies, facilitating commercial transactions and enabling the production and delivery of goods and other services. As companies learn to trade products and services in new ways, often through ICT, services have become a pillar of the global economy. A country with an open, dynamic and efficient service sector enjoys a competitive advantage in the production of both goods and services, as compared to countries with less developed service sectors.

The term "service" covers a broad range of that which produces value by providing solutions to problems facing customers, organizations, citizens and government. In today's interconnected, instrumented and intelligent world, better and smarter solutions are being provided across a variety of sectors, in particular healthcare, transport, energy and government services. The service sector includes everything from childcare, to legal advice, to custom software development and management consulting. In some cases, it is not easy to separate services from the goods with which they are associated, such as an extended warranty purchased with a consumer electronic device or the rental of an automobile. Services can also be embedded within a manufacturing process, as manufacturers procure inputs, such as inventory management and logistics services, from service providers, rather than performing these functions for themselves.

Furthermore, manufacturing industries are evolving to include services to a much greater extent. This may be partly explained by the fact that services are being increasingly incorporated into goods and products. Service packages covering installation, maintenance, updating, training and so forth become an integrated part of delivery. In many cases, the associated services become the main product.

The share of workers employed in services is now over 70% in most developed countries and catching up in developing countries. Services have been the primary source of growth in employment over the last decade. The service sector in the US represents the largest portion of employment and economic output – accounting for 90 million jobs and nearly 80% of US GDP – close to US$11 trillion.

---

[113] This chapter is based on a paper first prepared by Corinna Schulze for IBM, and later used as a contribution to the work of the Networked European Software and Services Initiative (NESSI) on developing a strategy to build systemic foundations for the service economy.
[114] With special thanks to her colleague Susan Tuttle, who helped tremendously with the preparation of this paper.

The development of services-based multidisciplinary skills is also gaining importance in developing economies - not only with a view to securing employment growth in the services sector, but also to enhance productivity. As part of China's 11th Five Year Plan, for example, they targeted accelerated development of the services industry (following India's lead). In particular, they are looking to move up the economic value chain, and hence investing accordingly in services-based skills.

One misconception concerning the growth of the service sector is that it is creating predominantly low-skill, low-value jobs as opposed to high-skill, high-value jobs. While the service sector includes some low-skill jobs, many other service jobs require high levels of skills or advanced education to perform complex tasks in the information economy. In fact, the percentage of employees with a college degree is greater in the service sector than in the manufacturing sector[115]. Despite their central role in co-coordinating economic activity, services have received little or no attention in terms of policy making.

When we think of services, we may not appreciate the breadth of economic activity they encompass: the engineer's network design, the barber's haircut, the doctor's diagnosis, the waitress's service, the architect's building plans, the carpenter's craftsmanship and the consultant's business strategy. Services have been traditionally regarded as the 'residual': a heterogeneous, 'left-over' collection of activities for consideration once innovation in the agricultural and industrial sectors has been addressed. Until recently, measurement of innovation in the services sector has been a neglected area of economic policy making (see Kanerva, Hollanders and Arundel, 2006), along with consideration of measures to support this innovation.

For the purpose of the recommendations made by IBM, we focus on innovation in ICT services, ICT-enabled services and knowledge-intensive services. The pace of growth in business services (i.e., those supplied to other firms, such as computing, financial, legal, consulting, advertising and marketing services), is spectacular, even when measured against the growth rate of other service subsectors. A European Commission communication (1998) on business services noted that they provide 8.5% of total employment in the EU, and 15.3% of value-added (more than banking, insurance, transport and communications services combined). Why are we focusing on ICT services? Because there are tremendous benefits to be derived from ICT – across all sectors of the economy, and these benefits are well-recognized.

More and more companies ask for more than products alone; they will buy solutions that allow them to modernise their business processes. Efforts for modeling business processes and implementing them as a value-added addition to software services will be necessary to support the competitiveness of industries.

Securing the transformation to a knowledge-intense, globally competitive services and software economy is far from straightforward, even with the appropriate investment in software and services research. Such a transformation requires a paradigm shift, facilitated complementary investments and structural change, e.g., in human capital, organizational

---

[115] OECD, Promoting Innovation in Services, p.26.

change, education, trust and security. It is paramount that economies manage the transformation to a services economy not only from a technological, but also from a socio-economic and human capital perspective. This will ensure sustainable change and growth in an increasingly globalized and competitive world in which services are already, and will increasingly be, a key determinant of economic growth.

B. THE STATISTICAL PICTURE

The lack of adequate data, indicators and methods to analyse services and service innovation, has been the constant refrain of researchers studying services over the years. Firstly, there is a challenge in analysing services and their innovative potential because services are simply too broad a 'sector' to be considered together in any meaningful or coherent form. The sheer size and significance of the sector within the economy has, therefore, been an issue in itself in terms of analysis and policy formulation. Services not only account for an increasing share of the economy, but are also characterised by a high degree of heterogeneity. In addition, they interact amongst themselves and with other sectors of the economy (notably manufacturing), in complex ways[116]. Thus, there is a significant challenge in reporting across the diverse activities comprising the services sector, and to provide an informed commentary on the innovation trends in such a 'top down' manner. Given such size and diversity, it is perhaps surprising that anyone could hope to satisfactorily cover such a heterogeneous and diverse set of industries with a single monomorphic model or paradigm.

Issues surrounding a lack of metrics, indicators and data also have crucial policy implications. Serious deficiencies in our understanding of the structure of the services sector and the factors influencing the growth of services enterprises remain. The available statistical material often does not reflect appropriately the dominant position of services in an economy.

However welcome subsequent initiatives have been, such as extending the European Community Innovation Survey beyond manufacturing to include services, insight into services and service innovation, and in turn policy formation, are still hampered by this lack of adequate basic statistics on services and service industries, which is a prerequisite for policy formulation, monitoring and evaluation. Therefore, there is a need for recognition among the key stakeholders associated with the analysis of services innovation that we need an improved understanding and measurement of the innovation process in relation to services. Innovation statistics are still strongly biased towards technological innovation, and the measurement of knowledge inputs and innovative processes and outputs in services is one of the key areas where initiatives are needed. Much remains to be done to compare service innovation between countries[117], but this has been hampered, among other things, by data comparability issues.

However, it is important to recognise that services and service innovation remain difficult to study and conceptualise. It is therefore more than 'simply' a matter of funding the collection of more data and the creation of new and more comprehensive datasets. Greater effort also

---

[116] See Hamdani, D. (2000), 'Measuring novelty of innovation: evidence from the Canadian Services Innovation Survey', paper presented at *The Economics and Socio-Economic of Services: International Perspectives Conference*, Lille, 22-23 June 2000.
[117] Kanerva, M. Hollanders, H. and Arundel, A. (2006).

needs to be deployed by the research community in developing new, more robust, indicators that better articulate and measure what service innovation is about, rather than simply seeking to adapt outdated modes of thinking in relation to innovation.

Services are becoming more R&D intensive: From 1990 to 2003, service sector R&D increased at an average annual rate of 12% across OECD members, compared to only 3% for manufacturing sectors. Services are increasingly innovative: the share of business service firms reporting that they were innovative in terms of introducing an innovation between 2002 and 2004 in the EU ranged from around 50% in Germany to less than 20% in Denmark.

We should be aiming for improved measurement and understanding of service and non-technological innovation. Statistics are of key importance in helping policymakers understand where growth is, and to justify expenditures. Statistics on services require further development.

Recommendations:

- Innovation statistics remain heavily biased towards technological innovation, and metrics to measure both inputs and outputs in service innovation need to be further developed and supported; and
- Support the research and statistical community in developing new, but robust, indicators to better articulate and measure what service innovation actually is.

C. THE IMPORTANCE OF R&D IN SERVICES

Government innovation policies, R&D budgets and programmes have historically focused on hard sciences and manufacturing. There is a need to address this imbalance, given the fact that services are the largest source of employment and economic activity. How these programmes are designed is important, because the innovation process in services can differ from that in manufacturing (although they can be linked, as previously mentioned.)

Over the past two decades or so, advances in Internet technologies, open systems and global reach have fundamentally shifted the way enterprises are managed. Many have moved from being centralised, monolithic organizations to being networked collections of firms collaborating and sharing services with specialized and niche partners and customers worldwide to produce goods and services more quickly, more efficiently, and more effectively than before. Enterprises that traditionally focused on in-house production now embrace partnering with specialists and service providers from different business ecosystems to provide critical and core products and services to customers. These complex business networks have only recently begun to take shape in many industries. This has led to increased complexity in harnessing the required services for value-creation, and a correspondingly increased need for understanding complex business services ecosystems.

In the context of service sciences, network dynamics depend not only on connectivity between firms and customers but also on connectivity within firms: that is, the socio-technical interface resides within and between firms, as well as at the point of service delivery. But what is the 'theory of the network' (or the 'theory of the ecosystem'), that is of comparable analytical value to the classic 'theory of the firm'? Understanding the rapid creation of service-chains and services networks, and understanding the value they provide to the ecosystem, is critical for current and future social and business environments.

IBM is addressing what it means to be in a world in which the harnessing of services systems is a complex problem. We envision a multi-disciplinary (anthropological, social scientific, economic, computational, management, and other), effort for tackling the challenges of understanding services and deriving principles for harnessing services for providing value effectively. We are not only focusing on enabling frameworks and technologies for business services in Europe, but also on long-term economic, social and organizational aspects of services. From a scientific perspective, the main challenge is to understand, model and validate the complex, networked services (whether for society, business or IT), that will provide a solid foundation for understanding networks of business collaboration, of social collaboration and of human interactions.

Non-technological aspects of innovation and research in services, aiming to integrate theories, methods and findings from a broad set of disciplines, are crucial. The overriding challenge will be to develop a complement to the classical theory of the firm that takes account of networks of relationships (among people and technology), within firms and across firms, and particularly how these affect service innovation and service delivery - and ultimately, create value.

A secondary challenge is to apply this new theory of the firm to shape policy and legal frameworks, aiming to place Europe in a position of economic leadership. Fundamental issues include whether legal barriers could prevent the development of new markets and business models, whether safeguards are required to make new economic activities acceptable, and whether policymakers will embrace the concepts and metrics of services science.

From a disciplinary perspective, a number of areas and issues readily suggest themselves, including, but not limited to:

Anthropology: What is going on? Who communicates with whom, and to what purpose? How is the communication changing (e.g., blogging)?

Sociology: How to conceptualize what is going on? What are the underlying social structures? Who are the new 'e-fluentials'? In which way and to what extent have societies already transformed (the gaming generation, second life gurus, etc)?

Economics: How to capture the value of what is going on? What economic activity is being supported by the social structures and what are the dynamics of the value flows? Do we need a strategic or game theoretic analysis of network dynamics? How can viable business models be built around this?

Mathematics: How to model what's going on in reality? Can we build predictive models of the structure, dynamics and value of networks and their constituent components? Can we appropriately capture the socio-technical interface?

Engineering: How do we build the systems? Can we design and construct systems to deliver complex, composite services that embody our understanding of networks and address socio-economic challenges, as described above?

Research funding plays an important role in stimulating service sector innovation. Research could help solve problems that ICT service providers face in managing the reliability of complex service delivery systems. Research should also aim at better understanding the non-technical aspects of service sector innovation, in particular organizational innovation, drawing on advances in the social and managerial sciences.

Service related R&D reflects the heterogeneity of the sector itself. Hence, there is a need to develop a better understanding of the nature of services innovation and related R&D in connection with different types of services. For instance, service related R&D can be very close to basic research (e.g., insurance/ actuarial modeling and financial analysis), or close to market activity (e.g., hotel reception process design).

Above all, we need to ensure that the research theme and project assessment criteria do not form a systemic barrier to services research. The inherent bias towards the manufacturing industry and technology-based projects needs to be addressed. For instance, typical service innovations are multidimensional, including organizational, service concept, business model, customer interface and delivery systems, as well as technological elements. This exerts a significant influence on the R&D activities in services, which also have a number of distinct features. Such features include: The informal nature of services R&D, the importance of customer interaction and, overall, a breadth of services related R&D that ranges from close to market activities to basic, research type activities.

Recommendations:

- Research support should be provided and actively promoted. Inter-disciplinary research should prioritise the development of metrics and indicators for service activities in both the public and private sectors. Collaborative research based on, for example, behavioural sciences, mathematics and modeling should be actively encouraged.
- Interdisciplinary studies, in particular between the Humanities and Social Sciences and Science, Engineering and Technology, should be central to any funding initiative.
- Funding programmes for enterprises are primarily aligned with technology-based research, which is often reflected by eligibility criteria. Risk aversion by researchers in services will be more prevalent, and require a greater degree of flexibility. The levels of research funding available need to be adjusted, while funding sources should be open to non-technology based research, paying particular attention to eligibility and bid evaluation criteria.

D. EDUCATION, LEARNING AND SKILLS FOR AN INNOVATIVE SERVICE ECONOMY

Skilled and creative employees are a fundamental factor in the innovation process and a major source of competitive advantage. In the pre-industrial, agricultural age, land and farm production defined competitive advantage. In the industrial age, it was raw materials and manufacturing capability. Today, it is the ability to create and apply intellectual capital based on multidimensional expertise – increasingly in the area of services.

Workforce skills must include both technology and strategic expertise. An understanding of technology – its current capabilities as well as its future potential – is now integral to business decision-making. Importantly, these skills are not static, and need to be continuously refreshed through life-long learning and retraining. Technology and skills in relation to innovation is not an either/or decision. The majority of service firms attach equal importance to investing in new technologies and in skills.

In the past IT services were all about "repair and maintenance." Today, these services are about optimising business performance. At the international level, there is a lack of labour supply with the necessary IT and business skills together with an understanding of the new role of IT services. This is probably the biggest challenge: the creation of a mobile workforce with the capacity to operate across cultural and language barriers. Despite the crucial role played by services, we are not producing graduates with the requisite skills for services jobs in the 21st century. We need more skilled professionals able to apply technology, management and knowledge to modern service architectures in industries like health care, financial services, retail, government and transportation.

Consequently there is a need to adapt educational and training policies to meet rapidly evolving needs for new skills, and create a new discipline for services science. Services science is a multidisciplinary field that seeks to bring together knowledge from diverse sources to improve the service industry's operation, performance and innovation.

In essence, services science represents a melding of technology with an understanding of business processes and organization. It is a shift from a technology-centric view to a holistic view that encompasses both technology and business. Professionals need new skills and education in a variety of fields to yield the best results in service industries. It is critical to develop and foster a broad perspective that includes research from many areas, including economics and law.

IBM is reaching out to universities and governments worldwide and there is a growing recognition of the critical importance of multidisciplinary services-related skills – but we need to move much more quickly if we are to meet our current and future skills needs.

Recommendation: Governments, industry and universities must together enable the creation of a new academic discipline in Service Science to bring together ongoing work in computer science, operational research, industrial engineering, business strategy, management sciences, social and cognitive sciences, and legal studies and develop the skills required in a services-led economy. Secondary schools should also be involved in this process. There will be an evolution from ICT workers with specialized technical skills towards hybrid professionals with competencies in business or scientific areas beyond traditional ICT who will be able to respond to the challenges of a more dynamic, service-oriented economy. Well targeted education policies would have a significant positive effect on the competitiveness of ICT and knowledge-services providers, given the sector's dependence on highly skilled workers.

E. CREATING NEW WORKING ENVIRONMENTS & EMPLOYMENT

In OECD countries, the large majority of employment growth over the last decade came from the service sector, and in particular business services[118]. The service sector is the only part of the European economy to have generated a net employment gain over the past two decades and now accounts for over 70% of total employment. However, it is important to recognize that the ICT marketplace continues to evolve – and dramatically so – and the skills and working practices needed in that changing marketplace require further development. Changes are occurring quickly, and in multi-dimensional ways.

ICT customers and clients increasingly base their purchases on business value, as opposed to technology. This will result in a major restructuring of enterprises in Europe including an increasing trend towards the virtualisation of businesses. Labour will be increasingly mobile, migrating back and forth between centres of activity as people with the required skills migrate to where they are most in demand. In this context, the modernization of working practices will be critical.

A greater proportion of the labour force will work flexibly, including self-employment and teleworking. This could present challenges in a range of policy areas, including employment legislation. It will be crucial to anticipate and facilitate change to improve our competitiveness, while also enhancing quality of general working life.

Recommendation: Governments should promote employment policies that facilitate increased flexibility on the part of both firms and workers to anticipate and facilitate change. In securing the transformation to a service economy, we will move 'up market' to secure higher level jobs in management, problem solving and creative thinking.

F. LEGAL AND REGULATORY FRAMEWORKS FOR SERVICE INNOVATIONS

Greater transparency in the market for services is a key challenge that bears significant influence on innovation activity. It is important that governments press ahead with their efforts to identify regulatory problems that discourage the development of service markets and innovations. Policy benchmarking should also be an important tool for governments as they develop their services innovation policies.

One factor underlying the success of the service sectors is that growth has generally been facilitated by a relatively unregulated and non-interventionist climate. It is therefore necessary to place great weight on getting the environment right – particularly regulation with a light touch.

---

[118] OECD, Promoting Innovation in Services, October 2005, p.9.

We caution against a presumption of going down the regulatory route unless there is a very clear need, and then only in tightly defined areas. Standards may, for example, support innovation if business driven, but inappropriate regulation of professional standards could also serve to reduce competition.

Services typically display rapid growth in transition economies, often fuelled by inward investment, innovation and deregulation. There will be a need to take account of the business model driving enterprises providing services.

Both the regulatory and legal frameworks need not only to be aware of this, but also work proactively with the enterprises concerned. Service provision often requires short term access to specialized activities, and depends on a high degree of flexibility, often provided by small-to medium-sized SMEs. Their *modus operandi*, for example through a combination of SMEs and disaggregate consortia, will provide significant challenges for all stakeholders in terms of the legal and regulatory framework.

Meeting this challenge will require a change of culture that is far from straightforward to accomplish. Consequently, there is considerable scope for governments to consider how best to implement this in the context of their own work as initiators and guardians of many of the regulatory processes. Governments can send a powerful signal in showing that being supportive and creative in services innovation does not necessarily involve any weakening or compromise of regulators' primary objectives.

Recommendation: We would support an approach that encourages effective self-regulation, with centrally imposed regulation being the last resort. Best practice should be encouraged in a system of self regulated professional standards, as this has the benefit of being industry driven, flexible and facilitating choice with regard to both quality and cost of the service provided.

G. REMOVING BARRIERS TO THE GLOBAL MARKET FOR SERVICES

Despite the service sector's large share of the economy, trade in services at a global level accounts for only 20% of total exports. One reason for the low level of trade in services is the existence of significant trade barriers across a range of services sectors in many countries.

ICT is enabling the trade of many knowledge-based services and creating tremendous opportunities for gains from trade. Many successful services companies owe their existence and success to the opening up of markets. Opening services markets will create fresh opportunities for firms to develop new, often ICT-related services and meet emerging global demands. In many ways, business services companies are the model enterprise in the new economy – they trade heavily in 'knowledge' products, are often built primarily from intangible assets (such as people), and are particularly well placed to exploit the potential of the new ICT marketplace.

We need to achieve a legal and administrative framework that allows for cross-border movement of services at the global level, ideally enabling enterprises to easily export innovative services business models beyond national borders. Governments should pursue an ambitious free trade agreement on services under the umbrella of the WTO.

Recommendation: Governments need to secure an ambitious outcome in the WTO Doha Round, including significant market access commitments in services from as many countries as possible. In recent decades, services' share of GDP has grown significantly, yet the growth in services as a share of total exports has failed to keep pace with this. This implies that there is tremendous opportunity for expanded trade in services as the global economy grows, particularly considering how many IT-enabled services are now more readily tradable. Lowering or eliminating existing trade barriers should spur further growth in the sector, by creating new opportunities for entrepreneurs to start up companies, compete and create jobs. Businesses and citizens will benefit from a greater choice of quality services, increased market opportunities and improved employment prospects.

H. SUPPORTING IPR FOR SERVICE INNOVATION

Informal Intellectual Property (IP) protection has a key role to play in the service innovation context. Importantly, IP protection in services is not limited to formal Intellectual Property Rights (IPR) protection methods, which tend to be more suitable in an industrial manufacturing context.

In contrast to technology-based innovation, innovation in services is more likely to be protected by non-patent IP processes as opposed to patents. Any IP mechanism and support for the protection of innovations in the provision of services will need to be flexible, take account of the perishability of services, facilitate the very short delay between innovation and delivery to market, and recognise that being 'first to market' often makes the difference between success and failure.

Open standards provide technical specifications for implementing features and functions developed by impartial, consensus-based organizations in an open and participatory environment, and made publicly available for all to implement on equal terms. Open source refers to software code that is publicly available in a readily comprehensible (source code) form, enabling anyone to copy, modify and redistribute without payment of royalties or fees. Development of open source software is a powerful example of collaborative innovation. Typically, open source programmers collaboratively create software, improve it and constantly share code changes within the community. Open source software can accelerate open standards by serving as a basis for common implementation. Open source stands in contrast to proprietary software in which one company or organization controls the development of the software and makes it available in object code form only.

We believe that both open source and proprietary software are important parts of a contemporary IT marketplace. Open source communities quickly deliver to market the innovations that can be adopted by companies, which may then use them as a basis to build additional, proprietary offerings. Both types of solution should continue to coexist and complement one another. Governments should ensure that their policies - including IP policy - do not discriminate against either software development model.

Knowledge is becoming increasingly global in its scope, as is business. We believe that policy goals should be framed to allow companies to prosper on the basis of new technology not only in Europe, but as leaders in the world market. It is therefore vital that IP regimes are formulated in such a manner so as not to inhibit researchers and developers from participating in global knowledge communities.

Unlocking innovation also demands an up to date IP policy, particularly with respect to patents, enabling both strong IP ownership as an essential driver of innovation, and fundamental technological advances that today are dependent on shared knowledge, open standards and collaborative innovation. IBM believes that a strong, global, intellectual property system encourages innovation. But the strength of that system depends on the quality it produces. Perhaps the greatest threat to innovation is that of low-quality patents – patents that are granted to inventions that are not genuinely new or useful. Governments should be sure to grant only high-quality patents – those for ideas that embody genuine scientific progress and technological innovation. Improvidently granted patents on old inventions or overly broad concepts remove from the public domain the very tools of innovation an effective policy framework should be seeking to nurture. Low quality patents can unjustly reward the patentee and make it difficult for competitors and innovators to use patented techniques to achieve meaningful advances.

In this context, we urge policymakers to grasp the thorny issues within current patent regimes in the context of international discussions. This is essential if we are to avoid a divergence of rules at the international level, which would significantly increase costs for companies seeking international growth.

Recommendations:

- Governments should take account of the implementation of open standards and the importance of interoperability when formulating patent policies seeking to promote innovation.
- There is a need for governments collectively to take the initiative to ensure cross national compatibility, whilst accommodating national, legal and cultural variability. In developing any IP mechanism for services it is important that service activities are acknowledged across all sectors, rather than taking a "silo" or compartmentalised, service sector specific approach.

I. THE ROLE OF DEMAND IN STIMULATING INNOVATION IN SERVICES

Public procurement can provide a lever to increase the demand for innovation in services. Public procurement is, however, faced with the dichotomy of risk aversion (accountability) versus the incentivisation of creative solutions, and the need to overcome the dilemma of extreme uncertainty around unproven and untested products, where even the relative likelihoods of success and failure may be unknown. Demand-driven research in this context may encourage early stage risk sharing, thereby reducing subsequent uncertainty.

As a general principle, policies promoting demand-driven innovation in services present a highly pertinent perspective, as described in the Aho report and several other recent documents[119]. Public procurement-related standards and regulations are another promising area where demand-driven policy measures can stimulate innovative services. At present, the extant range of demand driven policy measures is highly limited, and they present an area with much scope for further development.

Governments ought to adopt new innovative policy programmes to promote demand for external expertise in innovation projects. One means of achieving this is to offer demand-stimulating incentives for those who can make use of expert services. By stimulating demand, the supply and quality of expert services can be expected to improve endogenously. Voucher schemes offer one example of such activities, although comprehensive evaluation of the results of such schemes is not yet available.

Regional clusters represent the operational environment where service innovation policy can be tailored to meet the particular needs of the economic environment. Such a regional approach can form the basis for effective 'bottom up' developed service innovation policies that can stimulate demand as well as the supply of innovative services.

Horizontal policies also play an important part. Regional policies and service innovation policy, for instance, should support one other, and thus facilitate the effective delivery of policy measures.

Public procurement can be a driver for business investment in innovation. Private suppliers of services react and interact with their customers and their demands on a daily basis, regardless of whether the customer is a public purchaser or private business.

Governments also act as consumers in their own right, and should seek ways to become more innovative procurers of services. As such, governments are in a unique position to support service innovation by acting as lead customers with ambitious requirements when procuring services. Governments should be encouraged to develop and share their experiences of innovative procurement policies.

Recommendations:

- Governments should foster greater experimentation in developing demand-driven R&D programmes and promote the introduction of advanced education and training in public procurement for civil servants of contracting authorities and suppliers.
- Address the problem of risk aversion. Innovation may be considered in pilot or short-term projects, but often this is not followed through into longer-term projects, as there is often a preference for the lowest risk solutions.
- Support innovation by acting as an early adopter of new ideas. Early adoption of ideas can have a major impact on supply-side business. Providing firms with their first significant customer for a new innovation can form the reputational platform from which further sales and long-term growth can be achieved.

---

[119] Council of the European Union (2006), PRESS RELEASE, 2769th Council meeting Competitiveness (Internal Market, Industry and Research), Brussels, 4 December.

- Use procurement more strategically to stimulate innovative firms. For example authorities could promote the use, by public purchasers, of innovative criteria in the award of contracts.
- Put forward legislation that will encourage public purchasers to draft procurement policies and share these with private suppliers. Early stage supplier involvement in the procurement process is critical if innovation is to be fully captured.

J. SOFTWARE AS A SERVICE AND THE NEED FOR INTEROPERABILITY

An increasing number of services are being realised through the use of software as the technical means to the solution. Different application domains - financial, legal, governmental, industrial, business and personal services - are converging. Companies will not be able to provide all the services required for particular applications - the collaboration of services coming from various sources, including large and small companies, is essential. Also, companies will have purchased software from a variety of sources. Organizations don't want to replace their existing inventory – they want to build on top of it. Therefore, interoperability (and standards) is imperative. Efforts are needed to ensure interoperability of all kinds of services, especially software services that will lead to standardization for interoperability.

The use of standards and regulation is a highly effective way to influence markets and the development of innovative services. At the same time, increasing regulatory burden may also present an effective barrier to innovation and the development of competitive services. Hence, standards and regulation need to be used in a highly specific and selective fashion, for instance in, a) sustainable energy production, and b) in connection with public procurement. Sustainable energy production and environmental issues represent an area where a supportive regulatory environment could effectively stimulate the development of innovative services. For the future, global markets for energy and environment-related expertise look to be highly promising.

Standards in the ICT domain are largely developed in industry standards organizations, consortia and fora. The majority of the time, these are specialized organizations with strong expertise in their respective technology areas, and hence best suited to their respective standardisation projects. The objective of such standards projects is always to develop global standards on a voluntary basis, and with a clear market application.

With respect to standards policy, there are two major areas for improvement:

1.   Public recognition of standards from consortia/fora:

Globally acting consortia and fora with strong representation of companies have been established as key centres of competence for developing standards in the ICT domain, e.g., W3C, OASIS, OGF (Open Grid Forum) or IETF. Such changes in standardisation frameworks will help to make high quality and state-of-the-art technology available for the global marketplace faster and will encourage participation by companies in the various global standardization activities, as they seek to increase their competitive advantage in the global marketplace.

2. Strengthened upfront communication between governments and industry on standards and mandate initiatives

Efficiency can be gained by early involvement and consultation with industry before a public standards initiative is started or a mandate is issued. The main purpose of such a consultation process will be (1) to jointly evaluate the market need for a particular standard and (2) to jointly evaluate whether international standards are already available or under development.

K. CONCLUSIONS

Services are an area where tremendous innovation and growth is taking place, and there is already considerable activity fostering this development. Much, however, remains to be done. To compete in the world economy of the future, understanding and management of the services business is vital.

Changing demographics, environmental concerns, increasing automation, the growth of the internet and its 'next generation' are key factors influencing the establishment of a services and device-driven world at a scale and pace never before seen in history. They are also, at the same time, establishing the 'grand social challenges' of our century.

There is a unique opportunity for many countries to get ahead of the curve and tackle the great challenges of today and tomorrow, provided industries and governments are quick to adopt a strategy finding innovative, smart and often technology-based solutions to these great challenges. This opportunity also applies far beyond business in general - to countries, regions and cities, which are increasingly competing on the basis of smarter physical and social infrastructure: From efficient transportation, modern airports, secure trade links and reliable energy grids, to transparent and trusted markets and the quality of life on offer [120].

---

[120] See http://www.ibm.com/ibm/ideasfromibm/us/smartplanet/20081117/sjp_speech.shtml

REFERENCES

Organisation for Economic Co-operation and Development (2005), "Promoting Innovation in Services", Working Party on Innovation and Technology Policy, Paris. http://www.oecd.org/document/57/0,3343,en_2649_34273_35396409_1_1_1_1,00.html

European Commission (1998), "Communication from the Commission concerning the Contribution of Business Services to Industrial Performance: A Common Policy Framework" http://ec.europa.eu/internal_market/services/brs/business-services_en.htm

Hamdani, D., 2000, "Measuring novelty of innovation: evidence from the Canadian Services Innovation Survey", paper presented at *The Economics and Socio-Economic of Services: International Perspectives* Conference, Lille, 22-23 June 2000.

Kanerva, M. Hollanders, H. and Arundel, A. (2006), "Trendchart Report: Can We Measure and Compare Innovation in Services? European Trend Chart on Innovation", European Commission, Brussels: http://www.proinno-europe.eu/sites/default/files/page/10/07/eis_2006_innovation_in_services.pdf

Aho, E, Cornu, J. Georghiou, L. and Subirá, A (2006), "Creating an Innovative Europe - Report of the Independent Expert Group on R&D and Innovation appointed following the Hampton Court Summit", January 2006, European Commission, Brussels.